CHICKEN SOUP FOR THE GRANDMOTHER'S SOUL

CHICKEN SOUP
FOR THE
GRANDMOTHER'S
SOUL

Stories to honour and celebrate the ageless love of grandmothers

Jack Canfield
Mark Victor Hansen
LeAnn Thieman

Vermilion
LONDON

We would like to acknowledge the following publishers and individuals for permission to reprint the following material. (Note: The stories that are in the public domain, or that were written by Jack Canfield, Mark Victor Hansen or LeAnn Thieman are not included in this listing.)

Babies, Boredom and Bliss. Reprinted by permission of Janet Hall Wigler. © 2004 Janet Hall Wigler.

By Any Other Name. Reprinted by permission of Carol McAdoo Rehme. © 2004 Carol McAdoo Rehme.

A Grandmother Is Born. Reprinted by permission of Sally Friedman. © 1994 Sally Friedman.

The Longest Week. Reprinted by permission of Teresa Horner. © 2004 Teresa Horner.

(Continued on page 357)

1 3 5 7 9 10 8 6 4 2

Published in 2009 by Vermilion, an imprint of Ebury Publishing
First published in the USA by Health Communications, Inc., in 2005

Ebury Publishing is a Random House Group company

Copyright © 2005 John T. Canfield and Hansen and Hansen LLC

Jack Canfield, Mark Victor Hansen and LeAnn Thieman have asserted their right to be identified as the authors of this Work in accordance with the Copyright, Designs and Patents Act 1988.

The Random House Group Limited Reg. No. 954009

Addresses for companies within the Random House Group can be found at www.randomhouse.co.uk

A CIP catalogue record for this book is available from the British Library

Mixed Sources
Product group from well-managed forests and other controlled sources
www.fsc.org Cert no. TT-COC-2139
FSC © 1996 Forest Stewardship Council

The Random House Group Limited supports The Forest Stewardship Council (FSC), the leading international forest certification organisation. All our titles that are printed on Greenpeace approved FSC certified paper carry the FSC logo. Our paper procurement policy can be found at www.rbooks.co.uk/environment

Printed in the UK by CPI Mackays, Chatham, ME5 8TD

ISBN 9780091923983

Copies are available at special rates for bulk orders. Contact the sales development team on 020 7840 8487 for more information.

To buy books by your favourite authors and register for offers, visit www.rbooks.co.uk

To Anna, Gertrude, Shirlee, Blanche, Rhoda
and all the grandmas
of the world who blessed
not only our heritage, but our hearts.

Contents

3. BLESSINGS

4. ADVENTURES WITH GRANDMA

5. THROUGH THE EYES OF A CHILD

6. GRANDMA'S LESSONS

7. GIFTS FROM GRANDMA

8. LEGACIES AND HEIRLOOMS

Acknowledgments

The path to *Chicken Soup for the Grandmother's Soul* has been made all the more beautiful by the people who have been there with us along the way. Our heartfelt gratitude to:

Our families, who have been chicken soup for our souls!

Inga, Travis, Riley, Christopher, Oran and Kyle, for all their love and support.

Patty, Elisabeth and Melanie Hansen, for once again sharing and lovingly supporting us in creating yet another book.

Mark, Angela, Brian, Dante, Christie, Dave and Mitch, LeAnn's devoted, loving, supportive family.

Our publisher, Peter Vegso, for his vision and commitment to bringing *Chicken Soup for the Soul* to the world.

Patty Aubery and Russ Kamalski, for being there on every step of the journey with love, laughter and endless creativity.

Barbara Lomonaco, for helping us select wonderful stories and cartoons.

D'ette Corona, for being coauthor liaison extraordinaire. Your knowledge, patience and dedication brought this book to fruition.

Patty Hansen, for her thorough and competent handling of the legal and licensing aspects of the *Chicken Soup for the Soul* books. You are magnificent at the challenge!

Laurie Hartman, for being a precious guardian of the *Chicken Soup* brand.

Veronica Romero, Teresa Esparza, Robin Yerian, Jesse Ianniello, Jamie Chicoine, Lauren Edelstein, Jody Emme, Debbie Lefever, Michelle Adams, Dee Dee Romanello, Shanna Vieyra, Lisa Williams, Gina Romanello, Brittany Shaw, Dena Jacobson, Tanya Jones, Mary McKay and David Coleman, who support Jack's and Mark's businesses with skill and love.

Bret Witter, Elisabeth Rinaldi, Allison Janse and Kathy Grant, our editors at Health Communications, Inc., for their devotion to excellence.

Terry Burke, Tom Sand, Lori Golden, Kelly Johnson Maragni, Tom Galvin, Sean Geary, Patricia McConnell, Kim Weiss, Paola Fernandez-Rana and Teri Peluso, the marketing, sales and PR departments at Health Communications, Inc., for doing such an incredible job supporting our books.

Tom Sand, Claude Choquette and Luc Jutras, who manage year after year to get our books translated into thirty-six languages around the world.

The Art Department at Health Communications, Inc., for their talent, creativity and unrelenting patience in producing book covers and inside designs that capture the essence of *Chicken Soup*: Larissa Hise Henoch, Lawna Patterson Oldfield, Andrea Perrine Brower, Anthony Clausi, Kevin Stawieray and Dawn Von Strolley Grove.

All the *Chicken Soup for the Soul* coauthors, who make it so much of a joy to be part of this *Chicken Soup* family.

Our glorious panel of readers, who helped us make the final selections and provided invaluable suggestions on how to improve the book:

Jean Bell, June Bell, Michelle Blank, Phyllis Bohannan, Kris Byron, Mary Clary, Helen Colella, Caryll Cram, Judy Danielson, Shirley Dino, Diana Duello, Richard and Deborah

Duello, Berniece Duello, Susan Goldberg, Tinka Greenwood, Kristine Harty, Barbara Hill, Tony Jaworski, Sally Kelly-Engeman, Karen Kishpaugh, Linda Osmundson, Mary Panosh, Carol Rehme, Christie Rogers, Ruth Shefcyk, Mary Streit, Stephanie Thieman, Terry Tuck and Suzanne Vaughan.

And, most of all, everyone who submitted their heartfelt stories, poems, quotes and cartoons for possible inclusion in this book. While we were not able to use everything you sent in, we know it came from your heart. We are truly grateful.

Because of the size of this project, we may have left out the names of some people who contributed along the way. If so, we are sorry, but please know that we really do appreciate you very much.

A special thanks to Amy Williams who keeps LeAnn's speaking business booming while she writes . . . and writes . . . and writes.

To Mark, LeAnn's husband, business partner, webmaster and best supporter.

And to Berniece and Nerine, who taught her by example how to be the best grandmother.

And to God, for his divine guidance.

Introduction

When our children left the nest, we breathed a sigh of relief for a child-rearing job well done. Thankfully that reprieve was short-lived, for just when we thought we could never love another as deeply as our own, our child places their child into our arms . . . and the lay-down-my-life-for-you love starts all over again. Nothing in this world can prepare us for this moment, and nothing can compare as this child of our child steals our breath and our hearts. Then we watch as the baby's great-grandmother—our mother—embraces this miracle, bearing witness to this ageless mystery of maternal love. Happily we resume the work of caring for a child—but this time with less stress and even more fun! The dance of life goes on—the family circle grows.

Chicken Soup for the Soul applauds how grandmas bless all our lives, and we are honored to bless theirs. These true stories bring hope and happiness to those who caress us, not only with their hands but with their hearts. *Chicken Soup for the Grandmother's Soul* celebrates the love and joy only a grandma can know. Whether she's rocking or rock-and-rolling, knitting or surfing, hugging or hiking, every grandma will find herself in these loving, laughing, even life-saving stories.

On behalf of all the lives they've touched and changed forever, we say thank you!

Share with Us

We invite you to send us stories you would like to see published in future editions of *Chicken Soup for the Soul.*

We would also love to hear your reactions to the stories in this book. Please let us know what your favorite stories are and how they affected you.

Please send submissions to our Web site:

www.chickensoup.com

or mail to:

Chicken Soup for the Soul
P.O. Box 30880
Santa Barbara, CA 93130, USA
Fax: +1 805-563-2945

We hope you enjoy reading this book as much as we enjoyed compiling, writing and editing it.

1

THE BIRTH OF A GRANDMA

Soon I will be an old, white-haired lady into whose lap someone places a baby, saying, "Smile, Grandma!" I, who myself so recently was photographed on my grandmother's lap.

Liv Ullmann

Babies, Boredom and Bliss

When a child is born, so is a grandmother.

Judith Levy

"We're not going in there, are we?" I asked, appalled, looking inside the baby store my friend was determined to enter. I'd come a long way to visit . . . hundreds of miles, and she wanted to shop in a baby store? Quite frankly, I found those kinds of stores boring, the way I found most babies boring. I'd never been accused of being enthusiastic over little creatures who couldn't walk, talk or do anything except scream, make a mess and demand all of one's attention.

Turning on the well-worn heel of her running shoe, my friend shot me a steely look. "We won't be long," she promised, striding into the store.

Unhappily I trailed after her. *She's changed,* I thought grumpily as I stifled a yawn and tottered through the crammed aisles on my high heels. *Definitely changed,* I thought sourly as she spent the next two hours oohing and aahing over everything to do with infants until I thought I'd go insane.

What can I say in defense of my once-glamorous friend, who now smelled of spit-up and stumbled tiredly through the store misty-eyed with joy?

She'd become a grandmother.

That fact was responsible for her gleeful preoccupation with the world of little things, the reason she didn't have time to dye the gray in her hair, the reason she'd traded in her classic clothing for jogging gear, the reason she didn't seem able to talk about anything. Except babies. And most particularly, one little grandbaby.

After helping cram purchases into every nook and cranny of her car, I reminded my friend of a lunch date with our high school girlfriends at a hot new restaurant that featured elegant dining in an atmosphere that catered to people like me—tourists with hard-earned time and money to spend, who wanted to be pampered in a child-free environment.

I squeezed into the passenger side of the car, holding a huge teddy bear on my lap, thankful that soon I'd be in a world of my peers where conversation would veer toward spas, salons and shopping.

But I was sadly, pathetically mistaken. No sooner did we get to the restaurant than my friend took out her wallet and proceeded to spread pictures of her grandson over the gleaming table, expecting us to ooh and aah over the bald-headed tyke with the toothless smile. Every woman did. Including the waitress.

But not me.

What's the matter? I thought, depressed. *Am I the only woman on the planet who dislikes baby talk?* It wasn't that I didn't like babies. I did. I'd borne and raised one myself. Lisa had turned into a lovely young woman. Intelligent, kind, ambitious. We had a good relationship based on respect, love and mutual interests. But I had never been what one could call maternal. And what's more, my friend never had been either, I thought, glaring at her over a glass of wine. I couldn't understand what had happened to her.

We'd been teenage mothers together. We'd married and grown up with our daughters together. Together as single mothers we'd struggled in a world where we tried to fit work and relationships and parenting all in one. We'd been the best of friends.

What had happened to bring us apart?

I could only think of one thing. One word. Actually, two words. Grand. Mother.

What was so grand about that? I thought irately.

Months later, my daughter called. "Mom, guess what?"

I was filing my nails with one hand and juggling the phone with the other, trying not to smear my facial pack.

"I'm going to have a baby!"

The phone slid down my face as visions of gray hair and sweatpants filled my mind, and the sounds of squawking at all hours of the day and night filled my ears. I tasted weariness as I imagined trundling after an infant who needed smelly diapers changed while testing formula to feed a hungry, wailing new soul.

New soul.

I burst into tears.

"Are you glad? Or are you mad?" Lisa shouted into the phone. With trembling fingers I juggled the receiver and said through a throat suddenly gone dry, "I'm not sure." Silently I tried out the unfamiliar label. Grandma. "When's the due date?" I whispered hoarsely.

"Christmas day!"

Christmas in Seattle.

I flew over on the twenty-third. Lisa met me at the airport. Beaming. Huge. I remembered how that felt. Remembered how . . . how wonderful it was! How joyful! How expectant! For the second time since I heard the news I burst into tears.

On December twenty-sixth Bronwyn entered the world and stole my breath, my heart, my soul. My entire identity. "Let Grandma hold her!" I shouted, almost knocking my poor son-in-law off his feet as I snatched my granddaughter out of his arms. I looked down into her precious, angelic face and . . . burst into tears.

Over the next few days I fought like a dragon to hold her, feed her, change her. I shopped in the local supermarket with my hair pulled into an untidy ponytail, dark smudges under my eyes from day-old mascara, sleepless nights and sentimental weeping.

As I sat in the market's deli, rocking Bronwyn in my arms and trying not to get spit-up on my jogging suit, I reflected on my new heart, new eyes, new senses. And I knew that up until the day she'd come into the world, I had been blind. The miracle of her birth had wrought a miracle in me, one I could not get enough of. Babies. I planned to call my friend to see if she'd be available to go shopping next time I was in town. There were some baby stores I was eager to visit. I hoped she'd bring photos.

I couldn't wait to show her mine.

Janet Hall Wigler

By Any Other Name

*What is in a name? That which we call a rose,
by any other name would smell as sweet.*

William Shakespeare

Contemplating my impending role as grandparent, I spent countless hours and multiple conversations debating what my new grandchild should call me. After all, this was a big decision: a sacred moniker—set in stone—to be used by countless future grandchildren.

I mused over the merits and disadvantages of various names, rolling them around my tongue, tasting them, savoring them—trying them on for size. *Grandmother?* Too formal. *Grandma?* Mundane. *Nana?* Nah.

From the quirky *Punkin'* to the colloquial *Gran,* the whimsical *Oma* to the formal *Grandma-ma* (with an elegant accent on the last syllable), I experimented with them all.

"Give it up," said my more experienced girlfriends. "That first grandbaby will call you what she will. And, anyway, the actual name won't matter. Why, you'll be so thrilled, it won't matter *what* she calls you. Trust us," they nodded in agreement. "You won't care."

Well, grandbaby Avery turned one and my daughter put her on the phone so I could hear her chatter across the two thousand miles separating us. I knew this verbose babe's burgeoning repertoire now included words like drink, ball, banana, hi and even the names of several animals. With any luck . . .

"Hello, sweet pea," I gushed. "Happy birthday!"

"Avery, say 'hi' to Grammy," my daughter coaxed at the other end. "Say 'hi.'"

And then it happened. It really happened. A precious, breathy little voice pulled together two words from her vocabulary and cooed into the phone, "Hi, dog."

My daughter giggled, then erupted into a full laugh— and baby Avery repeated her new achievement with enthusiasm, delighted that it appeared to make her mommy so happy.

"Hi dog, hi dog, hi dog."

Huh, I laughed, my girlfriends were wrong. I care. I care *a lot.*

Carol McAdoo Rehme

A Grandmother Is Born

Of all the joys that lighted the suffering earth,
what joy is welcomed like a newborn child?

Caroline Norton

It's the phone call I've been awaiting for nine long months, yet when it comes, it's still a shock.

"This is it," our son-in-law says with a certain catch in his voice. "Jill's in labor."

And so the adventure begins. On the ride to the hospital, my husband and I cannot speak. For a man and woman who are about to become grandparents for the first time, it's all been said. All the fervent prayers for a healthy, whole baby already have been issued up to a higher power.

So we ride in silence, the silence of apprehension, excitement and joy waiting to explode.

At the birthing suite, all is surreal. While the rest of the inhabitants of planet Earth go about their business and pleasure on this brilliantly sunny afternoon, the entire world, for me, is enclosed within the walls of this waiting area.

My husband tries to read.

I pace in an unlikely caricature of those fathers-in-waiting from the Neanderthal days when mothers labored alone. Suddenly, I understand how those fathers must have felt.

Every now and then the midwife appears with a "bulletin." Those bulletins take on the breathless significance of a pronouncement about the future of world peace.

An hour passes. Two. Three. "Soon," our son-in-law tells us breathlessly in his one and only break from being on-site labor coach.

And at 3:42 on an ordinary afternoon, standing at the door of a modern birthing suite, I hear a cry. A baby's cry.

My heart stops.

Nothing in the world could have prepared me for this moment. Nothing will ever be the same for me in this glorious universe.

Today, I am somebody's grandmother!

Hannah—all seven pounds, thirteen ounces of her—has burst into the world.

I meet her moments later and fall madly, desperately, hopelessly in love. Nestled in my daughter's arm is this child of my child, a perfect pink and white miniature. I weep and laugh and thank God for allowing us this moment, this gift, this day.

Time is suspended. It is the deepest, most profound privilege to watch these new parents as they cuddle their baby daughter and explore her incredibly sweet face, her silky skin, her downy head.

Our son-in-law's parents are as speechless as we are. Hannah is the "we" of their son and our daughter, made tangible. In this room, on this day, we all know that this infant is our link to immortality. And this gritty, urban hospital suddenly feels holy.

It is another spectacular moment when I watch

Hannah's great-grandmother—my own mother—meet her. I bear joyous witness to the awesome, incredible continuity of life's longing for itself.

Later, her new aunts and uncles greet Hannah, laugh joyously at her perfection, and touch her tiny, tiny hand.

We are dumbstruck, overwhelmed subjects of this tiny empress, and she seems to revel in the attention on this first day of her life.

This being, after all, the age of technology, the moments are dutifully recorded on video camera. Someday, we will watch—and laugh at our foolishness.

But for this day, it is totally acceptable to worship at the bedside of Hannah and to marvel at the new life that begins with the love of a man and a woman.

Despite all we enlightened moderns know of the biology of life—despite all the excesses of this Information Age—the wonder is the same. The awe remains undiminished.

A baby is born. The universal family of man—and our family—grows once again.

It is as old as time and as new as tomorrow's dawn.

The dance of life goes on. The circle grows.

And a dazed, overwhelmed new grandmother tiptoes out of a room where a miracle has happened, wondering how she ever got to be so lucky.

Sally Friedman

The Longest Week

A sweet new blossom of humanity, fresh fallen from God's own home, to flower the earth.

Gerald Massey

It was a wintry Saturday morning and I was still asleep when the phone rang, but the urgency in Matthew's voice startled me awake.

"Esmaralda's water broke," my oldest son told me. "We think she's in labor."

I felt my heart sink. As a longtime childbirth educator and breastfeeding counselor, I knew all too well the potential risks and challenges of a baby born two months early.

We spent the next hours walking the halls of the hospital as Esmaralda's contractions grew ever stronger. Finally, the midwife knelt in front of her, Matthew sat behind her supporting her back, and Esmaralda's mother and I took our places, one on either side, holding her legs. In just a few pushes, the baby emerged—pink and healthy, a beautiful boy.

Beautiful, yes, but oh-so-incredibly tiny. Sebastian Rhys Pitman weighed just four pounds, six ounces.

Esmaralda's face glowed with joy as she held him against her. But within minutes, his breathing began to falter. We could see him struggling to take in each breath, and newborn Sebastian was moved to the nursery and placed in an incubator.

I was a grandma! But although I'd been there to rejoice in his arrival, I had barely seen, let alone touched, my new grandson, and my heart ached with worry.

By midnight we had even more to worry about. His breathing had continued to deteriorate, and eventually the pediatrician decided Sebastian needed to be transferred to a larger hospital where he could be placed on a respirator. An ambulance arrived to take him away, and a team of health-care professionals put tubes down his nose and throat and hooked him up to monitors for the trip. It scared us all to see this tiny, scrawny baby with so much of his little body covered by tubes and wires.

There wasn't room for my son in the ambulance, so I drove him to the hospital, an hour away. Matthew's a foot taller than me, but he leaned his head against my shoulder and wept as we drove through the dark and snowy night.

We were fortunate there was a Ronald McDonald House next to this larger hospital, offering a place to stay for parents whose children had been admitted. It became Matthew and Esmaralda's home for the next few weeks as Sebastian struggled to stay alive. They spent most of their time sitting alongside his incubator, talking and singing to him so he would know he was not alone.

The nurses encouraged his parents to participate in Sebastian's care from the beginning. He was too frail to tolerate much handling and needed to be on the respirator to keep him breathing, but when his diapers needed changing or when he needed to come out of the incubator for a few minutes, Esmaralda and Matthew were the ones who changed and held him.

I longed to cuddle him just once, but I knew that it was far more important for his parents to have that connection with him. I remembered how hard it was for me, as a new mother, to hand over my baby to someone else. I didn't want to steal even one minute of the precious time these new parents had to hold their son.

I could be patient. But my arms ached to hold him.

I was used to being the mother—the one who had that very intimate connection with the baby. I didn't know yet how to be a grandmother, and it was hard feeling relegated to the sidelines. Maybe if I held him just once, I'd feel more like a real grandma.

But I could be patient. I saw the happiness in Esmaralda's eyes as Sebastian responded to her touch and her voice, familiar to him from the months before he was born. I would wait.

After four days, he was growing stronger. He began to breathe on his own, and the respirator tube was removed and replaced with a smaller oxygen tube. The nurses began to feed him the breast milk Esmaralda had pumped, and she was able to hold him longer each day.

I continued to drive there daily to encourage them and to marvel in Sebastian's progress. Sometimes, as Esmaralda cuddled him to her, I would stroke his tiny hand or gently touch a foot that peeked out from the blanket. But my arms ached to hold him.

When he was a week old, the nurses informed us that he was almost ready to return to the hospital in the small town where we lived and he had been born. Yes, he still needed to be kept warm and fed by a tube for a few more weeks before he could come home, but he no longer needed all the special equipment.

As we celebrated this good news with smiles and hugs, the nurse said, "Now that he can be out of the incubator longer, would Grandma like a turn holding him?"

Would I? Would I?! I'd dreamed of little else for the past seven days.

I settled myself in the rocking chair and the nurse handed him to me. He was so light in my arms . . . such a tiny bundle. But he nuzzled his face against me and snuggled close. I felt a rush of love and emotion surge through me, and the tears flowed down my cheeks. Here he was, my beautiful little grandson, in my arms at last, breathing on his own and healthy and one step closer to coming home. I couldn't speak. All I could do was cry. My arms no longer ached as I held him near and took in the magic of the moment as I held him for the very first time.

Teresa Pitman

She Looks Just Like . . .

A man finds room in a few square inches of his face for the traits of all his ancestors; for the expression of all his history, and his wants.

Ralph Waldo Emerson

As I gazed in awe at my newborn granddaughter, all I could think about was the wonder of God's handiwork—until I heard the words, "She's *all* her mother, even her toes." Each word was spoken with emphasis, followed by an echo, "Yes, even her toes," as if that was the final word on the subject.

I stood outnumbered in a sea of in-laws. Gazing at the ten tiny pieces of evidence before the court of family opinion, I failed to see the referenced genetic code etched in such delicate pink appendages.

Can't my son claim even one little toe for our family? I silently cried out.

I had no idea what it would be like to be a first-time grandma. All my friends said it was the most wonderful experience in the world. So far my experience wasn't going too well.

Slowly, the in-laws' convictions got to me. I left the hospital with one prevailing thought: *I guess I'm a grandma of another family's baby.*

The personal grandma chamber in my heart closed up. After waiting thirty years, it had flowed with grandma's blood for a brief thirty minutes only.

You need to pull yourself together, I thought as I climbed into the car. Suddenly, my first memories of the baby's mother flashed before my mind—how her smile illuminated the sanctuary when she was a high-flying angel at the Crystal Cathedral, how her fingers performed an Irish jig when she signed for the deaf, how her blonde hair and flowered skirt blew in the wind of the spirit when she worship-danced. A rare beauty, within and without, she had stolen my heart.

Even if my son hadn't married her, she would have been my friend for life. Of course it's a privilege to have a grandchild who resembles her!

With excitement, I hung out at the baby's house the next day and the next. I watched and waited for my granddaughter to wake up so I could make early eye contact with that beautiful face. Days turned into weeks, but eventually the bluest eyes, rosiest cheeks, blondest hair and most radiant smile greeted me. I beamed back at her until my smiley muscles ached.

In another few months, her fingers, like precise pincers, held the tiniest of objects. I clapped my hands with amazement.

In a few more months, she toe-danced, twirled and reached for the sun. Overjoyed, I spun around and around with her.

She was just like her angel mother—her smile, her hair, her fingers and yes, even her toes.

The grandma chamber in my heart pumped with delight—until one startling day. I looked in her crib and saw a different child gazing back at me.

What is going on, God? You gave me a granddaughter who looks like her beautiful mother. Now you steal her out of the crib one night and replace her with a child who looks like my son?

"Yes, she has her father's eyes and expressions," the court of family opinion confirmed.

I conceded. When she looked at me I saw her father's deep, contemplative eyes. When she said "uh-oh" as she picked up scraps from the floor, I realized she was a neat-nik like her dad. When her legs grew off the doctor's charts, I knew they were her daddy's long legs. When she became strongly independent, I remembered, so was her dad.

My grandma's heart thrived with this fresh supply of past and present memories, until it suffered a second shock, six months later.

"Your granddaughter looks just like you," someone said to me. Family opinion voted affirmatively.

Oh, no, poor kid, I thought. I couldn't believe that in less than two years she had gone through three distinct meta-morphoses, from a look-alike of her mother, a stamp imprint of her father, to a picture of me! What was she—a child or a butterfly?

Curious, I did some research. I learned that if I were to look into a cocoon in the early stages, I would find a puddle of glop that contains imago cells with DNA-coded instructions for turning cream of insect soup into a deli-cate, winged creature.

That's it! She's a child with the power of glop! She will change her identity many times, each time emerging like a beautiful butterfly. Yet I will be proud that this ever-changing display of beauty, in each stage of life, is my unique first granddaughter.

Margaret Lang

Someone's Grandmother

Blessed be the hand that prepares a pleasure for a child, for there is no saying when and where it may bloom forth.

Douglas Jerrold

I was a frustrated wannabe grandmother. Every time I saw a small baby, I'd hear the ticking of the biological clock. All right, I admit that it wasn't my clock. But our two adult daughters had healthy clocks that I could hear ticking, even if they couldn't. That the younger one had just reached adulthood and that neither daughter was married were beside the point. I wanted to be someone's grandmother.

One day Jennifer, our elder daughter, called with the news, "Mom, I'm getting married!" She followed this with more good news, "Chuck has custody of his two-year-old son. We plan to come home to Alaska for the wedding."

I was ecstatic to be an instant grandma. Then I had a moment's pause as I tried to figure out what to do with a grandson. We raised two daughters and I have a sister. It occurred to me that I had no idea how to entertain a small boy. Could I be his grandma? Would he accept me? Would Chuck let his son call me "Grandma"?

Jennifer, Chuck and Chase arrived in the spring, had a summer wedding and I officially became an instant grandmother. I tried to pace myself getting to know my young grandson. Over the summer we explored hiking trails along the Mendenhall Glacier and tide pools in Tee Harbor. We picked wild blueberries, watched tiny hummingbirds, baked cookies and had long talks in a child's language that I'd long forgotten. All the while I fretted over losing touch with him when Jennifer and Chuck moved south again. I knew I had only a few short months with Chase.

In late fall, fate stepped in. My carpenter-husband Bob took a fall. He had a double compound fracture of his right arm and would be off work for at least nine months. Winter loomed ahead. With the heavy snowfall would come snow shoveling, snow plowing, keeping the furnace running and other winter tasks around the house. Jennifer and Chuck decided to postpone their trip south until the next year so they could help us through the winter. I had another nine months to spend with my new grandson.

Over the winter Chase and I watched Disney movies together, sang during baths about tiny frogs and bars of soap, danced the hoochie-koochie, read stories by Kipling and built snowmen. Spring was coming, and I knew that soon there would be talk of Jennifer, Chuck and Chase moving south again. They had been with us nearly a year, and I knew we weren't the Waltons. It hadn't been an easy winter and some days our big house felt small, yet I fought tears whenever I thought of them leaving.

Once again fate stepped in. An injury to my back required surgery and held me prisoner in our bedroom for nearly four months. Jennifer and Chuck delayed their departure again. Since Jennifer, Chuck and Bob were now working, Chase went to day care. I would wait in bed, listening for the sound of him coming through the back door and pounding his way upstairs to my bedroom. I delighted in listening to him as he sat on the end of the bed and told me about his busy day at "school." He shared garbled stories of coloring, cutting and pasting construction paper.

That summer we watched and rewatched the *Princess Bride, Zorro, Rikki-Tikki-Tavi* and countless other favorite movies with heroes and villains. Chase was as content to read books and watch movies with me that long summer as he had been to berry pick and hike the summer before. Yet I knew that autumn weather would once again bring talk of a move south.

The day did come when Chuck gathered their belongings into the truck and left on the ferry, and a few days later Bob and I took Jennifer and Chase to the airport to join him. I blinked back hot tears as we checked them in for a flight to Seattle. They might as well be moving to the moon. I knew that we would be lucky to see each other once a year. Chase would turn four soon. I doubted that he'd even remember me in a couple of months. I was certain everyone in the airport could hear my heart breaking.

Our house was horribly quiet those first weeks after they left for Oklahoma. I spent time building a small photo album for Chase, hoping that he'd remember his instant grandma in Alaska. I called Oklahoma often, though it was difficult to have a long telephone conversation with a three-year-old. My heart broke as he asked, "Grandma, come see me now. When am I coming home to Alaska? How is Papa?" And, "Grandma, do you know that in Oklahoma you can't even grow blueberries? Could you please send me blueberry bushes to grow?" I treasured each little chat we had.

The months passed and we got photos from Jennifer, a

lot of e-mails and periodic phone calls from Chase. For his fourth birthday I sent him a video about a kangaroo in Australia. Chase loved the movie and hurried to ask Jennifer if he could have a kangaroo. After all, they had some acreage and enough room for a kangaroo. Jennifer wisely told him, "It's okay with me, but go ask your dad." A very disappointed Chase returned to the kitchen to tell Jennifer that his dad said "no." Then his face lit with a great idea. In a small whisper he said to Jennifer, "Let's call Grandma in Alaska. She'll send us one!"

When Jennifer told me the kangaroo story, I knew that I'd made it. I was someone's grandmother, not for an instant, but forever.

Valerie A. Horner

A Grandmother Again

Every child born into the world is a new thought of God, an ever-fresh and radiant possibility.

Kate Douglas Wiggin

Each time is like the first time. I'm a grandmother again.

Ryan was my first grandchild, and I thought nothing could surpass the feeling. He expanded my life the moment I felt his finger curl around mine. My world was never the same again.

Jenny blew in during a snowstorm, and the moment she set her dark eyes upon mine, I was her prisoner.

Jake's smile was in his eyes, and when he opened them during our introduction, I wondered how I could have thought life was complete without his presence.

And now my daughter-in-law Liz has given birth to Ben. I think of him as gentle Ben because, though his cry is gusty, his gaze is thoughtful and I sense a gentleness within his soul—one I can't wait to share.

I will need time with this fourth grandchild, for we have important moments to fill and life to study. The clouds especially. I have much to say about clouds. I don't think we pay enough attention to the sky. I want to look up with Ben and see what we can find up there. Raindrops can be interesting if you try to catch them in your mouth as they fall. Snowflakes can be just as enticing, especially when they add up to a snowman or a sleigh ride. And the wind—we can't forget the wind blowing an autumn leaf from a tree. Perhaps we could follow it down the path. Ben and I have a lot to do together.

Exploring is one of them. Growing things in the summer and chasing worms and ants, and playing with pebbles and dirt—we will find time for all of this, as well as sitting next to one another and just thinking. Or telling stories. Or sharing feelings. Ben and I can do that any time. I'll clear my schedule.

I don't want to rush Ben. But I have so much to share. A big porch with seashells on it. Rocking chairs eager to be filled. A first trip to the ocean. A walk through the sand. The search for sea glass.

I am not the only one waiting. My animal family waits. I have cats that will purr this baby to sleep and a dog that will wash his face with affection. My songbird will teach him beauty; the turtles, patience; the fish, serenity. I will show this child how animals love and give and share and take away loneliness. When he is old enough, we shall sleep in the big bed together. I will assure this new grandchild that when there is a nightmare floating around, the cats and the dog will chase it away.

There are limits to the things I can do. I cannot solve eating problems, sleeping problems, potty-training problems or disciplinary problems, except when they occur on my time and property. Instead, I shall concentrate my efforts on the really important matters in life. I shall make sure the outside birdfeeder is filled so Ben and I can watch the birds dine. I will make certain we have a full supply of coloring books and crayons. I shall always set aside time for the urgent business of sucking lollipops and slurping ice cream. And I shall try never to be too busy for a game of marbles, or too rigid to break a rule now and then.

Ben will remind me of the important matters in life, such as smiling and laughing and skipping and crawling and jumping and running and whispering special secrets to each other. We will explore winding roads and backyard mysteries, and each day will hold a new discovery.

For everything in this world, it will be his first time.

And a first time for me, again.

Harriet May Savitz

"Grandma, you play like you want to have kids
of your own someday."

What Will I Call You?

Children are God's apostles, sent forth, day by day, to preach love, and hope and peace.

James Russell Lowell

When he was seven years old Robbie came home with a sad little face and tear-stained cheeks.

"Honey, what's wrong?" I asked, gathering my son in my arms.

"Mom," he wailed, "tomorrow at school we're gonna talk about grammas and grampas. Everybody's got 'em but me. I wish I had some."

"Why, sweetheart," I said sympathetically, "you do have some. You have Mimi and Nonie, and Henni and Pa-Pa." Just saying their names allowed me to realize Robbie's dilemma, but I forged ahead explaining, "You just don't call them Granny and Granddaddy like the other kids do."

"Well, I wish I did," he hiccupped, wiping his eyes with his sleeve.

"I wish you did too. I guess they thought nicknames would be cuter and . . . sound younger." Pulling him into the kitchen I continued, "I'll tell you what. Let's have some treats and we'll plan something really good for you to say about your grandparents tomorrow. But first I'll make you a promise. When you grow up and have your kids, I promise you they will call me Grandma and call your daddy Grandpa, okay?"

I'd always remembered that promise, but hadn't had the chance to keep it. Robbie grew into a good-looking hunk of a guy with a marvelous personality but didn't marry until after he was thirty and even then didn't have children of his own. His job put his name before the public and required personal appearances, so he was well known. We were very close, even though he lived in another state.

One evening right before Christmas, my husband took a long distance call from Rob. After they had talked quietly for a long time I heard Don say, "Okay, Rob, if you're sure, I'll tell Mom."

I thought, *What's that about?*

Later that evening Don told me a secret kept from me. When Rob was eighteen, during spring break, he spent one of those wild, uncontrollable weekends with a girl he didn't know. One night—no controls—and a child was the result. That had been twelve years ago. The girl, ashamed of the event, refused to divulge any name and made no demands for eight years. Eventually she needed financial assistance and consulted an agency. They insisted that the father be found to help with expenses. Rob had been contacted and notified to report for a DNA test. For the last four years he'd known about his son. He was supporting the boy financially and saw him from time to time when his job brought him to their area. Robbie told his secret to his dad when he first found out, but made him promise not to tell me. Later he would confide, "Mom, I wanted what you wanted for me; the center aisle of the church first, then the picket fence and then children. I hated to be such a disappointment to you."

Incredibly, hearing that story was a Christmas present for me. Our grandchild lived in a small town not sixty miles from us. My first thought was how many years we'd all wasted and how deprived the child must feel. Of course I would accept and love him. I knew grandparents who had turned away from the identical situation. It was their loss.

"I can't wait to see him. Let's go tomorrow," I said to my husband. "What must that poor child think of his absentee family?" What had he said when he was seven years old and it was time to talk about his grandparents?

After calling first, we drove over the next day. I was as excited as though a baby were on the way. We drove into their driveway and I jumped out of the car almost before it stopped. On the front porch was a young boy standing beside his bicycle. I kept telling myself, *Slow down, don't smother him.*

I smiled as I approached him, "Do you know who I am?"

He nodded. Then he moved a little closer to me, grinned and asked, "What will I call you?"

With tears in my heart I said, "Grandma. Please call me Grandma."

And I opened my arms to him.

Ruth Hancock

Love at First Sight

In praising and loving a child, we love and praise not that which is, but that which we hope for.

Goethe

Renee was four years old when we adopted her. Cute, tiny, talkative and strong-willed are all words I used to describe our new daughter. "Prodigal" was not in my vocabulary.

But as the years passed, it became apparent that Renee had an insurmountable problem bonding. Her first four years of neglect had changed her irreversibly. I often wished I could have held her as a baby, rocking and singing her lullabies. Certainly she would know how to return love if she had been given love as a baby.

I often wondered what she had looked like as an infant. I knew she was an extremely tiny preemie, but did she have her same dark hair and olive complexion? I had no way to know; there were no pictures.

Most of all, I wondered how to cope with her refusal of our love, year after year after year. As a teenager Renee rebelled against all authority and eventually left home, calling only when she got into desperate trouble. Finally, I could no longer handle the pain of her coming and going, and our communication ceased.

So it was a surprise when Renee contacted me one December. She was married. She had a baby girl. She wanted to come home. How could I say no? Yet, knowing my daughter and our painful, tumultuous history, how could I say yes? I couldn't bear having a grandchild ripped from my heart, too, when Renee, tired of her present situation, would move on—her pattern of many years.

I tried to resist the urge to see her and the baby, feeling it was best for all of us, but something stirred in my heart. Maybe it was the Christmas spirit. Maybe it was my desire to hold the new baby. Maybe I just wanted to see my daughter again. All I know is I found myself telling Renee that she and the baby could come for a visit.

On the day they were to arrive, I grew apprehensive. *What if she doesn't come?* That wouldn't be a shock by any stretch of the imagination. In fact, it was the norm for Renee. Then I wondered, *What if she does come? What will I do? Will we have anything to talk about? Anything in common?* The hours stretched by, and I kept myself busy with the multitudes of things I needed to do before Christmas.

Then the doorbell rang.

I opened the door. Renee stepped inside, clutching a wrapped bundle in her arms. She pulled the soft blanket away from the baby's face and placed Dyann into my arms. It was love at first sight. This tiny baby—my granddaughter—grabbed my heart, never to let it go. She had dark eyes and a head full of straight, black hair that begged for a lacy headband. In her features I saw her mother's lips, her cheeks and her slight build, and instantly knew I was looking at an incredible likeness of the baby I was never able to hold—my daughter.

Dyann wiggled and made sweet gurgling sounds as I cuddled her to my heart, knowing she would be there forever, no matter what happened in the future.

In those first years of my granddaughter's life, I bonded with her in a special way, offering the security and unconditional love that she so desperately needed in her unstable environment. I bought frilly dresses and lacey tights, and I took hundreds of pictures and hours of video of this effervescent child.

Dyann is now thirteen years old, and I cherish her with all my heart. And though her mother eventually deserted her, Dyann still keeps a sweet spirit and visits us often. On those summer and holiday visits I often mistakenly call her by my daughter's name. Dyann giggles and asks, "Grandmother, why do you keep calling me Renee?" I tell her the words she longs to hear as she snuggles into my embrace. "Because you look just like your mother, and I'll love you forever."

Laura Lawson

Loving Lauren

But Jesus said, "Let the little children come to me, and do not forbid them; for of such is the kingdom of heaven."

Matthew 19:14

"This is my mother, and she's divorced." The tiny blonde six-year-old smiled up at my son. Before he could reply, his own six-year-old daughter jumped in to tell the girl's mom, "This is my dad, and he's divorced, too!" Three months later I became a step-grandmother to Lauren.

I had never seen her first tooth or watched her first off-balance baby steps. I had never heard her first words or seen her struggle to tie her shoes. What I did see was a spoiled only child. Both sets of her grandparents spent lots of money buying her many gifts, and she came to me suggesting I buy her this or that expensive toy. I declined to enter her competition. The name "Jesus" was alien to Lauren. She had never ever been to Sunday school. She was a stranger to my world.

While her features and hair color fit in with my grand-daughters', her personality didn't. She was easily offended. Minor teasing sent her sobbing into her room. I had roughhoused with my little tomboys since babyhood. Lauren cried if I even tickled her. It was easy to compare her to my granddaughters, and she always lost in the comparison. Wimpy. Touchy. Too sensitive. How could I love a child so alien, one I didn't even know?

The Lord whispered, "Rachel, Lauren needs your love."

"How can I love her, Lord? Every sentence out of her mouth starts with 'I want.' I can't even play with her. She cries over every little thing. I can't get close enough to love her."

"How can she learn about me if you don't show her?"

"I don't know! I'm trying, Lord. But all I do is make her cry!"

"You don't want to love her."

"Okay, you're right. I don't want to love her. I'm tired of tiptoeing around her feelings. But I am willing to see her with your eyes."

The thought came unbidden. "She has to share her mother with two other little girls."

He had me there. Lauren had not complained when she became the middle child after being the only child all her life. In fact, she was delighted to have ready-made playmates.

"She loves to help."

I had to give God a nod on that one, too. Lauren loved to "cook" and set the table and even clean up. In fact, when dinner was over, my granddaughters vanished, while Lauren happily cleared the table and helped me rinse the dishes.

A few weeks later my son called. Could I possibly watch Lauren overnight? My granddaughters were with their mother and he had won a weekend stay in a hotel. He and his bride had never had a honeymoon.

Lauren arrived with her doll and pajamas. We spent the

weekend playing dominoes, watching old Disney movies and eating popcorn. Lauren was enchanted. Spending time, not money, was a new and exciting concept. The weekend passed much too quickly. I began to see her in a new light. She was a loving child. As she became more comfortable with me, she blossomed, chattering about all kinds of subjects.

Lauren's seventh birthday arrived a few months later. I blinked twice and she was ten.

The phone rang. "Hi, Grandma."

"Hi, Lauren. What's up?"

"Oh, nothing. I'm just kinda bored."

"Where are your sisters?"

"With their mom."

"Isn't this your weekend with your dad?"

"Yeah, but he's on a business trip."

"Are you lonely?"

"Yeah. There's no one to play with." Lauren hadn't been an only child for a long time.

"Do you want me to come get you?"

"Yes!"

We stopped off at Target on our way back to the house. As we walked up and down the aisles of the housewares department, Lauren happily chirped, "My Grandmother Houston loves pretty china." She pointed at the picture frame display. "My Grandmother Willy loves picture frames like those."

Grinning down at her I asked, "And what does this grandmother love?" I hoped she'd say "Jesus," but she didn't.

Smiling shyly she answered in one word: "Me!"

Rachel R. Patrick

And Then There Was Hailey

The future destiny of the child is always the work of the mother.

Napoleon Bonaparte

It was a hot summer afternoon just before my daughter Julia's senior year in college when she called long distance.

"Mom, I'm . . . I'm . . . pregnant."

Dumbstruck, I could barely breathe, let alone talk.

My mind raced. *She'd only been dating her latest boyfriend for six months. How could this happen? How would she ever finish college?* I took a deep breath and listened to what Julia had to say through her tears.

Her words tumbled out as if she were a defense attorney addressing a jury. "His mom thinks we should get married, but I'm just not ready for that. I really don't know him well enough. I know we made a mistake and I'm very, very sorry, but. . ."

Oh no, here it comes, I thought.

"Mom, this is my baby. I am this child's mother. I know it won't be easy, but I know I can do it."

I sucked in a big gulp of air and whispered a prayer of thanks.

But then I started to worry. How would Julia be able to finish college? How could she attend classes, work her two part-time jobs and take care of a baby?

Julia loved college. She loved living in a big house off campus with five other girls. And most of all, she loved the parties and the social life. How could she possibly continue that lifestyle while she was pregnant?

The answer came two months later, just before school started, when Julia and her boyfriend moved into a tiny apartment off campus. He explained, "I know this isn't the ideal situation, but I have a responsibility to Julia and to the baby. I'm going to be here to help her through this pregnancy. I'll work while she finishes school."

The following March I received a phone call that woke me from a deep sleep.

"Hi, Grandma!" The words rattled through my brain like fireworks as I shot out of the bed. "Baby Hailey and Julia are doing fine."

Julia dropped out of college for two semesters to stay home and take care of Hailey full-time while her boyfriend worked at a lumberyard. During those carefree summer days Julia experienced the joy of motherhood.

Her phone calls and letters to me sang tales about Hailey's every little accomplishment, from rolling over to smiling, about their long walks with a borrowed stroller, and about rummage sales where Julia found "tons of great baby clothes and most of them are only a quarter or fifty cents!"

That summer Julia developed a sense of calmness and organization that I'd never seen in my partying college coed. She had been transformed into a mom who was spending every one of her summer days simply cherishing her new baby daughter. Not once did I hear her mention that she missed the college parties or the shenanigans with her old friends.

One day in September, after Julia started back to school to finish her senior year, she phoned. "Mom, there's a conference for people all over the United States who are experts in my major. My professors really want me to go. The hotel where it's at is just a few miles from your house."

Before she could even ask, I shouted into the phone, "Yes! I'd love to watch Hailey!" It would be my first full day alone with my only grandchild. I could feel a giddy sense of joy bubbling up inside.

As I watched my daughter prepare to leave her daughter the morning of the conference, I listened as she put the well-being and safety of her child ahead of anything else in her life. I nodded enthusiastically at Julia's long list of things to do and how to do them for Hailey.

That day was nonstop joy for me as I played with, strolled, talked to, laughed with, fed, took pictures of and rocked my baby granddaughter. I found myself just watching her sleep, as I had done so many times when my own children were tiny.

A few weeks later Julia called me again in the middle of the day, bursting with news. "Mom, I had a long talk with the head of the department today at school. She said she can't get over how different I am this semester. She said I'm so organized and my attitude is so positive and that the entire department is amazed at how much I've accomplished and how well I'm doing in my classes."

My mind and heart swelled with pride and awe at the way my daughter's life was unfolding right before my eyes.

When I look back to that summer day when my unmarried daughter told me she was pregnant, I knew our worlds were about to change drastically. But little did I know that Julia's unselfish courage to give birth to her unplanned child, at a time in her life when motherhood was definitely not on her list of things to do, would be a new beginning for our family.

I learned that one of the joys of being a grandmother comes from watching your daughter grow into a mother.

Patricia Lorenz

2

GENERATIONS OF LOVE

And now abide in faith, hope, and love, these three; but the greatest of these is love.

1 Corinthians 13:13

Oohoo

Love is all we have, the only way we can help the other.

Euripedes

The whole town called her Oohoo. Until the day she died peacefully in her sleep at the age of ninety-nine, many never knew her real name. I was the grandchild who coined the name when I was four or five. My mother would walk me the two blocks to my grandma's house and help me climb the steep steps to her massive front door, which she always left unlocked. As Mom turned the knob and opened the door she would sing out, "Ooooooo hoooooooooo." Almost immediately, the beautiful, stately, white-haired lady with the big smile would come running down her staircase and scoop me into her arms.

I was a chubby, awkward, middle child, growing up in a small town in the 1950s where everybody knew everybody and all of their business. For some unknown reason, I experienced in my youth what too many kids are still experiencing today. If it hadn't been for Oohoo and the safe haven of her loving home, I might have fallen through the cracks. By age ten I had learned to "stuff down my feelings and insecurities," and by sixteen I was one hundred pounds overweight. But at Oohoo's house I never felt judged. At school I was a well-known troublemaker who had been in and out of the principal's office and suspended many times. But Oohoo loved me unconditionally and expected only the best from me.

My sister, Donna, was my hero and role model. She was four years older and had always been everything I wanted to be: head cheerleader, prom queen, valedictorian, yearbook queen, size eight. My younger brother, Duke, was just as admirable: star athlete, A+ student, Mr. Popularity. Then there was "Poor Debbie." I heard that name applied to me so often that I lost count. Eventually I began drinking and smoking and trying anything I could sniff or swallow. The label "at-risk youth" had not yet been coined, but I could have been the poster child.

Oohoo kept her door unlocked for a crying ten-year-old when she was called "Fatso," for a fifteen-year-old who wasn't chosen for the cheerleading squad, for a seventeen-year-old who wrecked the car and was afraid to tell her parents, and for a twenty-one-year-old who didn't want to live anymore.

My poor parents took me to counselors and doctors and were always trying to pull me out of my abyss. Upon the advice of a child psychologist, they agreed to let me stay with Oohoo temporarily. She never mentioned my weight, never condemned me and always treated me with respect and dignity. She was tough on curfew and following house rules, but she immersed me in love and became my role model.

Every Sunday from as early as I can remember, Oohoo picked me up for Sunday school. She taught there for seventy-eight years and practiced every word of what she preached. I never heard her say one unkind word about anyone; she was a friend to people of all backgrounds, cultures and races. Oohoo taught me the meaning of selfless giving, generosity and unconditional love. It is life's tests that make us either bitter or better. Oohoo taught me to be better.

I didn't know at that time about Oohoo's own broken heart or her problems with my grandfather. Against all odds, my precious grandmother had graduated from the University of Missouri in 1919, and she inspired me to stay in school and go on to college as well. Her house was filled with poetry and literature from her own classes. Her old trunk was filled with costumes from her days in Hollywood when she boldly accepted a journalism assignment where young women then were not encouraged to go.

Oohoo had been a teacher and a journalist, and I became a teacher and a journalist too. Who would ever have thought I would be an English and drama teacher using some of the old books and costumes I carried from Oohoo's house?

I am so grateful that Oohoo lived long enough to see me marry my college sweetheart, lose one hundred pounds, return to my family as a prodigal daughter and become Teacher of the Year. I got to tell her that she was my hero on the celebration of my grandparents' sixty-fifth wedding anniversary.

She stayed with my grandfather when she had reason to leave, but he, too, turned around later in his life, realizing what a gem he had in Oohoo.

I began my career with an advantage because Oohoo taught me unconditional love and empathetic listening skills I would never have learned elsewhere. Having served now in the field of education for over thirty years, I can honestly say I believe most "problem children" could be turned around if they had a caring grandparent, an

"Oohoo," in their life. As high school and university instructors, we are told to call home at the first sign of any problem behavior, academic or otherwise. When my students' parents aren't home, or are too busy or just don't know how to help, I have the alternative solution. Invariably there is a caring, knowing, loving person already waiting to help. All I need to do is ask, "May I speak to your grandmother?"

Debra D. Peppers

One Lonely Little Boy

You save an old man and you save a unit; but you save a boy, and you save a multiplication table.

"Gipsy" Smith

When I was twelve years old I was locked up in juvenile hall after being released from a Florida reform school. I refused to return to the Children's Home Society where I was raised. I was never going back to that orphanage, even if I had to spend the rest of my life locked up in a small cage at juvenile hall.

I had been there for several months, and I had flatly refused even to walk out the front door to help them clean up the streets for fear they would take me back to that awful orphanage.

It was a Wednesday morning, and a man named Burt who worked for the court came into my cell and asked me if I wanted to go somewhere special for Thanksgiving dinner. I told him that I did not want to go outside of the juvenile shelter. I liked Burt because he was a nice man. Burt's brother had written a song, which they played on the radio, called "The Lion Sleeps Tonight."

Burt kept going on and on about Thanksgiving dinner and how a kid should not be locked up on Thanksgiving. So I finally told him that I would go.

The day before Thanksgiving, an older woman came to the shelter. She talked with me for about ten minutes. She told me that she wanted to take me to her house for Thanksgiving. She also said that no child should be locked up in a cage. Before we left I made her promise that she would bring me back the very next day.

Mrs. Usher and I walked out of the juvenile hall together and got into her car and drove to her house. As we walked in I was really surprised at what I saw. Her house was really small inside. Not like the big dormitory house that I had lived in at the orphanage—you could sleep thirty or forty people in our house at the orphanage. I was even more surprised when I went to their bathroom. I saw right away that they were not rich at all. They only had one toilet and one sink in their bathroom! They were really poor—and they did not even know it.

Of course, I had never been in a regular house before, and I did not know that regular people only had one toilet and one sink in their bathroom. That is one of the hazards of being raised in an orphanage—you never get to see what life is like in the real world. Then one day the orphanage shoves you out and everyone treats you like you are an idiot. They think you are stupid because you do not know anything about real life outside the orphanage.

Wednesday afternoon and evening were very difficult for me. I wanted so badly just to get out of there and go back to my cage at the juvenile hall. There must have been fifty people going in and out of that house, each doing this and that, all getting ready for that big Thanksgiving Day dinner the next day.

I was really scared, too. I didn't like people very much.

Especially grown people. They can do some really bad things to you when you are a kid. I hardly moved an inch because I was so scared. I never got out of my chair, nor did I move in any direction until almost all those people were gone late that afternoon. Mrs. Usher came into the living room and asked me if I wanted a bottle of Coke. I told her thank you, but that I did not care for anything. I wanted that Coke real, real bad, too. But I was just too scared to take it. I thought about that Coke all day long, and how good it would have tasted.

Late that night, when everyone was asleep, I snuck into the kitchen real slow and quiet-like, and I took a cold Coca-Cola out of the refrigerator. I drank it real fast, in about five seconds, and then hid the bottle cap behind the refrigerator. After that I warmed the cold bottle against my stomach so it would be warm like the other bottles, then put it in the bottle carton so no one would ever know I drank it.

The next day was almost as unbearable for me as the first day, all because of the strange people coming for the big dinner. I would rather have died than to have gone through such a horrible experience as that dinner. All those big, strange people laughing and joking and making all kinds of noise. I had never been so embarrassed and so scared in all my life, and that is the God's truth. Not scared like being scared of the dark—scared in a different kind of way. I cannot explain it, not even to myself.

I hardly ate anything that day, even though I had never seen so much food in all my life. I sure was glad when it was finally over.

Later that night, after everyone else had gone to bed, Mrs. Usher took me out onto her front porch and we talked for hours and hours. She was a real nice lady. I had never once just sat and talked with anyone in my whole life. It was my first "nice and slow time," as she called it, and I really liked it.

I will never forget her kindness and her warm smile. But what I could not understand was why she was doing all of this for me. It was very difficult for me to understand why anyone would be kind to me. So I kept one eye on her all the time.

Mrs. Usher got up from her chair and went into the kitchen. She returned with a small bottle of Coke for each of us. She smiled and handed one to me. I will never forget that, either. That was the best Coke I ever drank in my whole entire life.

The next morning we ate breakfast together. Then she told me to go into the bedroom and get my things together so she could take me back to the juvenile hall, like she promised.

While I was in the bedroom packing I heard her in the hallway talking on the telephone to the authorities. She asked them why I was being sent back to the reform school. She wanted to know what I had done that was so bad that I had to be sent back there. They told her that I had done nothing wrong, but they had nowhere else to put me. I heard her get very mad at them and tell them that she was not going to bring me back to the juvenile hall to be "locked up again like an animal."

God knows I loved that woman for saying that! That was the most wonderful thing anyone ever did for me as a child. That, of all the things in my life, was the one thing that made me want to become somebody someday. That one little sentence was the small and only light that guided my life for the next forty-five years.

I stayed there with Mrs. Usher for several weeks, and then I turned thirteen and left to go out on my own. I continued to see the Usher family on and off for the next twenty or thirty years, until their deaths. I know they wanted to adopt me. But when it was discussed I told Grandma Usher that it was too late for me. She placed her hands over her face and cried. I told her, "I have to make it on my own now, 'cause I'm a man."

I just wish that I could have shown her how much I really loved her, but I did not know how to show love. I didn't even know what love meant or what it felt like.

Grandma Usher is now in heaven. I hope she knows how much I love and respect her. I think she knows how much she added to the life of one lonely little boy that nobody else in the world wanted by teaching me "nice and slow time" . . . and love.

Roger Kiser

The Lincoln Zephyr at Midnight

I was only three years old when my world crumbled.

I knew my mother was sick, but I did not know how seriously ill she really was.

One day a big black car came to our house and took her away to a dark, stone hospital high on a hill several miles from home. It was a tuberculosis sanitarium. Daddy could go inside the building, but we children were not allowed to enter. I remember standing by the somber building and looking at a small window high above me. Grandma and Daddy would say, "There's Mama; wave to Mama."

I waved, but all I could see was the faint flutter of a small white hand in the window up there.

As time went by, my father and grandma decided it was too difficult to maintain our large home and family. So the household goods were stored in a relative's barn, and my three brothers each went to a different sympathetic family member's home to live. I stayed with Grandma. We traveled all over Iowa. We would stay in someone's home for a few weeks, then Grandma would pack her small black satchel and stow my things in a pillowcase and we'd go someplace else for a while. Thankfully we had a lot of relatives and friends eager to help.

Daddy rented a room in the town near the hospital so he could be near his beloved Gracie. He got a part-time job driving a milk truck. I was bewildered and sad. I did not understand what had happened. Where were my parents? Where were my brothers? And where was my sweet little dog, Jiggs?

Through it all, Grandma was my savior. She comforted me as no one else could. One day we boarded a small train and rode one hundred miles to her son's home by the Mississippi River. What a thrill it was to ride on a real train with Grandma beside me! My uncle met us at the depot and drove us in his Model A car to his farm a few miles away. We were happy there. I almost forgot about my real family . . . until around midnight every night.

There was a railroad track across the road from the farmhouse. I loved watching the trains roar by in the day-time. But in the dark of the night the mournful wail of the whistle on the sleek new Lincoln Zephyr would waken me as it sped down the tracks on its mighty trek from Chicago. As it faded away into the darkness, I remembered. . . . I was in a strange bed, in a strange house, and I didn't know why my family wasn't there.

But Grandma was. She would hold me in her arms and soothe me with her lovely voice until I drifted off to sleep once more, the sound of the whistle ringing in my ears.

After my mother recovered and our family was together again, Grandma lived with us until the end of her days.

She has been gone for over sixty years now, but to this day the sound of a train in the darkness takes me back to those lonely nights when I was three, and I still yearn for the comforting, warm arms of my grandmother.

Kathryn Kimzey Judkins

The Fabric of Love

Nothing is so contagious as example.

Francois Rochefoucauld

As a child, I memorized the months: May, June, July, Grandma. During the hottest days of summer, Grandma rode the train from Boston, bringing a suitcase of kosher food, her own special dishes, her sewing box and a bulging sack of remnants. She collected the cloth to create outfits for me.

While Grandma sewed, I fingered the hill of bright fabrics and made rows of her spools. In Russia, Grandma told me, she wore dingy brown so she blended in under the bed when she hid from the pogroms. She wanted me, her first granddaughter, to stand out.

Haloed by a bright floor lamp, Grandma's thick glasses glinted as she pushed the needle in and out, each stab deliberate and focused. In Russia she had sewn near the dying fire, squinting in the dim light. When she came to America, Grandma sewed in a sweatshop lit by pale ceiling bulbs.

"Maybe I married your grandfather for the light," she told me. "He promised we'd have enough money for lamps in every room." My grandfather kept his promise: Grandmother's house was fine and bright. She sewed her son sailor suits of thick navy wool and flossy white piping. She sewed her husband linen shirts. For herself, she made serious cotton shirtwaists that nipped her wrists and circled her throat.

I watched as she gathered turquoise cotton in a pleated quartet, then let it flow into the stream of thread. I swayed along with the rhythm of the gather and release, holding my breath to count how many folds the needle penetrated.

The year I was twelve, Grandma broke her hip and did not come to visit. I began junior high school wearing hand-me-downs, fabrics that had stretched and faded on my older cousin's body, then sighed and adapted to me. I liked the quiet anonymity of blouses and skirts, too big, yet vaguely resembling the other girls' outfits.

Then Grandma sent me a box of clothes—dumpy flowered skirts that were for a baby-faced girl, not a teenager.

"Nobody wears these kinds of clothes," I told my mother.

"You will wear them," she informed me.

The day I wore my grandmother's skirt, I sank into the back of my classrooms so no one would notice me. During English, I spilled ink on the cloth petunias. On my walk home, my hem got splattered with mud. During dinner, spaghetti sauce stained my lap. Gradually, I eased out of Grandma's childish clothes and back into my bland disguise.

That summer, we drove to Boston to visit Grandma.

The brown houses were glued together with no patches of grass between them. Grandma's apartment was at the bottom of a steep hill. When she answered the door, her eyes were clouded, her fingers curled.

But her hug was fierce and strong.

Piles of fabric adorned her apartment: a scrap of cerise

silk here, a heap of lemony taffeta there. Her narrow bed was a pile of pink checked cottons, slinky purple rayons and sturdy burnt orange wools. Beside the small television, her sewing machine wore a frothy green net petticoat.

My mother looked inside the refrigerator. My father looked inside the medicine cabinet.

"Stay with your grandmother while we go to the store," Mother told me. I followed my parents, wanting to go with them, but they closed the door behind them.

"Sit, darling," Grandma said, patting the sofa. I perched on the worn brocade cushion and she brought me an ancient seafoam green dress from the hook on her bathroom door.

"Try this on," she said. I turned my back before I slipped out of my cousin's navy blue cotton jumper. Gingerly I slid the fragile dress over my head and felt it wrap me snugly.

"Ahh," Grandma said, folding her good hand around the stiffened claw of her other hand. She motioned me to the bathroom to have a look.

I balanced on the edge of the tub so I could see myself in the splotchy mirror. I turned sideways, awed at how the dress hugged my beginning body. Ahh, I looked sophisticated and alluring.

"Here's another," Grandma said, holding out a burgundy moiré.

For an hour colors spilled and sang, the fabrics like foreign children, each whispering in a different language. As I wiggled into the slinky dresses, I saw myself, a character in a long story of thread and fabric, a story unraveling into many different endings.

My mother wouldn't let me wear the dresses Grandma had given me.

"Too tight," she said.

So I decided to sew my own clothes.

The fabric store smelled of something new and barely opened. The bolts were alert soldiers. The clerks raced around armed with scissors, dripping with remnants, their mouths prickly with pins. I selected a shiny orange, purple and black pattern, something surreal that I would never find in Sears. From the easy-pattern booklet I chose a fitted waist and plunging neck.

At home, I rolled out the fabric and stared. I could not remember what to do, so I dialed Grandma.

I heard the murmur of television in the background while she thought about my questions.

"First make yourself a nice cup of tea," she said, her voice halting and dusty. "While you drink it, see yourself wearing this dress. Then, take your scissors and cut."

I found some Lipton's behind my mother's Nescafe. As I sipped, I saw myself sauntering through the hallway at school, a vision of color and style. Boys paused by their lockers and watched silently as I walked past.

But once I broke into the cloth, my scissors bucked, the fabric fought. Once I inserted the needle, insinuated the thread, my seams squirmed and refused to lie flat. Despite all my work, my dress wore a prissy, puckered look. Then I saw my mistake: when I had gathered the fabric, I'd yanked the thread too tightly. The dress had no room to stretch and grow.

A month after Grandma died, I received a battered cardboard box filled with scraps of material: a length from a dotted swiss I'd worn when I was three, a scrap from a fiesta dress I'd swirled in at age five, forest green velveteen from my cousin's wedding. I fingered each remnant of cloth and imagined the vest I might make. I knew just how to do it: I would sit in front of the light gathering and piercing, gathering and binding, gathering and, finally, letting go.

Deborah Shouse

A Legacy of Love

It would be more honorable to our distinguished ancestors to praise them in words less, but in deed to imitate them more.

Horace Mann

"Who's that, Grandma?" Four-year-old Taylor pointed to a delicate gold photo frame I'd carefully placed atop my new oak desk. I pulled my oldest grandchild into my lap so he could peer closer at the face of the woman smiling back at us. "That's Mam-maw Gladys," I replied.

I reached for the picture, my fingers carefully tracing the outline of the soft countenance returning my gaze . . . her clear blue eyes, the wrinkle lines that creased her forehead and the soft smile that always brought me peace.

My mind filled with remembrances of my mother. Always the peacemaker, it seemed she never made anyone angry. Even though she was barely able physically, she baby-sat my young daughter so I could work. She always made time for her grandchildren. When she wasn't with them, she was making something for them with her hands.

Then her illness progressed. She was in the hospital for three weeks, suffering complications from chronic lymphoma. The doctor wanted to experiment with a simple operation that might give her another year of life. She agreed so she could be around to greet her long-awaited first great-grandchild.

After the surgery failed, she had to depend upon a respirator to breathe. When the doctors determined she wasn't going to breathe on her own, the respirator was removed and she was moved to a private room. Mom died there the next day, exactly a month before Taylor's birth.

Still grieving, I traveled five hundred miles to be with my family and welcome my new grandson.

A few days later, my daughter asked me to sit with Taylor while she visited her doctor. As I rocked him and cradled him in my arms, suddenly I realized that my love for Taylor was the same that Mam-maw Gladys had for my children. At that moment, I felt so close to her. And through my tears, I understood why she had sacrificed and cared so much for her family. I realized her love for us was so deep, so wide, so unconditional—a love I was only beginning to learn to give.

"She looks like you, Grandma!" Taylor's voice jolted me back to the present. He touched the gold-framed photo tenderly. My eyes turned to his, and a soft smile came to my lips and heart, for then I knew my mother's love and peace.

Libby C. Carpenter

My Official Storybook Grandma

It is sweet to feel by what fine spun threads our affections are drawn together.

Lawrence Sterne

I spent most of my young life never having what I thought was a typical, storybook grandma. My dad's mother didn't live close enough, and my mom's mother died before I was born.

At the age of sixteen I lived in Alaska, where I met my future husband, who joined our mission team there. From the beginning, Mike talked about his grandma, who lived next door. She allowed him, his three brothers and sister to raid the refrigerator. She defended them ruthlessly. The more he shared about her, the more jealous I became.

After a year of long-distance romance, Mike invited me to his home in New York for Thanksgiving. I was so excited—until I found out I was going to be staying with the famous Grandma Reba. It was common knowledge that she had not liked most of Mike's girlfriends. I promised myself that I would not talk too much (impossible), swore I would not laugh too loud (unfeasible), but most of all I hoped she would love me.

I arrived and met his family, and then Mike and I walked across the street. I was more nervous about meeting Grandma Reba than anyone else. As soon as we entered, I felt the atmosphere change. Family pictures filled shelves. Homemade crocheted afghans dotted the living room furniture. Next to her chair sat a basket filled with her current afghan project and crochet hooks. A tiny lady, standing around five feet tall with curly gray hair and incredibly thick eyeglasses, came from the kitchen to greet us. She hugged Mike and I could feel her eyes moving over me. All I could think was, *Please like me.* She welcomed me warmly, and I began blabbing. She listened and smiled.

When Grandma Reba was able to interject a word or two, she told me that she would show me my room. Mike left, and she escorted me down the hall and opened a door. Inside was a bed draped in one of her homemade afhgans. She apologized for the room being so small, then asked me what I would like for breakfast. Desperate to please, I told her, "Anything is fine." Of course, true to form, I had to elaborate. "Eggs, bacon, sausage, cereal, bagel, orange juice, coffee, anything, really."

She smiled at my nervous chatter and said, "Okay."

We watched one of her favorite shows (I think it was *Wheel of Fortune*), then she went to bed. I already loved her but was certain she hated me because I had not shut up since she met me.

The next morning I was greeted by delicious breakfast smells. As I walked into the kitchen, I saw the table loaded with all the breakfast foods I had named. She stood at the skillet frying bacon.

"Oh, is everyone coming over for breakfast?" I asked.

She smiled and said, "No, honey. It's all for you."

For the first time since meeting her I was speechless.

After falling into my chair in shock, I glanced up.

"Aren't you hungry?" she asked.

I told her I would never be able to eat all of this and that I'd be too fat for Mike to date and what a sweetheart she was and how I couldn't believe she had cooked all this just for me. Obviously, I had found my tongue. She laughed and asked me what I wanted tomorrow. I told her cereal, coffee and orange juice was all.

After our visit, I knew I had experienced a storybook grandma. I was now as much a fan of Grandma Reba as her own grandkids. During the next year, I wrote her letters and sent her one of my high school graduation pictures.

The following year, Mike moved to Alaska and we became engaged. We decided to spend that Christmas in New York with his family. I decided to purchase my wedding dress there so his mom, sister and grandma would feel more included in the preparations. Unfortunately, Grandma Reba could not go shopping with us. When I greeted her this second time, it was as if she had shrunk. It was more obvious that her curly gray hair was a wig, her thick glasses looked thicker, and she had lost more of her hearing. It was hard to believe she was the same person, but she still had prepared my room, and each morning I woke up to cereal, orange juice and coffee—she remembered.

One evening while we were visiting her, she got up to go to bed, lost her balance and fell into the Christmas tree, knocking it over. Mike and his brother helped her up and teased her about drinking too much. She laughed, but we all knew that something was not right.

I bought my wedding dress and tried it on for her. I sang her the songs we would be singing at the wedding, and she cried. She told me how she wished she could come. I begged, but she said she would never be able to make a fifteen-hour flight.

"You'll be a beautiful bride," she beamed.

I hugged her. "I can't wait until we get married and you become my official grandma."

For Christmas that year she gave me an afghan that she crocheted just for me.

Two months after Mike and I left New York and six months before our wedding, Grandma died.

We received a box of things she wanted us to have. Apparently knowing that her time was short she'd spent her last months walking around her house, writing people's names on the things. Our trophies were a corner shelf that Mike had made for her in shop class, a picture that Mike had always loved, and my graduation picture that she had placed in a frame on one of her shelves. It was then that I realized she had told me in a very special way that she *was* my official grandma. Only family pictures were kept on her shelves. I was part of her family. I fell in love with Grandma Reba, but even better, she fell in love with me.

Michelle Rocker

"Grandma, you are always nice to us
from the inside out."

Deposition Stew

In the man whose childhood has know caresses and kindness, there is always a fibre of memory that can be touched to gentle issues.

George Eliot

The first time I saw her she was just a fat lady who served bread and soup at the shelter.

I didn't eat there all the time. Sometimes when Momma wasn't too bad, she was able to work and we had our own food. Now, don't feel bad for me and start saying things like "poor girl." I hate that. And don't start assuming that Momma is a bad person. I hate that more.

It's not her fault that Daddy lost his job and left town looking for work, never to come back. And it's not her fault she got sick right after she started working at the Food Lion down the road. People don't like it when a cashier coughs on their produce, so Mr. Ranier had to let her go. He said he would hire her back if she got rid of that cough. She was reliable, she never came in late and she never took a sick day. Maybe she should have. Maybe if she saw a doctor before things got too bad she might have gotten better.

"I have to work," she'd say, brushing off my worries as if they didn't count for anything.

Sometimes she knew a job wouldn't last. Like the time she took a position as a secretary for a lawyer downtown. Momma couldn't type and she couldn't spell, but she tried her best. When that man saw the deposition she worked on all week, he turned all red and fired her on the spot.

"That's okay, baby," Momma said. "I got paid, and I'll make some chicken and dumplings. We'll have a feast."

After that, whenever she got a good-size check, Momma would make some "deposition stew." That's what she called chicken and dumplings from then on. It was our secret recipe, and we always laughed when we ate it.

We hadn't had many reasons to laugh the first time that fat lady came to work at the shelter. She seemed nice enough though, until she started asking questions.

"How old are you, little girl?"

"I ain't little," I told her. "I'm five, and I'm big for my age."

"Yes, you are," she agreed, taking a step back to get a better look at me. "I would have guessed you were at least six," she told me, trying to get back on my good side.

I didn't trust her, but Momma said she was okay, just talking to pass the time, and I should be respectful from now on. After that, I didn't give the fat lady any lip. I didn't want her to think Momma didn't raise me right.

Momma took a bad turn soon after that; she got too sick to work. We moved into a homeless shelter and took all our meals at one soup kitchen or another. I heard someone telling her she'd better make plans for me. "Someone better be ready to take over soon," he said.

I didn't like that kind of talk.

"I make my own plans," I told Momma. "And my plans have me staying with you."

"That's what I want too, baby," she said. "And don't you ever forget that if anything bad happens, I'll always be with you, no matter where you go."

"And we'll have 'deposition stew,'" I laughed, remembering the wonderful smell of her chicken and gravy filling our old apartment.

"Deposition stew and homemade bread," she told me, giving me a hug so tight I could hardly breathe.

Then she died.

"Cold as ice" is what the paramedic said when they loaded her in the ambulance. I never saw her again. By the time anyone thought about me, I was long gone.

I wandered from shelter to shelter for a day or two, attaching myself to a crowd so no one would notice I was alone. I got by okay until I went into the place where the fat lady worked.

"Where's your momma?" she asked.

"She's not here tonight."

"I can see that. Where is she?"

"Can I please have some of that soup?" I asked, trying hard to remember to be respectful.

She poured a bowl, putting a big hunk of bread next to it before sitting me down for a long talk. "Now where is your momma? I know she wouldn't want you in here all alone."

"She's right here with me," I spit back at her. "Right by my side forever, just like she promised!"

"Is she now?" the lady asked, understanding and softening her demeanor. She had heard Momma's cough and knew she wasn't doing well. "Who will look after you now?"

"I'm not sure," I told her. "I haven't got it all figured out yet."

"Maybe I can help," she whispered. "You sit here and eat your soup, and I'll see what I can do."

A short time later, another lady, not quite as fat but otherwise looking a lot like her, came walking into the shelter offering to take me home. Seems she took in foster kids and just happened to have space for one more.

It took me a while to sort it all out, but the fat lady is momma to the one that I call Mom these days. I can't say Momma to her . . . that name belongs to my real momma, but she's okay with that.

"Call me whatever you like," she said, "just don't call me late for dinner."

That's funny, the way she puts it.

Tomorrow the fat lady is coming for dinner along with the rest of the family. Now I have a foster sister, two foster brothers and some cousins coming in from out of town. All that and a nice fat lady for a grandma. I'm pretty sure Momma will be watching, and she'll laugh along with us when my new mom and I cook up some deposition stew for everyone.

"Here Grandma, taste this," I'll say.

Bobbi Carducci

Thanks

*Letters are those winged messengers that can fly
from east to west on embassies of love.*

Jeremiah Brown Howell

Few things thrill this man more than the sight of my
grandmother's handwriting on an envelope. I always save
that piece of mail for last, saving it for when I am free to
pay it the attention it deserves.

I start with the many enclosures. My grandmother reads
at least three newspapers and clips the articles she thinks
may be of interest to family members. She prints the newspaper's name and the date the article appeared before folding the clipping so the headline is visible on top.

Today's batch includes a story about another adoptive
parent, an announcement about a book signing and tips
on defeating kidney stones. I read the clips slowly, knowing that she thought them important enough to send, and
her judgment was right on the mark.

Then I finally open my grandmother's card. She buys
discounted cards for their pictures and not the printed
text, which in this case congratulates me on a new job. The

words that matter are the ones she writes herself.

My grandmother starts where most people merely sign their name. She completely fills that page with her neat script, moves over to the facing page, and then finishes her note as the space runs out on the back of the card.

She is thanking me for hosting a birthday party. She doesn't simply say "Thanks," which would still be more than I received from others. My grandmother describes every detail she appreciated, mentions the news she heard and repeats the jokes that made her laugh. She recalls past parties I've thrown and dwells on the highlights.

Those who say that letter writing is a lost art never received mail from my grandmother, who has once again brightened my day and lessened my load.

Stephen D. Rogers

Aunt Tooty

Where there is room in the heart, there is always room in the house.

Thomas Moore

Her American name was Aunt Tilly; I don't know its Hebrew derivation, but to me she was always Aunt Tooty. She was the beloved substitute for my own grandmother, her sister Ida, who died before I was born.

Aunt Tooty was one of three sisters who immigrated to the United States just before the Russian revolution took place. Along with Ida and Tilly came Paulie; they were said (by their own account) to be the most beautiful, talented and sought-after girls in their shtetl. I believe it. The way they sewed and danced and laughed together, who wouldn't want to marry them? Besides, what other girls had the courage to secretly board a train and run away in search of a better life, as the three of them had when they were teenagers? For three weeks, until they were returned home, their mother thought they were dead. The three sisters were regal, imposing women. Tall and erect, their hair was swept up on their heads just like the empress's. They were formidable ladies who knew how to make themselves heard, noticed and respected.

But it was Aunt Tooty to whom I was truly drawn when I wanted a grandmother's love. It was to Aunt Tooty's house on Richmond Street in Philadelphia that I always wanted to go. It was Aunt Tooty's large hands and long fingers I wanted to feel caress me whenever I felt sad or scared.

Her house was really an apartment behind my uncle's appliance store. I loved the sitting room, with its bric-a-brac, teacups on doilies, silver inkwell on the writing table and sepia photographs, including one of my mother as a child with a gigantic bow in her black hair. I loved the smell of chicken soup simmering in a pot in the kitchen and the sound of Aunt Tooty pounding pastry on the wooden breadboard. I loved hearing her humming Yiddish songs as she danced around the room with me standing on top of her lace-up shoes. But most of all I loved the armoire drawer I slept in when I stayed at Richmond Street. It was the bottom drawer of a huge piece of furniture from "the old country" that pulled out to create a perfect sleeping nest for a three-and-a-half-year-old. Lined with a deliciously soft eiderdown and fluffy pillows such as you only find in Europe, that tiny space made me feel absolutely safe and loved. In the evening when I grew sleepy, Aunt Tooty tucked me in to my special bed chamber, and in the morning when I woke, she was there to greet me, her ample bosom already adorned with a cameo, a lace handkerchief tucked inside her dress for emergencies.

It was in just that place on one such morning that I awoke to my beloved Aunt Tooty singing, "I have a surprise for you!" Lifting me out of my drawer, she danced me around the room and then sat me in her lap. "You have a new baby brother!" she said. "Isn't that wonderful news?"

I knew that my mother was going to have a new baby, and I understood vaguely that its arrival was imminent when my father took me to Aunt Tooty's. I also knew that everyone waited with bated breath for it to be a boy. Mom was forty and had two daughters already, it was the least God could do for her. But I wasn't sure that it was wonderful news. I'd wanted the baby, and I was happy that my mother and he were safe. Still, what if Aunt Tooty loved him more than me? What if he got to sleep in the drawer, my drawer, and I had to be relegated to the couch, or worse, a bed! What if I could no longer dance on my Aunt Tooty's feet or if she stopped slipping me extra fresh-baked rugela or humentashen because she was too busy cooing over my new baby brother?

I needn't have worried. Aunt Tooty knew exactly how a little girl might react to news of a special sibling. "Now, you know," she said, pointing to my drawer-bed, "this is your special place when you come to see me. This isn't someplace anyone else can have when they come here. So don't think you can give this drawer to your little brother when he is old enough to sleep here. I'll fix a nice drawer for him too, but not this one. Oh, no, this one is just yours. Is that okay, *shana*?" she asked. (I loved when she called me *shana*; she told me it was Yiddish for "pretty". Then she swooped me into her arms and, humming a Yiddish melody, danced me into the kitchen for some milk and mundelbrot. The smell of simmering soup already permeated the little room. Pulling the lace hanky from her bosom, I began to suck my thumb, fingering her cameo with my free hand. The scent of her talcum reminded me of babies.

"When can I see my new brother?" I asked. I was ready to meet the long-sought-after son who I knew would never take my place, not in the drawer and not in Aunt Tooty's heart. "When can I see my new baby?"

"Today!" she said. "But first let's put away your bed. Next time you come, I want it to be all ready for you." She handed me a bag full of homemade cookies and I, in turn, relinquished her handkerchief. Together we prepared and stowed my bed, then went into the sepia sitting room to await the sound of my father's big, black Buick, the sight of my mother and the squalls of my new baby brother.

Elayne Clift

If It's Tuesday

*Few things are more delightful than grand-
children fighting over your lap.*

Doug Larson

From the kitchen I hear the crash and the baby's wail.
"Oh my gosh!" I shout as I reach the scene in the living
room. The bouncer is upended, baby and all, and her two-
year-old brother stands beside it, wide-eyed, lips quiver-
ing. I pull the baby into my arms and check her body for
welts and bruises. All clear. Hugs and kisses calm her, and
I turn my attention to the culprit, who stretches his arms
upward.

"Up," he cries. His eyes fill with tears. "Up."

I sweep him into my free arm. "It's all right, lovey," I say
between kisses. "You have to be gentle with baby sister;
you could hurt her."

It is Grandma day at my house, and I'm hoping my
grandson's rambunctious activity is a result of Easter
candy and not his recent second birthday.

I am not the kind of grandparent I intended to be. After
raising five children, I planned to model this phase of life

after my mother, who defined her grandmotherly intentions days after my first child was born. "I will not baby-sit. In fact, I'll be happy to hire a baby-sitter for you, but I will not baby-sit."

There was no doubt my mother loved the children, and they loved her, but all were content to sit across the table from one another sipping tea and eating oatmeal cookies for an hour twice a week. There was no diaper changing, lap sitting or neck nuzzling in my mother's house. Just short, polite visits and occasional dinners, always with me in attendance, the keys to the car in my pocket in case someone forgot the rules.

It worked for my mother, and I imagined it working for me. But when my son placed my first grandchild in my arms, I fell in love. Defenses melted, and the hardness in me turned to mush.

"Do I have to give him back?" I asked.

My waking hours following the birth of this baby were filled with a longing like one feels for a new love. Dropping by for baby hugs became part of my daily routine. It was a gift to hold this new little life close and breathe in his newness, to watch his face when he slept and his eyes wander around the room when he was awake. I couldn't get enough of him.

And so when it was time for my daughter-in-law to return to work, I found myself offering to baby-sit one day a week.

"Are you sure?"

I wasn't really, and I thought of telling them I'd changed my mind. *What are you thinking?* I asked myself. *This is your time. You've raised your children, cut back on work. You're free. You have time to write, read, do whatever you want. Don't you remember how old you are?*

"I'll give it a try," I told my son and his wife. "We'll see how it goes, whether it's too much."

That was the beginning of our Tuesdays together. They belonged to little Gordie and me. Everything else was put aside—appointments, phone calls, bills. I fed, diapered and cooed. I reveled in his smiles and tickled him into giggles. We played peek-a-boo and so-big and read *Goodnight Moon.* I searched his gums for budding teeth and watched as he took his first wobbly steps between the couch and coffee table, applauding himself when he reached his goal. We went to the beach and threw rocks in the water and went "so high" on the swings in the park. We stopped at the bakery and ate cookies before lunch. I heard his first words. And then words formed sentences.

The mother/disciplinarian in me from years ago no longer exists. I stand by calmly as he empties the ice tray in my refrigerator or the bowls from a kitchen cabinet. I get down on my knees with him to wipe up the water he spills from the cooler. Cheerios on the floor, a broken dish are no problem. I don't scold. I am Grandma.

Now there is a little sister who joins us on Tuesdays. Caitlin is a chubby baby who spends her days eating, sleeping and smiling. She is the promise of more firsts.

So every Tuesday my son pulls his SUV into my driveway and unloads babies and bags of diapers, clothes and bottles. A little boy strolls up my walk, smiles and holds out his arms for me to pick him up. Behind him is his father carrying an infant seat overflowing with baby girl. Her eyes crinkle in recognition when she sees me.

"Any time you feel it's too much, just let us know," he says.

Not a chance.

Alice Malloy

A Day at Grandmom's House

The chief pleasure in eating does not consist in costly seasoning, or exquisite flavor, but in yourself.

Horace

My eleven-year-old grandson Ryan was on his way to the school bus when, as he told his mother, his stomach began to bother him. It felt queasy. He didn't feel he should go to school. My daughter had a doctor's appointment in another city, so Ryan came to Grandmom's house.

He looked a bit pale when he walked in, and a bit taller, as if he had grown inches during the night. I settled him down in my big, king-sized bed, put on his favorite TV cartoons, puffed up his pillows as I once did for my own son at his age and asked him if he was hungry. That's the first thing grandmoms ask under any circumstances.

"I think I could have an orange," he said listlessly. Usually he was full of energy. Today, his body seemed limp, unable to withstand any physical activity.

So I cut up an orange and delivered it to him on a plate. He gulped it down.

Soon after I asked him again, "Would you like something else to eat?"

"I think I could have two pieces of toast," he said. "And maybe two hard-boiled eggs."

"Wonderful," I responded. I boiled some eggs, buttered some toast, put some jelly on the side and carried it on a tray to his bed.

He gulped it down.

An hour later we were both munching on our favorite cookies.

Followed by potato chips.

Followed by pretzels.

We finished just in time for lunch.

"Would you like a turkey sandwich?" I asked about noon. "With sliced tomatoes?"

"That would be great," he said.

He had some color in his face now. In fact, he seemed quite content. He lay beneath the blankets, my dog at his feet, the cats by his shoulder, the cartoons playing in the distance.

When lunch was over we attempted a game of cards, but we didn't have an entire deck. Usually, we find something to talk about, sharing things we don't share with anyone else. Today, neither one of us seemed in the mood for conversation. So we turned the cartoons back on and had an ice pop, a few more cookies, some water and some cold cereal.

He didn't move for eight hours. He just ate. And ate. And ate.

It occurred to me during this eating orgy that I had witnessed the same behavior with my son at the same age. I called it the growth spurt. He would complain about his stomach, saying that he didn't feel good. And he would stay home from school. And then eat for an entire day. It seemed he grew taller as he devoured the food. Just sprouted up. When you're eleven, it's difficult to understand that growing taller takes energy. And food. Grandmoms know exactly what to do about growth spurts—and eleven-year-olds whose bodies are changing as rapidly as the world around them.

An apple, watermelon, lollipops . . . all followed.

My daughter called to inquire about Ryan's health. "How's his stomach?" she asked.

"Fine," I answered.

"Be careful what he eats," she cautioned.

"I'm being very careful."

We ended the day with a game of Scrabble. Finally, he turned to me and said, "I'm feeling better, Grandmom. I think I've got to get out of here and get some air."

I smiled. I had done my job. Ryan was ready to go out and face the world again.

Probably two inches taller.

Harriet May Savitz

This Ain't No Bull

Every house where love abides and friendship is a guest is surely home, and home, sweet home; for there the heart can rest.

Henry Van Dyke

My grandson, Danny, looked in awe at my elbows. He couldn't understand why or how, when he pulled the skin, it remained out. "That's cool, Grandma. How do you do that?"

These questions and numerous other adjustments were to follow when our son realized I was getting "up in years" and offered to build me a new home near him on his farm. "Then when you get old, it will be easier to take care of you," he said politely. He invited me to live with him, his wife and their four children during construction.

I accepted the offer, but I worried what it would be like living with the kids on the farm. I'd had no experience with farming.

On my first day they showed me to my room. Granddaughter Heather had given up her bedroom for me and moved in with her sister, Kari, a sacrifice for both teenagers. "Mom just wallpapered my bedroom, Grandma. Don't you just love it?" Near the ceiling, a border of horse heads stared down at me.

French doors opened out of the bedroom onto a balcony where the view was spectacular. I watched the horses graze, and I could see the cows, pigs and chickens. A creek wandered into a pond at the bottom of the hill, which a blue heron, geese and ducks shared as their home. Life on the farm, living with the kids began.

I used to sleep in until 8:00 A.M. Life here began about 5:30 A.M. Have you ever heard four hair dryers all going at the same time? Then kids running downstairs, kids running upstairs, then down again? You can't beat it. So I'd wake up, stretch for a few minutes and say hello to the horses on the wall. They made me grin.

In the evenings in front of the TV, every sofa and chair was filled. On the floor, kids lay in all different directions, along with their dog, Annie, and two cats, Cupcake and Ziggy. Who would have thought those cramped circumstances would be enjoyable? Yet that scene became a lasting memory for me, like a scene from a Norman Rockwell painting.

Being the hip grandma that I am, I thought I ought to learn some of the chores around the farm so I could be of some help. My oldest granddaughter, Shannon, agreed to show me the ropes.

"Come with me, Grandma. We'll start with the chickens."

That seemed easy enough. We entered the coop and I immediately noticed a rather large rooster with a big plume on his tail eyeing me, but I continued into the pen. All of a sudden that rooster made a beeline for me and chased me around the pen. He pecked at my ankles, and I screamed. Shannon came after the rooster with a stick to scare it off. I made a huge jump for the fence and hurtled over it . . . landing in a nice mushy pile of cow manure!

Shannon wore a sheepish grin. "Wanna try feeding the horses?"

Granddaughter Kari had put her mare out to be bred a few weeks before. The time came for the vet to visit the farm to perform a pregnancy test. I wanted to be right there to see how this was done. The old vet drove up in his truck and went to the back, I supposed to get what he needed to do the pregnancy test. Now I'm not too smart when it comes to the farm, but I knew he wasn't going to get that horse to urinate on one of those chemical sticks to watch what color it turned! But when he came out from behind his truck with his arm in a rubber glove up to his shoulder, I gasped!

In this house, the kids did the laundry. I've never seen so many pairs of tiny bikini panties, except in department stores. I chuckled when I overheard one of the girls giggle as she unloaded the dryer, "Wow, Grandma wears big underpants!"

One weekend when the family went away, I stayed by myself. While walking down by the pond, I heard a mournful moo-o-o-o come from one of the cows. Upon investigation, I found she had just presented me with a little calf! Sheer excitement! When the family returned, I proudly informed our son that the cow had a calf while they were gone. I'd seen an appendage on the calf's underside, so I told my son it was a boy. He took me at my word and called a friend to come castrate the little guy, as was routinely done on the farm. He raised the calf's tail and said, "Uh-oh, guess what? This ain't no bull, it's a little heifer." Everyone looked my way for an answer, but I couldn't sputter one out.

As you can see, life is not boring when you live with your kids. Eventually my new home was finished and I moved into it. The Norman Rockwell picture changed. Although I am happy, I miss the laughter and fun of my son's household.

As you get older, if you are faced with living with your children, don't be afraid of it. Hang on! Perhaps Rockwell has already painted a picture of the pleasing life you are about to experience. Or maybe you'd like to paint your own picture. Either way, it will be as good as you make it—or better.

Joanie Gilmore

Everything but the Kitchen Sink

We are all here for a spell; get all the good laughs you can.

Will Rogers

By my teenage daughters' standards, her purse was huge. Theirs were tiny things that could barely hold a lipstick and compact; they wore them on their shoulders just under their arm. Grandma's handbag, suspended by thick, black leather straps, hung down on her hip. It was big enough to hold everything you could possibly want.

One day we were all in the car when my daughter Shazara spilled some drink on the back seat. "Mom, do you have any napkins?"

"No," I replied.

Suddenly, Grandma reached for her handbag on the car floor near her feet and opened it wide. Her head almost disappeared inside as she rummaged around, pulling out a handful of napkins.

"There you go, sweetheart," she said as she handed them to Shazara.

In my rearview mirror I could see my two daughters

sitting there with a huge grins on their faces.

"Mom, there's a thread hanging from my T-shirt," Reece called out.

Again opening the jaws of her handbag, Grandma rummaged in the darkness of her purse and retrieved a pair of scissors.

"There you go, love, " she said, handing it to the girls in the backseat.

They sat with wide grins on their faces that itched with orneriness.

"Mom, I need a knife and fork! " said Shazara, trying hard to sound serious about her request.

Again Grandma opened her bag and her head disappeared into its depths. She handed Shazara a neatly wrapped plastic knife and fork in a white napkin. "Here you are, Shazara."

I could see the girls' faces, looking quite amazed. Surely they weren't going to ask their Grandma for anything else.

"Oh no, my hands are sticky," Reece complained. "Have you got anything that I can wash my hands with, Grandma?"

Again, she delved into the black handbag. I could see the girls waiting in anticipation to see what Grandma was about to produce from her bag this time.

"Here you go," she said, passing a wet tissue in a sealed packet to Reece.

We all laughed out loud when Reece joked, "For a minute, Grandma, I thought you were going to bring out the kitchen sink!"

Nadia Ali

Trying Times and Dirty Dishes

The flower that follows the sun does so even in cloudy days.

Robert Leighton

I cleared the table and stacked the breakfast dishes on top of the dinner dishes still in the sink from last night's feast of macaroni and cheese with carrot sticks. I braced myself for the cold, clumpy feeling of the dishwater, then plunged my hand deep into the sink, searching for the plug.

"Yuk! Why didn't I do these last night?" I asked of who knows who. The only people around to hear me were my kids, ages six, five, three and two, and my six-week-old baby.

It wasn't just the dishes. The dryer had gone out that morning and sheets were drying over every available chair and table—to the great delight of my sons, who were playing fort all over the house. I would have hung the sheets outside, but it was ten degrees and the path to the clothesline was under a foot of blizzard snow.

The living room was an explosion of toys, and the way

things were going it would be lunchtime before breakfast cleanup was done or we were even close to being dressed. The flu that had run through the family had finally caught me after six nights of little sleep while I cared for each of their needs. It caught me the same day my husband, recovered and healthy, flew out of town on a business trip.

The hot water bubbled up the dish soap and encouraged me a little. "I'll have these done in no time." But before I could finish my pep talk, my newborn began to cry. I turned off the water and dried my hands, doubting that I would get back to the sink before the water was heavy and cold again.

I changed the baby's diaper, stepped over the basket of clean clothes that had sunk into wrinkled neglect, pulled one of the almost-dry sheets off the couch, swept away the full collection of my sons' horses, and settled in to nurse my baby.

Idyllic moment? Hardly. As soon as I sat, my lap was tumbled full of books. My kids' thought was that if Mom was sitting, she might as well read to us. So, balancing the four toddlers and protecting the baby from their commotion while trying to turn the pages with no hands, I began to read. I read over the phone ringing and over the TV set clicking on and off at full volume because one of them was sitting on the remote control that I couldn't reach and they couldn't reach under them to hand to me.

I read over my pounding headache, around the errant thought of what to make for dinner and over the doorbell ringing. The doorbell ringing! Oh no! All but the baby and me were off the couch and to the door before I could grasp a moment of hope that whoever it was would give up and go away, never to see me at my unshowered, unkempt worst.

"Grandma!" the children chorused while doing the Grandma-is-here dance of anticipated hugs and candy.

Grandma coming was always good news, but it couldn't be my mother. It couldn't be today. She lived three hours away. She never just dropped by. What would she think? I scanned the room and sighed. There was no way to recover this, no way to quickly put things right.

Cold, fresh air rushed in ahead of my mother, making me realize how stuffy and sick my house smelled.

"Cindy?" My mother called my name, startling the baby and making him cry. I wanted to join him. I heard my mother's uneven steps as she navigated around and over the things on the floor.

"Cindy?" she said again before spotting me among the Spiderman sheets.

I was stricken. I was embarrassed. I had forgotten it was Thursday. I had forgotten that my mother had planned to stop in on her way back home from the city.

"Oh my, have things gotten out of control around here," she surveyed the room and started laughing when she saw my nightgowns drying on the bouncing horse that was wearing one of my nursing bras for a hat, its ears sticking through the drop down flaps.

Her laughter filled the house with the first ray of sunshine to make it through the winter gray of the last mucky week.

I giggled, then laughed out loud before I teared up in my fatigue.

My mother cleared a space beside me. "Cindy, weren't you raised in my home?"

I nodded, unable to speak around the choking of my tears.

"Was my house always perfect, always clean?"

I shook my head no.

"Did you think I was a failure as a mother or as a homemaker?"

Again I shook my head no.

"And I don't think that of you. I have sat where you are sitting now." She grinned, then she reached over and pulled a horse from under my hip.

We chuckled together.

"Cindy, I can tell you one thing and you listen to me." Her voice became solemn. "These mothering days are the ones you'll etch into your heart, and when the years have passed and your time becomes quiet enough to roam its memories, they are the ones you'll hold most dear."

I recognized the love and truth in her words. I wrote them on my heart and contemplated them when my mothering days were calm and sunny and when they were hectic and never ending.

Now the years have passed and my time has become quiet enough to roam my memories. It is the mothering days that I open in my heart and smile fondly on.

And when my daughters and daughters-in-law are pressed in and overwhelmed with the making of their families and homes, I tell them this story and say to them, "These are the days you'll hold most dear." And they recognize the truth and the love of their grandmother's words, and they etch the memories into their hearts.

Cynthia M. Hamond

A Thank-You Note to Grandma

*Those who make us happy are always thankful
to us for being so; their gratitude is the reward of
their benefits.*

Madam Swetchine

Dearest Grandma,

I have always loved you, Grandma, for your sweet and
    loving ways.
You always had the knack of brightening ordinary days.

You are a sincere and honest woman, beautiful, kind and
    true.
Since I was a little girl I have always admired you.

You have given me many special gifts, but the most
    valuable that I recall,
Is a gift that I have treasured since I was very small.

This wonderful, lovely present was not a pearl or piece of gold.
It was not a diamond or precious gem, nor could it be bought or sold.

It was not a lucky charm that could be tucked inside my pocket.
It was not a silver necklace or an expensive golden locket.

It did not have a price tag. Its worth could not be measured.
Throughout my life, it is something that I have always treasured.

This gift is unique, one of a kind, its beauty beyond compare.
It fills my life with hopes and dreams and takes away my fears.

It was given to you quite long ago, sent by the Lord above.
He entrusted you to care for it and nurture it with love.

I thank you for my favorite gift worth more than any other.
I received it on the day that I was born, my beautiful, precious mother.

Gina Antonios

"Don't forget to send an e-card to your grandmother thanking her for the stationery."

3

BLESSINGS

*Some great moments occur from time to time
in life. When you do all you can to enable
others to have great moments, you'll be
blessed with some matchless moments
yourself.*

E. H. Kinney

A Holy Moment

Holiness is not a luxury for the few; it is not just for some people.
It is meant for you and for me and for all of us.
It is a simple duty, because if we learn to love, we learn to be holy.

Mother Teresa

No one feels very holy at 4:00 A.M., especially not me. Normally I would be fast asleep at this time, but a family emergency made it necessary for me to set my alarm and arise at this dark hour. I trip over my shoes as I round the foot of the bed and head for the hall bathroom to put on my glasses and begin the treatment regimen.

Two-year-old Andrew has pneumonia again. Having never fully recovered from it four weeks ago, Andrew had an asthma attack, tonsillitis and a relapse of pneumonia accompanied by bronchitis. His parents, my daughter and son-in-law, are exhausted. The treatment plan calls for breathing treatments every four hours around the clock, so we are taking turns. Melissa stays up for the midnight treatment, I do the 4:00 A.M. and

David gets the 8:00 A.M. just before leaving for work.

I look in on Andrew. He is sleeping peacefully as I prepare the vials of medication and pour them into the nebulizer. I must make sure he breathes the healing vapors until they stop steaming. This usually takes thirty minutes. The steam begins, and with it are my prayers for his recovery.

Andrew opens one eye. He sees "Mimi" and goes back to sleep. Sometimes he will mumble something about Rock City or the fish zoo (aquarium). Andrew is a trouper. He isn't alarmed at having his sleep disturbed. He's had scores of breathing treatments in his young life. He is all too familiar with having them, yet, gentle soul that he is, he makes no resistance. At two years, one month old, he weighs a whopping twenty-six pounds. We call him our "sunshine boy" because when he begins to have breathing problems, his mother holds him close, singing "You are my sunshine" to calm him.

As I hold the tube with healing vapors close to Andrew's nose and mouth, I remember that God is always hovering over me, especially when I am at my lowest point. His spirit broods over me, acting as a healing agent to cover me with a vapor of prayer. Too often, I am unconscious of the effort God is making, just as Andrew is unaware of me holding life-giving fumes to his nostrils. He is relaxed and rested, trusting in the care of those who love him.

Andrew's lungs will heal with proper treatment, medication and time. Doctors assure us that he will outgrow the asthma to become a strong young man. The pediatric pulmonary specialist has every confidence that the asthma attacks will lessen with age. That's what we pray for.

Becoming a grandmother has opened my soul to God's heart. Things that previously made no sense are now clear. But I suppose mortality is easily felt and moments treasured at 4:00 A.M. Before today I wouldn't have considered lost sleep a gift. But to kneel by my grandson's bed and minister to him at 4:00 A.M. is a special moment, a chance to talk to my Father and an opportunity to serve. I never felt more holy.

Sheila S. Hudson

Grandma's Prayers

Prayer should be the key of the day and the lock of the night.

Thomas Fuller

It was a very hot July evening in Illinois, and our family was enjoying ice cream on the porch together. I was only eight years old, and my father was teasing me when I jumped backwards off the railing and caught my leg on the porch step. The deep cut required stitches and a trip to the hospital.

My doctor was out boating, and since it was 1947 and there were no cell phones or other means of communication, we had a three-hour wait in the emergency room. Finally, he arrived and began stitching with my mother's help. With my leg fully bandaged, I was sent home to recover. By Friday, something was terribly wrong. My temperature climbed to 103, and a quick call to the doctor revealed I had gangrene. On Sunday morning I had my second dose of antibiotics, but by afternoon I had a violent reaction, leaving me with a very high fever, delirious and completely covered with hives.

The doctor met us at his office and, after a brief exam, looked very grim. Taking my parents into the other room I heard him say there was nothing more he could do and no other drugs available for him to use. He further informed them that I had not received enough penicillin to fight the gangrene that had already eaten away the stitches, leaving a gaping hole in my leg. The only way to save my life was to amputate my leg, and he immediately scheduled surgery for the following morning.

Needless to say, all of us were in shock. No one wanted to face this. My father was especially devastated and called for the church members to come over and pray. Even though I was burning up with a fever, in pain, itching and delirious, I cried out, "I just want Grandma to come and anoint me with oil and pray for me! I know if she prays everything will be just fine."

Grandma and Grandpa Ozee lived just around the corner from us, and I spent many hours at their house. Grandma lived what she believed, and I had absolute confidence that her prayer on my behalf would certainly touch the heart of God. Whenever I visited her at 9:30 in the morning, I always found her sitting in her rocking chair with her Bible in her lap. At 10:30, I knew she would be on her knees in prayer. I often sat quietly as she shared the Bible with me. I watched as she prepared meals for the transients who rode the boxcars into our town and somehow knew their way to her door. While she cooked, they were required to read a chapter in the Bible before they could eat. While they were eating, she would gently present the salvation message and they always left with a prayer and a New Testament. I have no idea what happened to any of them, but I am confident many left knowing they had met a very special lady who not only gave them physical food but "living water" and hope for a better life.

I knew Grandma prayed for everything from a sick parakeet to the terminally ill. I remember being amused when some of the ladies from the church came to her house complaining about the church problems and the preacher. Very few words had been spoken when Grandma had them on their knees and praying for the preacher and all the problems involved. She had great faith and believed God answered prayers. She taught me the Lord was faithful and interested in even the smallest details of life.

Grandma never missed an opportunity to take any situation and turn it into a learning session. I vividly remember the time we visited the old, rickety, smelly outhouse at Great-Grandma's farm. There, in that most unlikely place, was one beautiful flower blooming through a crack in the floor. Grandma quickly explained that no matter how bad the situation or how dark and dismal things might look, there was always hope. Just as the flower could bloom in the most difficult circumstances, so could we, because God was faithful and could make something beautiful from the ashes of our lives.

That is why I was calling for my grandma in my hour of need. Soon she appeared at my door with the bottle of anointing oil in her hands. I had no doubt God would hear her simple prayer for my healing and grant her request for a miracle to save my leg. When Grandma finished praying, I knew I had been healed, and I fell into a beautiful, peaceful sleep, not at all worried about tomorrow. I had a deep abiding peace that my life would be spared and I would always walk on two legs.

The next morning at the doctor's office, my parents anxiously waited while the doctor unwrapped the bandage. All eyes were on him as he stood in obvious amazement. Slowly he shook his head and said, "I have seen a miracle. There is no way the small dose of penicillin could have

done this. There had to be a power higher than me working on this leg."

The surgery was cancelled, my leg rebandaged, and I
went home to recover without need for further antibiotics.

Today, I still have the ugly scar to remind me of this
very traumatic time in my life. But I also still have two
legs, which reminds me of God's healing power, a praying
grandma, and that flowers bloom in the most difficult
circumstances.

Sharon Ozee Siweck

"Grandma, can you bounce me on your knee,
or is it too busy praying?"

Angel in the Clouds

The guardian angels of life sometimes fly so high as to be beyond our sight, but they are always looking down on us.

Jean Paul Richter

The anesthesiologist covered my face with the mask while I counted one-hundred, ninety-nine, ninety-eight, ninety-seven. . . .

My ordinary world was gone.

Seven hours later, I awoke under painfully bright lights. Through the confusion of tubes, monitors and beeping machines, I realized I was in the recovery room of St. Mary's Hospital. I couldn't feel my legs. Thunderous spasms of pain pelted my head. I couldn't talk. Something obstructed my throat. I tried to spit it out, but I couldn't. It was a tube. I thought my head would explode. Then blackness . . .

My dream world began.

My husband and kids, I heard them. But where were they? I tried to touch them, see them, but all went black. It seemed like only seconds later that beautiful, silver-flecked clouds billowed above me. A beam of white light shown about, and within its center I could see a human shape. It was my grandmother, whom I had cared for until she died in my home two years earlier. She wore a long white robe, soft and shimmering as pure silk. The wrinkles had vanished from her face, and the gray no longer mingled with her dark hair. A halo surrounded her, like sunshine glistening on a field of freshly fallen snow.

My grandmother reached out her loving arms. I yearned to go into them as I had done as a child. Mother's smile (I called her Mother) radiated an aura of absolute rapture such as I had never seen before. I wanted to go with her to that place that provided such happiness and held no pain. My body wanted to rise and lift toward the white-clad figure. The lights were enticing, and Mother beckoned me to her bosom. My body levitated, but my right hand clutched onto something holding me down. It was as if my husband and three children were an anchor, and I held its cable. As my grandmother summoned and the desire to release my hand from the heavy cordage grew greater, my body floated up, up, up—except for the right hand that held on tightly and refused to let go.

I desired the peace and tranquility that Mother in the billowy clouds offered, but the hand held on, and I dared not loosen it. Even in my unconscious state, I knew that by relaxing a hand muscle for only a second, the blinding pain in my head would be gone and I would join my grandmother in heaven. Yet the hand held on. Mother smiled, letting me know it was okay to hold on as she faded into the clouds.

I heard someone call my name.

Mother? I opened my eyes expecting to see my grandmother.

The lady standing beside my bed was dressed in white, but instead of a gown, she wore a nurse's uniform. "Welcome back. We thought we were going to lose you there for a while." She smiled. "Your husband and three children are here. They've been waiting for three days for you to come out of that sleep."

I tried to reach for them, but my right arm would not move. The fingers on that hand would not release their grip on the mattress.

The operation was an apparent success. The shunts drained the fluid in my spinal cord, yet my right arm was paralyzed. Deep within myself, I knew. Perhaps I could never explain it to others, but I knew I had made the choice. I elected to live, and Mother approved.

I also realized that I had the courage to undergo the second corrective surgery to stop the headaches. There was still the danger of death when the surgeon's knife would cut into my brain, but I knew I could not lose. Not with Mother and her tranquil beam of light waiting on the other side and a precious family, for whom it was worth giving one's right arm, waiting on earth.

Jean Kinsey

Parting Gifts

Prayer begins where human capacity ends.

Marian Anderson

Paralyzed with fear, I stood in the vacant dining room of a nursing home in Tennessee watching CNN track the approach of a killer.

It was 3 A.M., August 28, 1992. A night-shift attendant was keeping watch beside a wide-screen TV. I had come looking for a glass of water to sustain a vigil of my own, but was captured by a strange irony. Computerized weather maps were tracking Hurricane Andrew's relentless and deadly assault on the South Florida coast. No power on earth could arrest, avert or deter this category five monster from destroying everything in its path.

Down the hall my ninety-two-year-old grandmother was also fighting a formidable foe. As inescapable as that hurricane, there was no way to slow death or speed it up, we just had to face it . . . together. This would be our final memory—the hardest and the best.

"Mimi" had lived with our family for ten years. She watched our daughter grow up and fascinated her with stories about life on a southern farm at the turn of the twentieth century. She and Leina had been co-conspirators, faithful confidantes and pseudo-siblings. It was a rich and rewarding exchange.

At the age of ninety-one, however, Mimi suffered a series of ministrokes that ultimately placed her in a nursing home. After the last major stroke, she couldn't swallow.

This night, I was feeding her liquids with a syringe, measuring drops as she had once done for me as a premature baby. It was very difficult to see her this way. I had prayed every way I knew how and was almost prayed out.

Then insight spoke. What I needed was a prayer partner—someone to hold me up right then in prayer. Earlier I had sent my family home to rest. There wasn't a phone in the room, but I knew that God could prompt a heart to pray, so I asked him.

Thirty minutes later, the head nurse was taking vital signs when we heard a commotion outside the door. She slipped out, and through the cracked door I heard her calming one of the residents. A sweet, endearing lady, Miss Minnie was forever getting lost and confused looking for her room. Again the nurse tried to point her toward her room some distance away. Again the protest: "But I *need* to pray!"

Something propelled me toward the door, and as I opened it, the nurse apologized, "She says she has to pray *here . . . now.*"

"By all means, let her come in!" My response was automatic as I opened wide the door.

Miss Minnie walked in, not with her usual hesitant shuffle, but with a purposeful stride that took her right to the head of Mimi's bed. She laid her hand on my grandmother's head and issued the most beautiful, coherent prayer of healing I had ever heard. When she was done, I knew that whatever happened, everything was going to be all right. I looked into her eyes to thank her. The usual look of doubt and confusion was gone. There was a fire in her eyes, a commanding countenance of faith, purpose and resolve. I later learned she had once been a devoted person of prayer, but the next day she couldn't even remember that she had prayed.

During the remaining hours that night, Mimi slipped into a coma. I held her hand, asking God to gently shepherd her home, asking him to protect the people in Andrew's path. At times I wondered if this was how Jacob felt in the Bible the night he wrestled with an angel till dawn. Like Jacob, I was determined to wrest a blessing from this painful ordeal . . . a resurrection moment I could hold in my heart. Jacob got his blessing at dawn. For some reason, 7 A.M. was in my mind.

At 6 A.M. the nurses were unable to record vital signs, but Mimi's breathing was measured and methodical, as if she were running a race. I sat beside her, stroking her brow and speaking gently. As deliberate as a soldier's march was each labored breath. She slept on.

Suddenly, on impulse, I pulled back the window curtain and noticed a faint rosy glow on the horizon. I looked back at Mimi and . . . *as if arriving* . . . she took a deliberate, almost satisfied, last breath. Her journey was complete. Her rest was won. I glanced down at my watch and it was . . . seven o'clock! I just sat there stunned, unable to get up, somehow grateful to be alone.

My thoughts drifted to those who'd been wrestling with the reality of the storm, and my heart laid claim to a prayer that out of all their pain and suffering there would be an offsetting blessing too. I later learned that 7 A.M. was the official time of sunrise on Aug. 28, 1992, and the moment when Hurricane Andrew abated.

Marcia Swearingen

A Teenager's Song for Gramma

This world is not conclusion, a sequel stands beyond—Invisible, as music, but positive, as sound.

Emily Dickinson

As I sort through stacks of sheet music next to the piano, I come across an almost-bare sheet of music—only a few measures of notes scrawled in my own sloppy script. I stare at the unfinished waltz and my mind travels through the memories of my great-gramma Fritz.

I find myself standing in the huge garden next to Gramma's white farmhouse in rural Iowa. Gramma loved plants and flowers. She cared for them all and prayed for them individually. I see her kneeling next to a soft mound of soil where a seed has just been planted. Gramma makes the sign of the cross over it and says, "God bless you, grow."

Gramma Fritz was a creator. Nothing went to waste at her house. She used every scrap of fabric to make her famous quilts and "rag rugs." She made mats out of bread sacks and doll clothes out of flour sacks. Every scrap of food was eaten, every bone boiled for broth.

Everything Gramma used was an original—like her—the meat grinder her mother used and the foot-powered sewing machine. When I told her about microwave ovens she quipped, "That's all I need—some machine to help me get fat faster!"

That was Gramma. Witty, clever and a little sarcastic. I'd been told that "Little Anna Fritz" never outgrew her schoolgirl spunk. She could outwit anyone—like a "stubborn German"—and everyone loved her for it. She always had a quip or quote. She blamed modern commercial Christmases on "Those wise men who just had to bring gold into the situation."

After ninety years of strength and health, Gramma got sick. Sometimes she was winning her battle with congestive heart failure, other times she was not. When I realized that Gramma, like her beloved springtime, would not last forever, I wanted to do something really special for her, in honor of her. I wanted to write a song—more than a song, a beautiful piano piece. I wanted to capture my love for her and her spirit in music. It sounded easy, but it was not. Too soon I learned that composing the kind of music I wanted took a lot more than strong will and eight years of music lessons. I kept my goal a secret, though I don't know why. Day after day, I tried and tried, refusing to give up, while becoming increasingly frustrated.

One night we got the long distance call from Iowa. Gramma's condition was getting worse. I had to accept the reality, then, that writing her song would take a long, long time—perhaps longer than Gramma could wait. Still, I could not let go of my goal.

Finally I shared it and my frustration with my mom. She sat beside me on the piano bench and wrapped her arms around me, speaking with comfort and wisdom—with words I would have expected to hear from my wise gramma Fritz.

"Maybe it isn't the music you're afraid to let go. Maybe it's Great-Gramma."

She was right. I didn't want to let go of Gramma. As long as I was hanging on to my goal, I felt like I was hanging on to her.

That night in bed I thought about what Mom had said and realized I would never have to give up Gramma or the wonderful gifts she had given me. Hers was a spirit that would live forever. She was a special blessing, and blessings never really die. The fear of losing her vanished. I fell asleep remembering Gramma telling me how she danced when she was young. She and her friends never tired, they just kept dancing.

Now I sit next to the piano with my unfinished goal in my hand. Dance, Little Anna, dance. You have helped me to be free.

Angela Thieman-Dino
Age fifteen

Love and Water

Woman is the salvation or the destruction of the family. She carries its destiny in the folds of her mantle.

Henri Frederic Amiel

Mama died just days before my eleventh birthday, and my destiny careened dramatically from snug to loose-ended. Overnight, my childhood vanished. In those coming months Dad met Dot at work and began seeing her regularly. A year later, they married.

So much. So quickly. Another woman moving into our house stirred anew my still-fresh memories of Mama. At the same time, uninitiated Dot inherited a brood of three children, ages five, eight and eleven.

When alone, I listened to an old recording of "You'll Never Walk Alone," and I was convinced my mama sang those words to me from the other side. Yet, in moments of grief, I wondered, *How can she walk with me now?* My child's heart yearned for a mother's touch.

"Do you want the kids to call you 'Mama'?" Dad asked Dot one day. Something in me wanted her to say, "Yes."

Dot looked troubled for long moments, then said, "No. That wouldn't be right."

The *no* felt like a physical blow. *Blood's thicker'n water*, came my grandma's favorite litany. I'd not, until that very moment, grasped its meaning. My stepmother's answer seemed proof that blood *was* thicker, that I was merely Daddy's baggage—proof that, to her, despite the fact that she introduced me as "my daughter," I was biologically not.

I was of the *water*. So I distanced myself.

My sulky aloofness hid a deep, deep need for acceptance. Yet, no matter how churlish I became, Dot never hurt me with harsh words. Ours was, in those trying days, a quiet, bewildered quest for harmony.

After all, we were stuck with each other. She had no more choice than I.

I visited Mama's grave every chance I got, to talk things over with her. I never carried flowers because fresh arrangements always nestled lovingly against the headstone, put there, no doubt, by Daddy.

Then, in my fourteenth year, I came in from school one day and saw my newborn baby brother, Michael. I hovered over the bassinet, gently stroking the velvety skin as tiny fingers grasped mine and drew them to the little mouth. I dissolved into pure, maternal mush. Dot, still in her hospital housecoat, stood beside me.

In that moment, our gazes locked in wonder. "Can I hold him?"

She lifted him and placed him in my arms.

In a heartbeat, that tiny bundle snapped us together.

"Like your new coat?" Dot asked that Christmas as I pulled the beautiful pimento-red topper from the gift package and tried it over my new wool sweater and skirt.

In short months, Dot had become my best friend.

At Grandma's house one Sunday, I overheard her tell

my aunt Annie Mary, "I told James I didn't think it was right to force the kids to call me Mama. Irene will always be Mama to them. That's only right."

So that's why she'd said no.

Or was it? *Blood's thicker'n water.* Was Grandma right? Was that always true in matters pertaining to familial loyalty? I shrugged uneasily, telling myself that it didn't matter anyway.

Over the years, Dot embraced my husband, Lee, as "son," soothed me through three childbirths, and afterward spent weeks with me, caring and seeing to my family's needs. While grandmothering my children, she birthed three of her own, giving me two brothers and a sister. How special our children felt, growing up together, sharing unforgettable holidays like siblings.

In 1974, Lee and I lived two hundred miles away when a tragic accident claimed our eleven-year-old Angie. By nightfall, Dot was there, holding me. She was utterly heartbroken.

I moved bleakly through the funeral's aftermath, secretly wanting to die. Every Friday evening, I dully watched Dot's little VW pull into my driveway. "Daddy can't come. He has to work," she'd say. After leaving work, she drove four hours nonstop to be with me each weekend, a long trek that continued for three months.

During those visits, she walked with me to the cemetery, held my hand and wept with me. If I didn't feel like talking, she was quiet. If I talked, she listened. She was so *there* that, when I despaired, she single-handedly shouldered my anguish.

Soon, I waited at the door on Fridays. Slowly, life seeped into me again.

Nearly twenty years later, Dad's sudden auto accident death yanked the earth from beneath me and again I lapsed into shock, inconsolable. My first reaction was, *I need to be with Dot, my family.*

Then, for the first time since adolescence, a cold, irrational fear blasted me with the force of TNT. Dad, my genetic link, gone. I'd grown so secure with the Daddy-and-Dot alliance through the years that I'd simply taken family solidarity for granted. Now with Dad's abrupt departure, the chasm he left loomed murky and frightening.

Had Dad, I wondered, *been the glue? Was glue genetic, after all?*

Terrifying thoughts spiraled through my mind as Lee drove me to join relatives.

Will I lose my family? The peril of that jolted me to the core.

"Blood's thicker'n water."

If Grandma felt that way, couldn't Dot feel that way, too, just a little bit? The small child inside my adult body wailed and howled forlornly. It was in this frame of mind that I entered Dot's house after the accident.

Dot's house. Not Dad's and Dot's house anymore.

Would Daddy's void change her? She loved me, yes, but suddenly I felt keenly DNA-stripped, the stepchild of folklore. A sea of familiar faces filled the den. Yet, standing in the midst of them all, I felt utterly alone.

"Susie!" Dot's voice rang out, and through a blur I watched her sail like a porpoise to me. "I'm so sorry about Daddy, honey," she murmured and gathered me into her arms.

Terror scattered like startled ravens.

What she said next took my breath. She looked me in the eye and said gently, "He's with your mama now."

I snuffled and gazed into her kind face. "He always put flowers on Mama's grave. . . ."

She looked puzzled, then smiled sadly. "No, honey, he didn't put the flowers on her grave."

"Then who . . . ?"

She looked uncomfortable. Then she leveled her gaze with mine. "I did."

"You?" I asked, astonished. "All those years?" She nodded, then wrapped me in her arms again.

Truth smacked me broadside. *Blood is part water.* Grandma just didn't get it.

With love blending them, you can't tell one from the other.

I asked Dot recently, "Isn't it time I started calling you Mom?"

She smiled and blushed. Then I thought I saw tears spring in her eyes.

"Know what I think?" I said, putting my arms around her. "I think Mama's looking down at us from heaven, rejoicing that you've taken such good care of us, grandmothering my children, doing all the things she'd have done if she'd been here. I think she's saying, 'Go ahead, Susie, call her *Mom.*" I hesitated, suddenly uncertain. "Is that okay?"

In a choked voice, she replied, "I would consider it an honor."

Mama's song to me was true: I do not walk alone.

Mom walks with me.

Emily Sue Harvey

The Perspective of a Pansy

What we call wisdom is the result of all the wisdom of past ages.

Henry Ward Beecher

In Atlanta we have the luxury of planting pansies in the fall and viewing their curious faces all winter long. That is how my grandma described their blooms, as faces. She was right. If you look into a pansy's velvet petals you can see its eager expression peeking out at you. It was my grandmother's love for this flower that drew me to *Viola tricolor hortensis* when I was a little girl. My favorites were the white petals with purple centers, or "faces." They remain my favorite flowers today.

Since pansies are annuals, last year's flowers had long since died and been pulled from the ground, never to be seen again. I hadn't taken the time to plant even one flat of pansy seedlings that fall. Actually, I hadn't found the time to do much of anything but work since September. My job had become especially demanding due to a project that required me to fly weekly to Washington, DC. Between airports, delayed flights, cancellations, taxicabs, trains and countless hotel rooms, I hadn't spent enough time with my husband, hadn't returned phone calls from my parents, hadn't sent birthday cards to my dearest friends, hadn't taken the necessary time to come to terms with the death of my grandma and certainly hadn't made time to put pansies in the ground.

Perhaps by skipping the whole pansy planting process that autumn I was putting off facing the reality that Grandma, the only grandparent I had ever known, had died.

My connection between her and the flowers was so strong. I told myself I was too busy for gardening so many times that I convinced myself it was true.

As I drove home from the airport one chilly November evening, I was overwhelmed by an empty pang in my heart. It had begun as a slight ache and built up to a deep, hollow throb after five straight days of deadlines, lists, conference calls and meetings. I hadn't allowed any time for myself, to read, to visit with friends and family or even to pray. I had tried to ignore this vacuous feeling. I had just kept going and going, like a robot following pro-grammed commands, forgetting about all of the things in life that gave me deeper meaning. The pain was especially great this particular evening due to a canceled flight that delayed my getting home until long after my lonely hus-band was already in bed.

After fighting eight lanes of stop-and-go traffic for over an hour, caused by what appeared to be a fatal accident, I arrived frazzled and tired in my suburban neighborhood. As I pulled into my driveway, my headlights shone into the empty flowerbeds. I glimpsed something white rest-ing on the ground. I parked my car in the garage and walked around to the front yard to collect what I assumed was a piece of garbage to throw away. But I did not find trash. Instead I found a lone white pansy with a purple face flourishing by itself in a barren bed of pine straw.

The determined flower had fought all odds to spring from a ripped-up root, which is not bred for regrowth, to return another year. It didn't seem possible, and maybe it wasn't. Yet here was a perfect pansy grinning at me and asking me from its remarkable face why I too couldn't break through the dirt and let myself bloom.

Touching that flower, I knew this was Grandma's way of letting me know that although she had left this earth, she wasn't really gone. Just like the pansy that had been pulled from the soil yet was still blossoming, my grandmother's spirit would always flourish inside my heart. I sighed, recalling that Grandma would have never put work first. Her family and friends were the priorities in her world. She didn't know the meaning of timetables or deadlines. Although her life was simple, she was always happy and saw only the good in others and the beauty in the world around her.

It was time to open my heart and my eyes to the important things around me, to fill up the empty hole inside me with the nourishment that only God, family and friends could give me. Work could wait. Life, as the pansy showed me, could not.

Laura L. Smith

Red and White Carnations

This was the first Mother's Day since Grandmother passed away. I dreaded going to church and seeing families sit together with their moms. I hated being in church alone, and especially today I hated admitting to myself and others that my mother left and my parents were divorced. I never talked much about it, but I realized everyone in the church knew more about it than I did.

"Maybe I should have stayed home," I said to myself as I walked up the church steps.

"Good morning, and happy Mother's Day," a greeter said to several churchgoers in the narthex. "Please take a red carnation if your mother is living and a white one if she has passed on."

I must have stood in front of the large basket of flowers for several minutes. I couldn't decide which one to take.

My real mother is alive, but dead to me. I reasoned. *She left when I was two years old, and I've only seen her twice in all of my sixteen years.*

The first time she showed up was two years ago. It was my brother's high school graduation. A teacher came to me and said, "Barbara, this is your mother."

"My mother!" I snapped. "What is she doing here?" Behind my teacher stood a brown-haired, short lady with a warm smile.

"Hi, Barbara. You've turned out to be quite a young lady," she said.

"Hello," I managed to respond. She looked at me and waited for me to say something else. I didn't know what to say or do. The seconds seemed like hours. I just stood there and looked at her. *Do I look like her?* I wondered. One of my classmates rescued me from the awkward moment by asking me on the stage to have our pictures taken. I excused myself and made sure I got lost in the crowd.

The second and last time I saw her was at Grandmother's funeral. She tried to talk to me then, but I just looked down. I didn't feel like talking to anyone.

I have no memories of anything my mother and I did together. To call her "Mother" seemed strange because Grandmother Benedict took care of me, went shopping with me and saw to it that my homework got done.

"I really should take a white carnation," I rationalized. Grandmother was the real mother to me and she was gone. She was there when I needed to talk. She taught me the art of homemaking. She instructed me in cooking and baking the Hungarian way.

I have fond memories of Grandmother sitting by her quilting frame and singing hymns in her native tongue. I would sit and listen to stories of how she immigrated to America and how God kept her safe, providing for her needs. She always said, "Use what God gives you wisely. If you pray for your daily bread, then don't waste it."

Looking back, I knew her faith and the time I spent with her passed on influences that were like the quilts she made. There were many fragmented pieces that, when sewn together, formed a complete pattern. The dominant pieces were love, joined by threads of laughter and tears.

I pulled a white carnation from the basket and took a seat in the back pew. The organist began the prelude and quietness settled over the congregation. I sat clutching the white carnation while my heart held tightly to the past. Grief surfaced again, and I saw nothing promising in my future. Most of the people around me knew that my real mother was alive. *Would they understand why I took a white carnation? Does God understand?*

The choir began to take their seats. The organist played softly. I raised my eyes and focused on the large wooden cross behind the choir loft.

Oh, Jesus, you do understand, don't you? You were hurt. You were rejected by those you loved. Yet you chose to forgive them. Help me to do the same with my mother.

The organist continued to play as the pastor took his seat behind the pulpit. I looked back in the narthex and noticed the basket of flowers. I quickly, but quietly, walked back to the flower arrangement to put the white carnation back. I wanted to prove to God and myself that I was willing to deal with the past and the future.

All of the red carnations were taken, but my eye caught a glimpse of one single red and white carnation lying on the table. It probably had been taken out of the basket because it was neither all red nor all white.

God does understand my feelings, I thought. *The florist didn't make a mistake. This carnation is just right for me on this Mother's Day.*

I took the red and white carnation back to my seat, thanking God that I would forgive the mother who was alive, and love forever the grand"mother" who would always be alive in me spiritually.

Barbara Hibschman

The Feeling

*A*nd *whoever receives one little child like this in My name receives Me.*

Matthew 18:5

I sat in a beautiful city park one day watching my three-year-old granddaughter swinging when I felt this take-your-breath-away feeling. It was a feeling I had often experienced on our own little piece of land out in the country.

It is strange how we ended up buying that place. We were looking for a place to live and finally discovered an old farmhouse on an acre and a half thirty minutes from the city. The house had been built as a one-room schoolhouse in 1911, and the basement was still a dirt cellar. Looking at this old place, I regretted the thought of giving up my beautiful home in the city, with wall-to-wall carpets, a lovely fireplace and a bay window. I knew my husband wanted a country place, but giving up my city home was not going to be easy. Then we walked out across the land, and this beautiful feeling hit me. I commented to my husband, "It feels so good here."

We looked through the old place and once again walked out in the yard, and as we traveled down a wee slope to a tree-lined enclosure this wondrous feeling again came upon me. "Honey, it feels so good here!" I guess I told him that at least three or four times that day and again in the weeks and months that followed our purchase of the home. I received that glorious feeling each time I walked into a small enclosure we called our Secret Garden.

But I was not the only one to feel this warm energy. Each time we had company I encouraged them to spend some time alone in the Secret Garden, and every single person said the same thing. They felt a good, warm feeling come over them.

Now here I was in a park with my granddaughter and I had that same amazing feeling. I called to my rambunctious little granddaughter, "Jani, come over here and sit with Grandma."

She climbed up on the park bench and managed to slow her energetic little body long enough to listen. "Jani, will you sit here with me and just close your eyes and see if you feel anything?"

Bless her; she didn't question my weird request. She merely closed her eyes and sat perfectly still. I waited to see if she would experience what I did. And then I kept on waiting, as she seemed in no hurry to open her eyes. This was surprising for such a lively little bundle of energy.

Finally I could wait no longer. "Jani?" I touched her shoulder, gently encouraging her to open her eyes. As she did, I asked her, "Jani, did you feel anything?"

She beamed a beautiful, radiant smile and said, "Oh Gamma, it feel like God giving me a hug!"

Ellie Braun-Haley

Picked Just for You

Flowers are love's truest language.

Park Benjamin

"I'll call you right back, Marge," I told my friend on the phone. "Someone's at the door. Probably another salesman."

On our street we get salespeople of all kinds—remodeling, newspapers, entertainment discount cards, you name it—plus eager children with Girl Scout cookies, boxes of candy, gift wrapping packages and Easter eggs, all in the name of charity for more schools and clubs than I can keep straight.

This time my door opened to two little girls. I had met Alyssa, six, a couple of weeks before. Since then, she'd waved to me every time she struggled past my house on a pair of inline skates almost as big as she. Like most of the children on our street, she called me "Grandma Bonnie."

Now Alyssa smiled. "Hello, Grandma Bonnie!" she chirped. "This is my little sister, Ariana. She's three." To her very nervous sister, "It's okay, honey. She's nice people. You'll like her."

The three-year-old held a "bouquet" in one hand, and the other gripped a tiny notebook and huge broken crayon. "Go on," her big sister urged, "tell her."

Ariana looked at me solemnly. "I want to help raise money for my preschool," she said, holding out her flowers. "So I'm selling these for one dollar a bunch."

I had a hard time hiding my grin. I understood her notebook and crayon—a substitute for the record-keeping forms and pens she'd seen the older children lug door-to-door with their wares. She couldn't, of course, even print her own name, much less a receipt.

As for the bouquet, it consisted of seven scraggly oxalis blossoms. Now if you're a gardener, you're probably already cringing. If you're not, let me explain. Oxalis is a weed, a madly determined, clover-like plant that's almost impossible to get rid of. Worse than dandelions! Obviously Ariana had plucked these despised but thriving flowers from her own yard or a neighbor's—or maybe even mine.

Her big sister smiled. "Aren't they lovely, Grandma Bonnie? And they only cost a dollar for the whole bunch. It's all for Ariana's preschool."

Now maybe I was being played for the world's biggest sucker, but the girls' initiative did tickle me. "All right," I agreed, "one dollar coming up."

Alyssa tucked the bill in her sister's skirt pocket. Then Ariana handed me my purchase. "Uh," I suggested, "why don't you just keep the flowers and the money both? Then you could sell the flowers to someone else."

Both girls stared at me, horrified. "Oh, no, Grandma Bonnie!" Ariana cried. "We picked them just for *you*. See, they're *beautiful!*"

And so they were. Seven slender stems soon graced the bud vase by my kitchen window. A week later, they were still crowned with a tassel of perfectly shaped lemon-yellow bells of joy—twice as many as when my little neighbor handed them to me with dozens of new buds yet to open. What a bargain!

I had called these tiny plants "weeds"—disgusting, worthless things with no right to exist. But in their innocent hearts, those two little girls saw them as they really were—a precious creation of God's to treasure and share out of loving hearts to brighten the day of a lonely old "Grandma."

Bonnie Hanson

Shiny Red Shoes

*B*lessings *ever wait on virtuous deeds, and*
though late, a sure reward succeeds.

William Congreve

Caring for my tiny granddaughter for days, weeks and
then months at a time was one thing. But *permanently?* I
was bone weary with rearing kids alone, and now I had
my father as well.

I felt I had no choice, yet I worried, *could I do this?*

Two-year-old April quickly settled into our little single-
mom household and began to thrive. Already she was her
great-grandpa's "little buddy." He had recently moved
from a cane to a wheelchair, which he and April called
"Buggy."

April dressed each morning at one end of the large
house and skipped down the hall (April seldom walked)
and into our game room, which I had bartered for use as a
Montessori school. There, under the tutelage of a well-
respected headmistress, she received the one-on-one nurturing that I'd given my other children and reliable child
care so I could keep my corporate job a few miles away.

As Daddy grew weaker, affluent family members promised to pay my salary if I would quit my job to care for him. So I gave up the career for which I had worked so hard, sold the country home and the horses, and moved nearer to family, to a pleasant suburban neighborhood with a good elementary school nearby.

Before long, the promised financial help suddenly stopped with brutal finality. Yet I felt certain that God had called me to care for both father and grandchild, and he would show me the way.

We cut out all unnecessary expenditures, and my one teen still at home went to work part-time. I began a series of odd jobs that would take me from home only a few short hours at a time . . . window washing, cleaning houses and sewing.

When April was five, her favorite treat was a shopping trip to anywhere. I had squirreled away sixty-five dollars to spend on Christmas, including our traditional turkey and trimmings and token gifts for a few close family. "Honey," I told her, "we'll do most of our shopping at the church bazaar, then on Christmas Eve when things are on sale, we'll go to the mall, and buy anything you want that costs under twenty dollars."

That day the sky was full of rain clouds, and the parking lot was crowded. I tucked my checkbook, a snack and rain cape into a small backpack and started across the huge parking lot, little beribboned doggy-ears bouncing beside me. We heard the Salvation Army bell clanging noisily long before we approached the store's entrance. April tugged at my fingers, "Munner! I want to give some money to the needy children!"

A knot formed in the pit of my stomach.

If I had completed the paperwork lying on my desk at home, part of the money pitched into that little black pot would have been offered to us. I felt in my pocket. *Lord, like the widow's mite, please honor whatever we can offer.*

With great ceremony, I dropped a nickel and two pennies into the little outstretched hand. The coins rattled in the pot, and April clapped her hands, her eyes sparkling. The soldier rang his bell, smiling, "Thank you! Merry Christmas!"

Inside, we made our way through the noisy crowd, and April suddenly stopped, tugging me to lean down, "Munner, I want some shiny red Mary Janes!"

Red patent shoes? On Christmas Eve? If there were a pair of red shoes anywhere in the city this time of year, they would be expensive.

We giggled a lot that day, searching. I pleaded for a trip down toy aisles; she adamantly pleaded, "I want Mary Janes . . . ," then stooping to point, "with a shiny buckle right *here!*"

Between shoe stores and the inevitable, "Sorry, no red shoes . . . ," I guided her through every toy section in the mall, to no avail.

We said it together, "I'm hungry!" as we arrived at the fast food island, laughing and racing for an empty table. My backpack produced cheese, some crackers, her lunch Thermos filled with milk and two straws. She nibbled at the cheese and nibbled carrot curls off five slim fingers where she had carefully placed them like golden rings.

Meal completed and my energy waning, I wished she would choose something so we could go home. "Wouldn't you like this lovely doll?" Thoughtfully, she considered, her eyes downcast. Then, ". . . A buckle right here!"

The Shoe Box was the last store in the mall with possibility. I had once thought little of paying forty-five dollars for a pair of Buster Brown shoes in this very same store. I hoped yet feared we'd find the red slippers here.

We did.

The shiny red Mary Janes fit perfectly and April

marched up and down, up and down, before the mirrors. I dreaded asking the price. The clerk looked at the end of the box. "Just $34.98."

I've been told my face always betrays my emotions. April's eyes met mine as the disappointment rose, with tears not far behind. "But wait," said the clerk quickly. "Let me check with my manager."

"I want to wear them home!" April bent down and touched the buckle, satisfied.

Silently, I prayed.

After an agonizing wait, the clerk returned. "Since these are the last pair, how about half price?"

My tired feet and my heart were swollen with weary joy and gratitude to a benevolent God, and a compassionate clerk and manager. April skippity-hopped the red shoes all the way to the exit, where rain came down in torrents.

With britches rolled well above my tennis shoes, I drew up the straps on my little backpack as far as they would go, then strapped it on April's back. Next, I snapped and tied the rain-cape and hood securely about her neck and hoisted her to my shoulders. We proceeded like a hunkering giant into the downpour, waving to the missionary still ringing, ringing his bell, wishing all a Merry Christmas. With my grandchild squealing above me, I held tightly to her small knees. With shiny red slippers bouncing against my grateful chest, I knew.

Yes, I could do this.

I would not be alone.

Bettye Martin-McRae

Monday Night Tea

To everything there is a season, a time for every purpose under heaven.

Ecclesiastes 3:1

"Mom!" my exasperated eight-year-old pouted glumly. "That's your 'no' look. All the other kids go see the Cookie Lady every day. Can't I go, *please*?"

This same request had punctuated every afternoon since shortly after we'd moved to this new area of town. A lady who gave away cookies to small children made me wonder if we had made the right move. But surely, I reasoned silently, all of these children's parents must know this person if they allow daily visits. Sighing reluctantly, I looked at the five eager faces outside our screen door. I took my daughter's hand, bowing playfully. "Okay, Princess. I am your royal subject. Lead me to the Cookie Lady."

Giggling in delight, the children pulled and led me, like a Pied Piper in reverse, I thought, hopping and skipping down the street past other homes that were similar in size and status to ours. The children teased to see if I could identify their homes as we walked on, laughing and creating silly rhymes to help me remember whose home was whose, and making up names when I didn't know. Our entourage must have been quite the sight. "Blue, blues, that house is Sue's" and "Christmas red without the green, that house belongs to Imogene" were completed with groans and more laughter.

Looking up for the next home, I realized we were heading around the bend and stopped in my tracks, suddenly shy. Our family had walked the neighborhood and noticed the half-dozen imposing, column-fronted homes on the bend. We had not yet seen or met any of their owners, and my neighbors and I were in awe of the social and financial power these homes represented. It was almost as if the bend contained an imaginary boundary.

"Come on," the children urged, pulling me toward the most elegant home.

As they raced past me to the door, I was awed that the children had no concern of status as they listened to the beautiful multitoned chimes harmonize a welcome while I weakly compared it to the ding-dong of our doorbell.

I was completely disarmed, however, by the tall, elegant older woman who answered the door. *Loving.* The description came to me unbidden and remained as she gave us each an obviously homemade sugar cookie centered with a pecan half.

Business done, the little ones lined up on her porch and munched happily, allowing Magdalene Veenstra to introduce herself and smilingly guess whose mom I was. Imagined social barriers melted with her charming story of once offering "store bought" cookies, which were instantly rejected by several children who announced they would return "when you feel better and make Cookie Lady cookies again." Five minutes later I left, bemused and wondering over a warm invitation to join her for a cup of tea the following Monday.

A junior-high home-economics class was my only preparation of protocol for that first visit, and I wore a skirt to honor her generation and her genteel nature. I was grateful for the sense of smell when she opened the door; my aproned hostess did not need to tell me she had been baking. I followed her to the kitchen with an anticipation that never dimmed over the following fifteen years of Monday night teas.

Leading me past her blue delft collection and through a luxurious formal dining room to the kitchen, she directed me to a seat at a porcelain-topped table from another era. From there I watched "the ritual," as I came to think of her tea preparations, while drooling (inwardly only, I hoped) over the freshly baked delicacies that she'd placed on our English rose china plates.

A small but pleased surprise filled me as she sat and bowed her head in prayer. Realizing that this longed-for grandmother figure also shared my faith instantly drew our hearts closer.

From that Monday on, recipes filled our conversations—recipes for her famous pecan cookies and the almond-filled tarts known to other generations as bridesmaid tarts—then other "recipes," for living, for walking the faith, for loving our families and eventually even for dying. Each cup of tea opened a chapter of a living history book with tales of war, the Depression, numerous presidents, life on several continents and the inventions of radio, airplanes, automobiles and television. But history came only after our time of prayer for family, including present and future generations.

Being accepted taught me to accept others; her childlike faith ("I asked God to keep me safe while I slept—should I now insult him and stay awake worrying?") taught me to keep things simple. A favorite adage of hers, "Use it or lose it," gave me inspiration to utilize my talents and energy. It was this very adage that gave me a final lesson.

Grandma V, as I'd come to call her, had asked me to read. Her hearing and vision were now limited, so I was sitting on a cushioned footstool at her feet, but the book lay closed in my lap. She had recently ceased most cooking and had shocked the motor vehicle department by voluntarily giving up her license with a simple, "It's time." I was distressed by her inactivity, so I sat gently chiding her to "use it or lose it" when she caught me by surprise. She leaned forward until we were practically nose-to-nose and effectively stopped my thoughtless chatter. I gave her my full attention as she looked me straight in the eye, paused for effect and said, "You ever been ninety-three?"

We laughed the rest of the night over her remark and my shocked reaction. As usual, though, I was on the way home when I realized the lesson amid the humor. I cannot lead where I have not gone. Ecclesiastes' "a time for everything" formed the refrain to memories of ageless wisdom from the kids and the Cookie Lady.

Surely there is a time to walk before and a time to walk behind, but the time is always right to walk beside.

Delores Christian Liesner

4

ADVENTURES WITH GRANDMA

If I had known grandchildren were going to be so much fun, I would have had them first.

Erma Bombeck

Outing with Gram

If nothing is going well, call your grandmother.

Italian Proverb

The sight of our fourteen-year-old grandson Dave being violently sick from his first round of chemotherapy is one I will never forget. That single snapshot in time hovered like a dark cloud, even though his mom later found a remedy to control the nasty side effects. It represented the reality of an unexpected diagnosis—cancer in his right leg. He was home now between chemos, and today was my day with Dave.

A husky about-to-be freshman, Dave's precancer interests had focused entirely on sports and activity. How, I wondered, would I find something to do on this cool fall day with a young man on crutches, weakened and tired but still game for his turn to spend a day with Grandma? All past outings and ideas were scratched due to his limited strength. We would have to find something to do for an hour or two before returning home for medication. I was baffled.

Even when I saw Dave's eager glance as his mom knelt

to tie the shoe on his splint-protected leg, I had no clue what we would do. I prayed frantically for an idea, wondering, *What do teenage boys like Dave like to do?* All eight grandkids had enjoyed my past spontaneity, but this time I felt hollow.

Then, just as Dave stood and asked, "What are we going to do today, Gram?" it came. *Cars! Boys like cars!*

"It's a surprise, Dave," I smiled, now calm. "I think you will enjoy this."

We drove to Highway 20, which is lined with car dealers. Pausing expectantly before we turned onto the street, he eyed me. "So, Dave, see any cars you want to test drive?" Widened eyes and a happy smirk were my answer. He quickly chose a Cadillac, and we swung into their lot and parked.

A number of steps led to the office, so Dave waited while I went inside. My nephew Kenny calls me "General D" when I get this determined, and I chuckled as I climbed the steps, wishing I'd called ahead. Fortunately our arrival was at a quiet moment, and the salesman who greeted me was also a grandparent. A brief explanation that I was in no position to actually purchase a car but was requesting a ride for my grandson produced a hearty welcome.

"No problem," said the kindly salesman, who came out and greeted Dave eagerly. "I think I have an idea which car you'd be interested in," he said, pointing out a blue sporty model. A responsive grin, followed by the first of many sighs of "Sweet!" indicated full agreement.

Our butter-smooth ride through town was highlighted when Dave suggested we go by the house and show the family what we had "found." Everyone oohed and ahhed over the features, and his siblings hinted recklessly for their next outing. After returning the Cadillac and giving profuse thanks, we returned home for Dave's medication. His eighteen-year-old brother Mike greeted him with,

"After that, what will you do this afternoon—test drive a Hummer?"

"Yeah," Dave laughed, adding, "in my dreams."

I tore out of their house before I heard any more. The day was half over. Could it be done? I raced to my house and the Internet, punching in "Hummer." A yelp of joy brought my husband running. There was a dealership only forty minutes away! I called with trepidation and explained this time that I not only was not in the market to buy the vehicle, I couldn't even test-drive it.

"Come on in!" laughed the enthusiastic manager.

Dave was ready to go a few minutes later, eagerly wondering where we were going next. "A surprise in a half hour," was all I could trust myself to say, and we chatted about the Cadillac ride and other cars he thought were "sweet."

The final exit was on a hill and the Hummer showroom was visible at the bottom. "You didn't!" he said, gazing at me a moment and then back at the yellow and black signage. "I don't believe it."

In awe, we walked up the ramp to the futuristic building. Two men stood dwarfed behind massive glass doors, which apparently allowed the gigantic vehicles to be driven out. The manager and a salesman, Mike, greeted us and gave Dave the royal treatment, including a tour, history of the Hummer and a look inside both standard and luxury models before going outside for a ride.

Our guess that the erect, crew-cut salesman had been a serviceman was confirmed as he guided us to the silver Hummer he'd purchased after military use. Gallantly hoisting Grandma in the back, they circled the Hummer admiringly and then climbed in to inspect and discuss every minutia, from the "rotating gun" atop the vehicle to every dial and engine part. I am usually bored with such guy stuff, but time flew as I watched Dave's grin broaden time and again. When Mike asked, "Are you ready for a ride?" Dave turned, and I knew the look he flashed me would hold a lifetime of memories.

Oh, what a ride! Several times Mike or Dave glanced back and inquired if Grandma was doing okay. Gripping the seat stiffly, I did not enjoy riding up—or down—what felt like ninety-degree hills. But I was there for Dave and squeaked out, "Fine," to their chuckles, as Mike drove over and through every imaginable obstacle and finished with a road test on the freeway!

Later, buckling up to head home, I marveled at the answer to my prayer. An exhausted Dave placed his souvenirs and crutches in the back and tilted his seat for a rest. The quiet ride home was broken a few minutes later with a sleepy chuckle and music to a grandmother's ears. "You'll never be able to top this, Gram. . . . It was a Hummer of a day!"

Delores Christian Liesner

Grandma Days

There is nothing more properly the language of the heart than a wish.

Robert South

I was barely awake when the phone rang at 7:20 A.M.

"Hello?" I mumbled groggily, trying to clear the fog from my sleepy brain.

A little voice whispered, "Hi, Grandma!"

Suddenly I was wide awake. "Hi, Logan." I was surprised and delighted with the wake-up call because I knew his parents cautioned him not to call me too early in the morning. "How are you today?"

"Grandma," he continued to whisper, "Mom's still sleeping and Daddy went to get a newspaper, so I sneaked on the telephone."

I chuckled at the thought of this four-year-old waiting for an opportune moment to phone his grandma, knowing he can call me any time, day or night. There are no restrictions on our relationship, certainly not with something as mundane as time.

"Is today a Grandma Day?" he asked hopefully. Grandma

Days are the highlights of his young life.

"Yes, it is. Are you ready to come over?"

He assured me he was, and I was there at 8:30 A.M. sharp to pick him up.

"What would you like to do today?" I asked as we drove the few blocks to my home.

"Let's go to Goose Lake, Grandma." He giggled and said, "That sounds funny. Goose Lake Grandma!" He laughed as though he had made a huge joke and started chanting, "Goose Lake Grandma! Goose Lake Grandma!"

I got his tricycle out of the garage and we began the one-mile trek to Goose Lake, which is actually a man-made lake in a residential area. Its real name is Foxwarren Lake, but to Logan it is Goose Lake because of the numerous Canada geese that have made it their home.

As he pedaled down the sidewalk, he practiced reading street numbers on the houses we passed. Then he counted by twos, fives and tens, and then backward from 100. He had an obsession with numbers. The bigger the number, the more he liked it.

"See that tree?" He pointed to an elm tree. "It's going to turn into an apple tree soon. The apples might have little worms in them."

I smiled at the idea of an elm tree bearing apples.

"Look, Grandma, a zillion dandelions!" We stopped to stare at a field, covered in yellow and white softness. "Dandelions are weeds," he stated.

"Yes, they are," I agreed.

"But I still like them."

"I know you do," I answered. He picked a dandelion that had gone to seed, closed his eyes and blew the white puffy tendrils away.

"I made a wish. Do you want to know what I wished?"

"If you tell me, it won't come true," I said.

"But I want you to know," he insisted.

"Well, if you whisper it in my ear, then it should be okay." I bent down, and he cupped my ear with his hand and whispered his wish.

He stopped to pick up a feather, examined it closely, then put it into his bicycle basket. An unusual stone followed the feather, adding to his treasures from nature.

At Goose Lake we played in the park and watched the geese, which observed us, hoping for a handout. "Look at all the ducklings," remarked Logan, watching the fuzzy yellow babies waddle after their very protective parents.

"They're called goslings," I corrected. "Baby ducks are ducklings, and baby geese are goslings."

"Well then, they should be called gooselings! Look, there's Mother Goose!"

Disappointed that we didn't have food to offer them, Mother Goose gave a warning hiss and shuffled off with her little ones in tow, plunging into the lake. I guess they couldn't read the sign that stated "No Swimming".

On the way back home, Logan recited the house numbers on the other side of the street. He tried to whistle and when a faint sound came out, he announced gleefully, "I have magic lips!"

"Hold my hand, Grandma," he said, so I did. He pedaled his tricycle, steering with the other hand. I recalled what his mother said to him as we left that morning. "Have a good day with Grandma," she said, blowing him a kiss.

"I always do," Logan said. He paused, then continued, "And I always will!"

As he pedaled along, I squeezed his chubby hand in mine, remembering his dandelion wish . . . that every day be a Grandma Day, and "a grillion days more."

I knew I'd hold his hand for a while but his heart forever.

Maria Harden

Afternoon Delight

A grandmother is a little bit parent, a little bit teacher and a little bit best friend.

G. W. Curtis

Mishelle's brown eyes sparkled during the entire ceremony. She couldn't wait for the day she graduated from kindergarten, and had talked about it for weeks. Now she was standing on the stage with her classmates. Twenty five-year-olds wore blue graduation caps with tassels brushing against rosy cheeks flushed with excitement.

I snapped several pictures throughout the morning ceremony, capturing her big smile during each song that had been carefully rehearsed for parents, grandparents and family members. The highlight of the ceremony arrived when my youngest granddaughter marched across the stage to receive her kindergarten diploma.

She is quiet by nature, but I noticed she had little control over the spring in her step, almost skipping to reach her long-awaited certificate. I thought how beautiful she looked in her new pink-and-white flowered dress and patent leather shoes.

Following the ceremony, assorted cookies, frosted cup-cakes and red fruity punch was served to the young grad-uates. While munching on sweets, Mishelle introduced me to several classmates in frilly dresses. Her chatter was excited. And rightly so. This was the biggest day of her life.

Arrangements had been made for the children with working moms to spend the afternoon playing games in a supervised classroom until their parents picked them up. My granddaughter was prepared to join the other chil-dren when her mother had to return to work.

I had an idea. Speaking to her mother, I said, "Rather than stay at school, can Mishelle come home with me?"

My daughter-in-law thought for a moment.

"We'll have lunch together," I said, quickly adding, "and you can pick her up after work."

The instant her mother said yes, Mishelle began jump-ing up and down, clapping her hands.

A passerby, noticing her exuberance, said to Mishelle, "I see you're very excited about graduating today."

"No, not that," she answered.

The bystander looked puzzled, and my heart soared when my granddaughter said, "I'm going to Grandma's house."

Diane M. Vanover

Two Dedicated Grandmas

A laugh is worth one hundred groans in any market.

Charles Lamb

Who would have ever imagined they'd do such a thing?

Joel, my son, was celebrating his fourth birthday. Our family and friends gathered at the local Discovery Zone to party. After pizza and presents, it was time to play.

The kids crawled into the ball pen, where they literally swam through hundreds of balls. A large tunnel wound up and around the building. One by one, children crawled up and through the tunnel and traveled down its slide, shooting out the end straight into the sea of balls.

I never saw them make their move; finding their way into the balls. I didn't even see them enter the tunnel that climbed up to the top of the slide.

But I heard them!

My head turned. *It couldn't be . . . they couldn't have!*

But they had!

My jaw dropped as I looked up and saw Grandma Mary

Lou and Grandma Joyce on all fours, cramped inside the tunnel at the top of the slide.

"You go first," Grandma Mary Lou insisted.

"Well, I have to!" Grandma Joyce replied. "You couldn't get around me if you wanted too!"

And then giggles and laughter, like that of schoolgirls, streamed out of the tunnel . . . but no grandmas followed.

I maneuvered closer and positioned my camera, getting the perfect picture of two dedicated grandmas in ever-so-compromising positions.

"Are you gonna go?" I asked while looking up the tube. "You two are holding up the line."

Within seconds, Grandma Joyce made a splash as she flew down and out the tunnel and was buried beneath the balls.

"Are you okay? Lady, are you okay," a bystander asked.

I held my post and looked up into the tunnel again. Instead of shwooshing down the slide as Grandma Joyce did, Grandma Mary Lou sought a more sophisticated way. With her appendages spread-eagled and securely pressed against the sides of the tunnel, she sought to inch her way down the slide. Her body shook with laughter. Several children, strangers and family members, stood watching to see the last grandma propel from the slide. Wanting to savor the moment, I took more pictures of Grandma Joyce wading through balls and Grandma Mary Lou struggling to maintain somewhat of a ladylike position while contorting down the slide.

Within minutes, two grandmas emerged from the ball pen. Immediately, they headed directly to the little girls room, no doubt to gather their senses and pull themselves together. I marveled at them as they passed me. Grandma Mary Lou and Grandma Joyce, truly two dedicated grandmas—and certainly the life of the party!

Janet Lynn Mitchell

"Let's come back tomorrow with the grandchildren."

Go-Cart Grandma

The best hearts are ever the bravest.

Lawrence Sterne

When Grandma Emma Kobbeman's husband died during the Great Depression in 1932 she was just forty-two years old with five children ranging from twelve to twenty-three years old. From that day on, she struggled with poverty, single parenting and trying to find work with a fourth-grade education. She struggled, but she never lost her sense of humor or her spirit of adventure.

By 1960 Emma was a grandma with twenty-four grandchildren, all of whom lived close to her in northern Illinois. During the late forties, fifties and early sixties we'd gather often for a huge family picnic in a park not far from her home. This beautiful park along the shores of the Rock River was filled with Indian lore and bordered the home of Grandma's oldest child, my aunt Helen, and her six children.

One of those family picnics remains crystal clear in my memory. As Grandma's five children, their spouses and her two dozen grandchildren arrived, carrying enough food for Chief Black Hawk's entire army, we spread out among the tall pine trees to enjoy the day. Grandma, of course, presided over the festivities from her folding lawn chair, giggling at the antics of whatever baby happened to be the youngest member of our sprawling family.

Perhaps she ate too many sweets that day and was on a sugar high, or maybe it was the sight of her entire immediate family gathered together that made her feel especially frivolous. Whatever it was, we held our breath when Grandma made the announcement with her hands on her hips and a twinkle in her eye that she was going for a ride on my cousin's go-cart. She walked straight over to the go-cart and announced in a loud, clear voice to her eldest grandson, "Larry, show me how to run this thing."

Larry had built it from scratch. The body looked rough, but the engine was a piece of mechanical art that would have made Mario Andretti proud. When Grandma Kobbeman plopped her ample backside down onto the wooden seat and then stepped on the accelerator with her heavy brown oxfords, that little engine threw itself into world cup competition.

We cousins watched from a distance as she outran us in the first ten seconds. Grandma whizzed past three dozen giant pine trees, flew across the makeshift track Larry had made and then sailed right into the park's baseball field. She would have made a home run except she missed second base by fifty feet. She barely missed the popcorn stand and then headed straight for a forested area that led directly to the river. Both arms flailed in panic as Grandma's heavy oxfords pressed even harder onto the accelerator. She yelled, "Stop this thing! How do I get it to stop?"

As she headed for a row of poplars, narrowly missing two oversized oak trees, she must have experienced total body panic. Both of her legs shot out in front of her as she released them from their death-grip on the gas pedal. She quickly came to an abrupt halt in front of the sacred Indian mounds at the edge of the water. Chief Black Hawk would have been proud.

Grandma walked back to the picnic area, gathering up steam for the next two hours, during which time she barely took a breath while she told and retold the story of her go-cart adventure to all the relatives and even some strangers who happened by.

For a woman who grew up on a small farm in Illinois and watched our country change from horse-and-buggy to men-on-the-moon, Grandma had adapted remarkably well. The automobile, airplane, indoor plumbing, industrialization, mass production, frozen foods, space travel, civil rights and women's rights were all born during her lifetime. From horse-carts to go-carts, Grandma displayed a keen sense of humor, an unbridled spirit of adventure and a deep faith in God that I will always be glad is part of my heritage.

Somehow, as I walk through this world as a single parent, I draw strength from Grandma Emma. I have raised four spirited children of my own and am now a single grandmother of eight. I've ridden an alpine slide down a steep mountain, put my life in my daughter's hands on the back of her motorcycle on a busy California highway, snorkeled in two oceans, taken a sunrise flight in a hot-air balloon over the Arizona desert, and traveled alone for two days on two planes and two buses to arrive in Kuala Lumpur, Malaysia, to attend the wedding of a woman I'd met only once.

As far as I'm concerned, I've just begun. I think Grandma Kobbeman would approve heartily that I hope to go parasailing, explore the African continent, hike the Great Wall of China and go white-water rafting. I can almost hear Grandma up there cheering me on, "There's no way we want to stop this thing!"

Patricia Lorenz

Surf's Up, Grama

The purpose of life, after all, is to live it, to taste the experience to the utmost, to reach out eagerly and without fear for newer and richer experience.

Eleanor Roosevelt

My forty-five-year-old daughter, Sue Ellen, had been surfing for a couple of months, trying to entice me to go to the coast to try it. I kept putting her off, thinking, *Why would they want their almost seventy-year-old mother tagging along on this younger person's junket?* "It will be a great girls' weekend out," Sue Ellen coaxed.

The plan intrigued me . . . and scared me half to death!

I kept being wishy-washy about the possibility, hoping Dad and I would follow through with our plans for a fall trip and I'd have a good excuse. When this didn't seem to materialize, however, I reluctantly penciled in the date on my calendar.

My forty-one-year-old daughter, Diana, and two grand-daughters, ages eighteen and twenty, were all psyched up to go as well. But Diana kept saying, "You're nuts to try this, Mom; even I'm afraid of getting hurt." Sue Ellen, on the other hand, was saying, "Go for it, Mom. You can do it, and you'll always be able to say that you surfed for your seventieth birthday."

Well, that did it. My better judgment took a back seat, and I was determined. My husband just rolled his eyes and said, "I hope you know what you're doing!"

In the weeks to follow we all did our exercises and lifted weights to strengthen our wimpy muscles. One day when I stopped at Sue Ellen's, she motioned me into the dining room, where she had tape on her hardwood floors marking the foot placement on a virtual surfboard. She demonstrated the "pop up" procedure, where with one motion you pop up from a flat position on your stomach into a crouched position on the surfboard. Next thing I knew she had me on the floor doing a paddling motion with my hands and arms, then shouted, "Pop up!" Well, let me tell you, I felt like a newborn calf trying to stand!

The actual day arrived and, with gear and food packed in the car, we drove to Cannon Beach on the Oregon coast. We headed for the local surf shop to get outfitted—wetsuit, booties and gloves first. Next, a surfboard to suit one's size and ability. A short board is for the more experienced surfer. The long board gives a longer surface to manipulate, which was more my speed. This whole idea was becoming more of a reality every minute.

The surf coach we hired met us at the shop. Tony, a rugged, blond surfer type, was very laid back and comfortable to be with and seemed to enjoy our little group.

We followed him a few miles down the road to North Beach, which was in a more protected cove where the wind wasn't as strong and there were not as many rip tides with their strong undercurrents. We each unloaded our surfboards, strapped on a backpack, and hiked a mile or more down a trail, through the woods to the beach, pairing up to balance two surfboards between us.

It was a beautiful, warm, sunny weekend, and the area was crawling with funny-looking people in form-fitting wet suits. We donned ours there on the beach and draped all of our clothing over huge driftwood logs that had rolled in.

Tony was very safety conscious and spent a lot of time on the sand teaching us safety measures and surfing techniques. We learned how to lie on our boards, pop up to the crouch position and do a little two-shoe shuffle to balance and stand upright.

The waves were four to six feet high that first day, so I opted to stay on the beach and video the others. The second day, the waves had subsided to two to three feet high and I was ready. "You'll be up and surfing in no time!" said Tony.

He led us out through the surf and into the swells and held my surfboard while I got on. Lying on my stomach, I started paddling like mad. He gave me a push just as a big wave hit me. I remembered to pop up into my crouch position and I sailed like a bullet in a big whoosh of water toward the beach. I squealed with delight that I was still on my feet—that is, until the fin on the bottom of my board hit the sand, landing me right on my rump. I came up sputtering and coughing like a wounded pup, still leashed by the ankle to my board. Sue Ellen was on the beach filming me coming in. The girls and Tony were all clapping and cheering me on as I limped back to the beach, stifling my sobs of pain.

Gingerly, I perched myself between two logs so I wouldn't have to sit on my tailbone, which was steadily pulsating and throbbing. After collecting myself for a while, I thought the cold seawater would help, so I very slowly made my way across the beach and back into the water.

Standing sideways to the waves so as not to jar my posterior, the cold felt good on my bruised bottom. Just about then, Diana came sailing by on her board, thrilling to her latest ride in on a big wave . . . on her belly! "Diana," I said, "I can't bend over to get my board, but if you can get me headed right in the waves, I bet I can do that! I didn't come here to sit on a log all day."

I caught a few good waves belly-boarding, then was happy and proud to leave it at that. Tony said he was surprised that I'd gotten up the first time and stayed up that long; many of his students didn't even make it up the first time. A little praise did wonders for my bruised ego, if not for my bruised bottom.

After several hours of fun in the surf, it was time to leave. We trekked across the beach, up over the rocks on the bluff, and hiked the mile through the woods. It hurt to lift one leg up over the moguls, but with Sue Ellen giving me a pull from her end of the board, we got to the car and were mighty glad to be there. Those pillows for the ride back to Portland felt mighty good.

After about a week of a painful posterior, I checked in with the doctor. "Just badly bruised," he said. I've had a lot of fun telling the story, from my doctor who said, "You did this how?" to the nurse at the injury clinic who said, "At your age? Wish I dared to try that!"

A sensible senior perhaps I'm not, but in spite of having to sit on a pillow for a couple of weeks, I'm glad my good judgment temporarily took a back seat, that I took the challenge and had this fun "senior moment." I read somewhere that "Life is not a journey to the grave with the intention of arriving safely in a pretty and well-preserved body, but rather to skid in broadside, thoroughly used up, totally worn out and loudly proclaiming, 'Wow! What a ride!'"

It certainly was a ride to remember with daughters and granddaughters. They're each ready to ride the waves with gusto at the slightest mention of "Surf's up, Grama!"

Pam Trask

Grandma and the Snow Bank

Grandmothers are a special gift to children.

G. W. Curtis

Brian banged the door behind him and ran into the kitchen holding his new toy. "Grandma! Come outside and try my pogo stick!"

I shook my head. "Grandmas are breakable, Brian. I'd better not."

Disappointment drowned his hopeful expression, and he slouched out of the room. As I watched him go, my memory rewound to my own childhood.

In 1952, I'd been sent to stay with my grandparents. My little sister was gravely ill with something called "acute hemolytic anemia," which I could barely pronounce, much less understand. Mother's hands were full as she juggled nursing chores and chasing after my brother, an active preschooler. At ten years old, I was deemed responsible enough to travel alone the length of the state and not be "too much trouble" to Grandma and Grandpa.

I'd never traveled by myself, never been away from my family and never attended a city school. But there I was on an airplane bound for Portland, where my grandparents were waiting.

Grandma looked the same every time I saw her—round, firm and fully packed into a corset. She wore dresses and "sensible" black lace-up shoes, and she confined her flyaway hair in a bun at the back of her head. Born in Sweden some seventy-odd years before, she never quite conquered her Scandinavian accent.

Once we arrived at my grandparents' house, I settled my belongings in the familiar upstairs guestroom. The thought of having to make new friends and fit in with a strange fifth-grade class dimmed the joy of being at Grandma's without having to share her with my brother and sister.

The night before I started school, Grandma rolled my straight brown hair in rag strips so I'd wake up with curls. As I fell asleep, my head felt lumpy and so did my insides.

The next morning, jagged icicle teeth grinned at me from the eaves outside the bedroom window. Rattling and clanking, the radiator hissed in the chilly room. I huddled close to it and reached for warm clothes.

Grandma had laid out a brown plaid skirt and yellow sweater, along with a pair of brown wool kneesocks. I pulled on the skirt and sweater, but left the kneesocks untouched on the bed. Everyone at my old school wore anklets. Grandma's arguments couldn't persuade me to change my mind. I was sure I would be branded as weird if I showed up wearing stockings cuffed at the knee.

When it was time to leave, Grandma went along to enroll me in school. We walked to the corner of her block, then headed downhill on an icy sidewalk, following the same route my mother had taken when she was my age. All too soon the building loomed—three terrifying stories of stone, with a fenced playground facing the street. I watched children arriving ahead of us. They were cutting around the end of a wrought-iron fence and scooting down a snow bank onto the playground.

Suddenly I didn't want to continue on the shoveled walk that bisected the fence and led to the wide front doors. Everyone on the playground would see me and know I was a stranger.

"Please, Grandma, let's go this way." I tugged her toward the shortcut. "All the other kids are doing it."

She didn't hesitate. "Come on then," she said, easing around the end of the fence.

We traipsed to the snow bank and together plowed down it full force. Grandma slid on her backside, then sprung to her feet at the bottom, never missing a step. Clutching the strap of her handbag, she kept pace with me as though we were both ten years old. My bare legs were cold and wet; my Buster Browns filled with snow.

Our descent probably lasted just seconds, but those seconds were enough to install me in my new world. I walked proudly across the playground with Grandma and up the steps into the school.

Thanks to Grandma's courage and sense of adventure, I belonged.

Now, standing in my kitchen, I reconsidered my grandson's request. I called out the window, "Brian, let's play on that pogo stick!"

Grandmas aren't so breakable after all.

Ann Kirk Shorey

Grandma's River

*Happiness consists in being perfectly satisfied
with what we have got and with what we haven't
got. It is not how much we have, but how much
we enjoy, that makes happiness.*

Charles Haddon Spurgeon

Throughout my youth I treasured the hot summer days
spent with my grandma. Every summer she transformed
her front yard into a summer utopia. She accomplished
this by utilizing only what she had on hand: her eroded,
sunken front yard, cardboard boxes, old lawn chairs, blankets and a water hose.

Grandma, despite her poverty—or maybe because of
it—knew what the real blessing of summer was . . . water.

Before lounging in the old, white wooden lawn chairs,
Grandma and I would begin the yard transformation. First
came the draping of the old, hard lawn chairs with soft,
colorful blankets. Then we hauled out our daily supplies
of favorite items—ice-cold Orange Nesbit pop; thick,
salted slices of watermelon; chilled, hard green apples and
frozen candy bars. The treats varied daily, depending on

how much of Grandma's Social Security check was left. The two constants, however, were Grandma's beloved *Reader's Digest* and her large blue washcloth dunked in a pan of cold water filled with ice cubes.

Once the transformation was complete, we each took our places under the weeping willow tree with everything we needed close at hand in cardboard boxes. The day included hours of visiting, laughing, eating and pans of icy water. Later in the day, Grandma read stories to me from her *Reader's Digest.* I loved those stories and was mesmerized listening to her warm colorful voice as she read.

As the temperature increased, Grandma would douse herself with a wet cloth, press it up against her forehead and exclaim, "Oh, honey, this feels so good! You know, Melodie, nothing cools you off like a cold compress, unless you go to the river."

When the heat lingered on and became more intense, Grandma would say, "If it doesn't cool down soon, we will have to go to the river."

My heart started to race at the mention of the river. I had waited all day to hear those words. Yesterday the river was so wonderful; to return would be grand.

It was always midday when Grandma made the big decision to go. Finally, she would give in and say, "Honey, let's go to the river. I can't stand this heat anymore."

I would leap from my chair and squeal with excitement, "Grandma! Grandma! Can we make the river deep today?"

Walking around to the side of her house in her worn-out rubber thongs, making a flapping sound as she went, Grandma answered me loudly, "Let's see how the water pressure is, honey. Maybe we can have a waterfall too!"

I ran alongside my grandmother as she pulled and tugged her long, tangled hose to the front yard. She looked at me lovingly and said, "You first, honey. Go get in your chair. Hurry now, get your shoes off, I'll go turn on the water."

Each time I'd jump into my chair and fumble at my shoelaces to beat the water. I always succumbed to pulling too hard on my tennis shoes until they surrendered and came off. I anxiously pulled on the toe of my white socks, stretching the cotton material beyond size. Finally, victory . . . I saw bare feet!

I could hear the surge of water in the pipes making its way to the faucet; soon it would be flowing in the hose. Oh, the joy of anticipation! My excitement grew as my naked toes waited in the green grass for the arrival of water.

Grandma always held the hose high, water spewing and splashing about. Standing above me, she laughed and sprayed my tiny feet. The cold water was exhilarating. I giggled and bounced in my chair with delight as the water touched my skin. Laughing and looking up at my grandma, I would shout, "Grandma, I love you and your river so much!"

My grandma's expression softened, as if realizing the depth of joy she was giving me.

After a few minutes I announced, "Okay, Grandma, it's your turn now. Sit down!"

Then, taking the thick green hose in hand, I would spray Grandma's large swollen feet and legs. Grandma laughed loudly and rubbed her chubby feet together in the cold surging water. After awhile she sighed with relief, exclaiming, "Melodie, what a difference this water makes. I can finally breathe, honey. Thank the good Lord for water!"

As the water rolled down Grandma's legs, I chimed in too, mimicking her tone perfectly. "Thank the good Lord for water!"

Grandma would let the water run until the sunken side of her lawn was completely flooded. Her concrete sidewalk held the water in place until it evaporated later.

After the lawn was flooded, we sat there dangling our feet in about three inches of water, enjoying our created surroundings of old lawn chairs draped with blankets and our trusted cardboard boxes holding all our daily treasures.

It never even occurred to me how ridiculous we might have looked to some. The only picture I recall in my head when remembering those glorious summer days spent at Grandma's are images of blissfulness and joy.

Yes, it was there in my grandma's run-down, flooded yard that I had my first taste of summer bliss. Many, many years have passed since, but I still long for those hot summer days shared with her. Some children had swimming pools; others had trips to lakes or the ocean; thankfully, I had "Grandma's River."

Melodie Lynn Tilander

Journey Home

As she glared at the Houston rush hour traffic, Grandma clutched her steering wheel as tightly as I gripped the map in my hand. That morning we had left Grandma's little cabin in the Ozark Mountains to move her in with my family in southeast Texas. I was her designated companion on the trip.

"Look at that sky," said Grandma. "Storm's coming."

I peered up at the sky. It was black, very black. Torrents of rain, hail and high winds hid in dark clouds like these. In my thirteen years of life I had watched enough newscasts to know that in the worst storms, Houston's underpasses flood up to six feet deep in minutes, road signs blow down onto the expressway and hail the size of golf balls dents cars.

Afraid, I said, "Grandma, we gotta get off this highway." I looked for an exit. Grandma was as worried as I was about the storm. From the inside lane of four lanes of traffic, Grandma spied an exit sign. With barely a glance over her left shoulder, she shot across three lanes of traffic. Cars honked. A few swerved. I closed my eyes until I could feel the car enter the exit ramp.

"Flip on the overhead light," commanded Grandma as

we slowed for a red light. "Find us a way home."

We started a new journey down two-lane roads. Every time we came to a four-way stop Grandma looked at me. Each time I studied the map silently. When I figured where we were and where we were going, I pointed the way. Grandma did not question. The crumpled map became damp in my clutches as hour after hour we drove through winding back roads and small towns. The houses we passed in the middle of the night were dark. The Texas landscape was silent. It seemed as if we were the only people in the world who were awake.

Finally, it began to rain. Together, we strained against our seatbelts to see the road ahead. I did not need the map anymore. We were on the last stretch of road before the turnoff to our home. My eyes shut briefly every few minutes as I dreamed of my soft, warm bed. During one of my dozes Grandma switched to the outside lane. I was too groggy to comprehend that there was no outside lane on that two-lane road. Moments after the "lane change" the rain fell faster. Tiny rocks dinged the windshield.

Mysteriously, the pavement suddenly became bumpy and uneven. I glanced out my window. We were rushing past tall weeds and bushes just inches from the window.

"Grandma," I yelled. "You're driving on the shoulder!"

"No, I'm not," she snapped.

A few moments later the shoulder of the road ended. A bridge abutment loomed in front of us.

"Get back on the road," I hollered.

Grandma swerved into the correct lane as the road funneled under a bridge.

We drove in silence, continuing to stare into the darkness, looking for our turnoff.

A few miles later I saw the exit to the road where we lived. Grandma slowed the car and turned off the lonely stretch of highway.

"There's our driveway," I announced wearily. She shifted into low gear, turned and missed the entrance completely. The car nosed into the ditch, the tires slowly sinking into the rain-saturated earth.

Grandma unfastened her seat belt. "Let's go," she said wearily. "We're home."

We staggered out of the car and up out of the ditch. Sliding in the mud, I tried to keep up with Grandma. The porch light was on. A faint glow came through the window from the living room lamps. Grandma trudged slowly in front of me, exhausted from long hours of night driving, narrowly avoiding a bridge collision and parking in a ditch at the end of her destination. Still, we beat the storm. We made it home.

I know now what I did not know as a thirteen-year-old girl that dark rainy night. Grandma had more to be afraid of than the black clouds that gathered against the Houston sky. At the age of seventy she left, leaving the Ozark mountain cabin that held countless memories of her late husband. She was on her way to a small town on the Gulf of Mexico. There she would start a new life with her daughter, son-in-law and six children—a new life at the age of seventy, when she should have been settling into the routine of her twilight years. Grandma, my grandma, took on a whole new challenge.

Today, as a middle-aged woman I can only say that I hope to grow old like her. I want to face each new bend in the road as it comes, just as she did on that rainy night so long ago. With courage and a sense of adventure, I want to face the journey home.

Renee Hixson

Getting directions to Grandma's in the computer age.

Travels with Grandma

Not a sentence or word is independent of the circumstances under which it is uttered.

Alfred Lord Whitehead

My daughters, Linda and Leslie, never called my mother anything but Honie. Mother announced early on that she was much too young to be a grandmother, and Honie was the closest derivative of her name Helen, so Honie she was to all of us.

Honie was an inveterate traveler, and fortunately for us, she derived great pleasure from taking us on her journeys. Although Linda was fifteen and Leslie was twelve and I was thirty-five, Honie always referred to the three of us as "her girls" and treated us as if we were all the same age. And on her trips, since she was well read and very knowledgeable about everywhere her travels took us, we all acted childlike. No matter what the country, every morning Honie would determine our destination and our destiny for the day, and we would follow like dutiful little ducklings wherever she led. For one so small (she was barely five feet tall) she was a born leader and not to be deterred in whatever she determined to achieve.

Her notion of speaking a foreign language was to speak English very slowly, very loudly and act out the words as one might in the game of charades. We would stand aside as she went through her convolutions, and although we might risk a whispered "Is it bigger than a breadbox?" we generally shut up and let her elicit whatever answers she could with her dramatic efforts.

Our first Sunday in Lisbon, she approached a Portuguese gentleman on the street, pulled on his sleeve, pointed to the heavens, then folded her hands in supplication and said, "God—pray, God—pray?" The gentleman looked at her quizzically, and then as the light dawned, responded, "You want a church, lady?"

Honie beamed in pleasure as he pointed out the nearest church and went on his way. She had already mastered Portuguese. We rolled our eyes in despair and followed her into the church, not sure whether to pray for indulgence or beg for forgiveness.

In our week's stay at the Avenida Palace, there was scarcely a morning that she did not have a request for the front desk, and to their credit, they were always tolerant and usually accommodating.

One morning as we rode down to the lobby in the big iron elevator, Honie was doing her usual "tch, tch," as she decried the fact that European hotels "never, ever, ever supplied washcloths" and announced that she would just stop by the front desk to request three for the next morning. Approaching the desk clerk, she said slowly and distinctly, "Excuse me, but we . . . don't have . . . any . . . ," and folding her hand into a ball, she vigorously scrubbed her cheek.

"Soap?" he asked.

She shook her head in irritation. "No, no, washcloths."

"Ah," he nodded knowingly. "I will see to it, señora."

Mission accomplished, we were off to Nazare for a day of exploring. The next morning she informed us once again that she needed to stop at the front desk.

Timorously we followed and waited while she informed the clerk that we were out of Kleenex in our bathroom. This request included placing her hand over her nose, saying "achoo" several times and wiping her nose. Now it was the clerk's turn to roll his eyes, but he acknowledged her request and we were on our way.

The next morning we were halfway across the lobby and almost out the door when Honie stopped us. "Just a minute, girls. I need to tell the desk clerk that we're out of toilet paper."

The picture of how she might dramatize that request was more than any of us could face. We were out the door in a flash, leaving Honie to face the clerk on her own. There is a limit to what even the most dutiful ducklings will endure.

Phyllis W. Zeno

Going Places

Fun *gives you a forcible hug, and shakes laugh-ter out of you, whether you will it or no.*

David Garrick

I've been to an N'Sync concert. I've snacked at Jekyll and Hyde, the popular theme restaurant. When Britney Spears was involved with a restaurant in Manhattan, I dined there. Am I a teenybopper? Ha! Far from it. I've visited playgrounds, amusement parks and Chuck E. Cheese's. Am I a toddler? Of course not. I've been at the huge kaleidoscope in the Catskill Mountains of upstate New York and visited Liberty Science Center where patrons are encouraged to touch and test the museum exhibits. Okay, now you've probably guessed it. I'm a grandmother.

You'll find there are many perks to being a grandparent . . . once you recover from that initial shock. And I say shock, because no matter how lovingly anticipated, the birth of a first grandchild is a milestone moment. Many of us become grandparents when we're not quite ready. It seems like only yesterday we were caring for our own babies, and now one of them has a child.

But soon we learn that grandchildren look upon the world with new eyes and that it's quite possible to share that gift. They're great company; they inspire us to go on quests without traveling to exotic lands and foreign shores. I've taken a couple of young ones on an elephant safari . . . on the Jersey Shore. Thanks to my pitiful sense of direction, we wandered about before finding our quarry. And there we were, looking at Lucy, the Margate elephant, a historical structure, once a publicist's ploy to urge folks to buy property, then a tourist camp and restaurant, and now a fascinating building, complete with howdah atop. We climbed into one huge right leg, went to the upper story, looked out Lucy's eye at the ocean and then climbed up to the howdah.

On a recent off-season visit to the giant kaleidoscope, we lay on the floor and looked up as the world changed before our eyes. Would I do that if I didn't have a kid next to me? I'd love to say I would, but I doubt it.

Grandchildren allow us to enjoy the things that either weren't around when we were kids or things we never got to see. Sure, I did some of this stuff with my own kids, but life was so busy then. Now I can enjoy all these little pleasures.

Merry-go-rounds—I've always loved them. I enjoyed riding the horses that didn't move when I was a young child and riding the horses that went up and down when I was a teenager. Now I pretend I'm going just to take a toddler for a ride, but it's a sham. I love every minute of it. I've ridden merry-go-rounds at amusement areas and malls and on the historical flying horses carousel on Martha's Vineyard.

I've visited a simulated rainforest where butterflies flitted about, landing on our shoulders and backs. I've been to a small local museum where huge, mechanized dinosaurs roared and shuddered. I've ridden the rails on the Hello Dolly train in the Pennsylvania Dutch country and clambered aboard the swan boats in Boston for an old-fashioned ride.

I've tuned in Nickelodeon and the Cartoon Network. I find it wonderful that despite all the changes in the world my grandchildren often watch the same cartoons and shows that I did years ago. We can watch Bugs Bunny or *I Love Lucy* together and laugh at all the same things. I thought I'd be bored at kids' movies, but I've seen some truly original ones, like *Babe* and *Toy Story* and, of course, *Shrek,* while swiping a few handfuls of popcorn from my little compatriots.

There is always a grandchild willing to go for ice cream or pizza, and the kids love to traipse through the little candy store nearby and pick out penny candy the same way I did when I was a kid. There is always someone to laugh (and as they get older, groan) at a corny joke. And any grandkid under the age of eight is happy to be my dance partner when I have old-time rock 'n' roll blasting on the stereo in my living room.

Just about everything, from making cupcakes to painting ceramics, is more fun when there's a grandchild eager to learn how. All of sudden I'm an expert, despite my lack of skill in many such endeavors.

Dr. Seuss wrote a wonderful book called *Oh, the Places You'll Go!* and I'm grateful that I have grandchildren to take me along.

Thanks, grandkids!

Carolyn Mott Ford

Will He Remember?

What we learn with pleasure, we never forget.

Alfred Mercier

I have a confession to make. I am in love with a younger man.

It is a deep and lasting love unlike any other I have experienced. When we are together, all is well with the world. When we are apart, I long for his presence to fill the ache in my heart. For over four years, his unconditional love has completed me like the last piece of a puzzle. I now understand when poets and romanticists describe how they would lay down their life for someone they love. I would do the same.

The object of my affections is my only grandchild. I marvel at being a grandmother, but I wear it well, like a comfortable coat that feels right. I wonder why I do, since I have little experience of having a grandmother myself. My maternal grandmother died before I was born. My paternal grandmother lived in Europe, and I only recall her visiting us once. When I was about fifteen, my parents sent her a plane ticket to come to Canada for my sister's wedding. She came, but the language differences made it difficult for us to communicate. I wondered what she felt when her son packed up his family and moved across the ocean so many years ago. I wished I had known her better. I wished she had come with us. I wished I had memories with her.

I never knew what I missed until I became a grandmother myself. I can barely remember anything until I began school, and even then, they are only half-remembered fragments. My biggest concern is that my grandson will not remember our days together. Time is fleeting; it steals memories of yesteryear, evaporating with the dawn.

Our days together, grandmother and grandson, are filled with fun, learning and play. Some days we just sip at the day, savoring it slowly, and other days we take a deep swallow and taste all it has to offer.

With the consent of his parents, I have been fortunate to be part of many firsts in his young life. I was the first to take him to see Santa at the mall. I took him to his first movie, his first trip to the beach, his first haircut with "a real lady at a real hair-cutting place." We have enjoyed lunches at restaurants, visits with friends and excursions to museums. We have ridden the bus and the train. We have scoured the neighborhood for garage sales, played in parks, fed the birds, splashed in puddles, raked leaves, picked pine cones and built snowmen. Will he remember any of this?

I wonder if he will remember who taught him how to crack eggs and whisk batter nice and smooth for the pancakes he loves so much. Or how we built a secret fort under the dining room table with blankets. Will he remember who played endless games of Checkers, Candyland, and Chutes and Ladders with him, while teaching him how to lose gracefully? Will he recall who taught him to play "Twinkle Twinkle Little Star" on the piano, his little fingers stretching to cover the right keys, his face a study in concentration?

My grandson rejuvenates me. Seeing the world through his eyes is nothing short of wondrous. His energy is refreshing, and his infectious giggle makes me laugh. I pray he will remember the lullabies, the laughter and, most importantly, the love when he is grown and has a family of his own.

Will he remember me?

Maria Harden

5

THROUGH
THE EYES OF
A CHILD

I love these little people; and it is not a slight
thing, when they, who are so fresh from God,
love us.

Charles Dickens

Love Never to Be Blinded

The balls of sight are so formed, that one man's eyes are spectacles to another, to read his heart.

Samuel Johnson

"Mom! Come look at the sunset!" My six-year-old daughter called, running to the window at the retirement home. Mandy could be demanding and full of energy, and she seemed to be far more so when my attention was on someone else. Right now that attention was on my mother, frail and angry and sitting in the lobby of the retirement home we had placed her in.

"It's an institution! You're trying to put me into an institution!" Mother had declared when we first suggested the idea. But with her age and her blindness and our trying to raise two very active girls and balance jobs to pay the bills, she finally relented. I had tried to make her happy and feel at home, even taking time to make her a lavender and blue quilt, her favorite colors before she lost her sight.

So here she sat, huffy, gloomy and not talking to me. The caretaker of Suncrest Home came over with a cup of tea. "Now, Mrs. LeSage, how about a nice cup of tea? It's your favorite, Earl Grey with lemon."

"Mom! Come see! Come see!" Mandy interrupted from the corner by the window.

The caretaker smiled. Mother turned away and the tea was placed on the table beside her. I shrugged, not knowing what to do, how to cope anymore. I wasn't far from tears.

The caretaker pulled me gently aside. Away from the lobby and out in the corridor, she placed her arm around me as I collapsed into sobs. "I just don't know what else to do," I said, my voice breaking. "I know she hates me for it, but I don't know what else I can do. She can't be on her own, not with her blindness and . . ."

"Quit blaming yourself," she said firmly. "That won't help either you or your mother. Right now you have to be firm but loving. In time, she will adjust to her new surroundings . . . and besides, you're only a few miles away."

Not that it matters, I thought, remembering my mother's stony glare and silent face. She would probably never talk to me again. I was walking back toward the lobby when I heard the excited voice of a child. Mandy! I had left her in there with her grandmother and the other residents! What could she be up to?

"It is purple! Real, deep purple. Purple like the grapes on Uncle Willis's vines in September!"

"And what about the red? Is there any red?" an elderly voice asked.

"Red? Yes there is red in it too! It has all different kinds of red—like the bike that Grandpa gave me for my birthday when I was five. Do you remember, Grandma?"

I came in to see Mandy and her grandmother standing by the window as the warm sun set outside. Mandy gently pressed my mother's hand to the glass. "I know you can't see the red anymore, Grandma, but you can feel it, right? And the golden yellows and the orange and . . ."

My mother smiled and clasped Mandy's hand, then pulled her close for a hug. "Yes, I can. I can feel the colors of the sunset."

She let my daughter guide her back to a chair and hugged her once more. "And when you tell me what you see, well, it makes it all real for me." She turned to me and said, "Well, now it's your turn. Tell me, what color is that quilt that you made me on my bed?"

From then on, Mandy met with her grandmother at least once a week and phoned her often. She told her of the colors of her school—brown wood and bright yellow paint with a picture of a happy face on the door. She told her of the green of the ocean when she first visited it and how the stormy blue sky was the same color as her cousin Jennifer's eyes. She shared the dark black of her graduation gown and the glorious yellow rose corsage that Grandmother sent for her special day. She phoned her long distance to share the black sand of Hawaiian beaches and the icy crevices in the Yukon. She even told her the shade of hair of the boy she fell in love with—dark and wavy, just like the old pictures of Grandfather.

Mandy taught me a valuable lesson: that I could not give my mother her sight back, or the life she once had. I had to stop feeling guilty and focusing on what I couldn't give her but rather on what I could . . . time and the colorful sharing that comes from a love that is not blinded.

Nancy V. Bennett

Pennies from Heaven

You cannot teach children to take care of themselves unless you let them try. They will make mistakes; and out of these mistakes comes wisdom.

Henry Ward Beecher

"Nana! Help! I'm falling!" and suddenly the little girl with her new roller blades had fallen on the sidewalk for the one hundredth time.

"I can't do it!" the little girl cried as a tear rolled down her cheek.

"Don't worry. I'm here to catch you," whispered Nana as she wiped the tear away. "Remember, when it rains, it rains pennies from heaven!" Nana hugged the girl and started to hum the song.

From the time the girl was six weeks old, Nana took care of her in every way. She fed, rocked and played with the girl. She never seemed to mind when the little girl smelled dirty. She was always there with open arms when the little girl was wobbly or unsure of herself. She smiled and encouraged her when the little girl couldn't talk well and told her to keep practicing.

"You can do anything you want to do. Just put your mind to it," Nana would say to her.

Nana taught the little girl to play the piano. In Nana's shaky handwriting, she would write songs for the little girl to play on the piano. Every Christmas they saw *The Nutcracker* together. Nana would cheer and clap when the little girl would try to twirl and dance like the ballerinas.

"Remember, never give up. Just feel the music in here," and she would point to her heart. The little girl understood, because when she was with Nana she felt she could be and do almost anything.

During this time the little girl didn't notice how Nana's hands and head shook for no reason at all. She didn't notice, and she didn't care. Nana loved her and was her very best friend.

Soon the little girl went off to school. She got new friends and became busy with all the things school brings. She had less and less time to spend with Nana. Nana's shaking got much worse, and soon the girl felt strange being with her. The little girl found out that Nana had a disease called Parkinson's, which is a disease that takes over a person's body. This disease forced Nana to move to a nursing home to be taken care of.

One day the girl went to visit Nana. Everything about the nursing home gave the girl a strange and uncomfortable feeling. She noticed the small, bare room. She noticed that Nana didn't smell as good as she used to. The girl heard Nana's teacup make a clinking noise against the plate as her Nana slowly took a sip. The girl could hardly watch as Nana got up and slowly, oh so slowly, tried to take a tiny step. The girl felt sad as she watched her Nana fall back on her bed. And then suddenly the girl saw a picture in her mind.

The girl remembered how Nana had gently encouraged

her when she was learning how to try her new roller blades. She remembered how Nana would hug her and smile whenever the girl felt she couldn't do something. And then she realized something else Nana had given her. Nana had taught her what to do for someone who needed to feel safe, secure and loved.

The girl took her Nana by the hand and slowly helped her to her feet.

"Well, I can't walk as good as I used to. I don't feel so sure of myself," Nana slurred.

"Don't worry, Nana, you can do it. You know, when it rains, it rains pennies from heaven."

Emily Erickson
Ten years old

Dusting in Heaven

Heaven, the treasury of everlasting joy.

William Shakespeare

My eight-year-old son, Jonathan, is an exceptionally inquisitive and cheerful child who must have an answer for every question that enters his mind. I truly admire this awe-inspiring quality in him. However, I'm stumped when I do not have an answer for him.

While tucking him into bed one night I faced the hardest question he'd posed to me up until then.

"Mommy," he said, "where is my granny now, and what is she doing there?"

I was entirely lost for words. There was a long pause as I searched my heart and soul for an appropriate answer.

My mother-in-law had been diagnosed with lymphoma and suffered through two long years of chemotherapy and radiation. Our family, being very close, prayed together as we watched this horrible disease claim her life twenty-six months later. My son was very close to his grandmother, and her death was a great mystery to him. I always knew this time would come, but how to prepare for such a question was a mystery to me.

Granny must have been listening to the conversation between her only grandson and me because my answer to him came out as if someone was talking for me.

"Jonathan," I began, "Granny has gone to live in heaven." Recalling the special care and tidiness she took with her home, I added, "She is dusting the clouds and keeping them shiny white."

After a brief thought, Jonathan smiled as if he could imagine Granny working hard in heaven, and he kissed me good night. Relieved that I had satisfied his curiosity, I let out a breath of relief. I, too, missed her, and was happy I had moved through the interrogation without tears. Jonathan fell asleep, happily as always.

The next morning he ran through the house and jumped into bed with me. "Mom!" he said, "please come and look out your window!"

I half opened my eyes and gazed at the rays of sunshine filtering into my bedroom. "Yes, Jonathan, it is going to be a beautiful day."

Jonathan had a glow about him as he looked at me with his wide-open eyes. His face beamed like a shaft of light as he glared out the window where the sun came shining in. He said, "Granny is doing a great job up there in heaven. Just look at those clean, white, fluffy clouds!"

Denise Peebles

Healing

You must do the thing you think you cannot do.

Eleanor Roosevelt

Grieving deeply, Grandma Dunkle refused to sleep in her bedroom after Grandpa died. To everyone's surprise, her four-year-old granddaughter, Robbi, adopted the mission of reacquainting Grandma with her king-sized bed again.

"Grandma, we sleep in your bed tonight," Robbi would say.

"No," Grandma replied, her eyes filling with tears. "Not tonight."

And so it went, one weekend trailing after another during sleepovers, with Robbi's plea rejected time and again.

One night, after changing into their pajamas, Robbi simply led her grandmother by the hand down the hallway to the master bedroom. Grandma paused in the doorway for a long while, tears welling up. Robbi jumped onto the bed and flipped back the covers.

"It's all right, Grandma," she said, patting the space next to her.

Like swallowing medicine whole to avoid the bitter taste, her grandmother quickly scooted under the covers. There, they held each other snug in the middle of the huge bed, where for the first time in weeks her grandmother slept without nightmares.

Through the wisdom and sensitivity of a child, a grandmother had taken the first tentative step toward a healing journey.

Once again, as a teenager, Robbi perched on the edge of the king-sized bed, caressing her grandmother's hand. There were only a few months left. Robbi tended to her in those few precious months, massaging her with a wealth of love and tenderness. Studies and boys and other high school commitments were relegated to the back burner.

And for the second time in her life, Robbi's heart broke when her beloved grandmother was laid to rest.

But it didn't stop there.

As a young woman, Robbi, continues to make ever-widening ripples within the older, more fragile generation. One can see her today as a college student working in a nursing home, changing a feeding tube, cupping an elderly resident's hand while he reminisces, reading letters for eyes that can no longer focus.

And to think it all began with a four-year-old rising above her own grief to reach out and heal her grandmother.

Jennifer Oliver

I Will Remember

If becoming a grandmother was only a matter of choice, I should advise every one of you straight away to become one. There is no fun for old people like it!

Hannah Whithall Smith

Until I was eight I thought Sunday was called Sunday because you had to spend it in the sun. I thought that because I spent every single Sunday outside in the garden with Nana. The zucchini plants quickly became my favorite. It was the way the tiny little delicate tendrils reached out and wrapped around the lattice, like tiny fingers holding on as tightly as they could. They seemed so helpless. I would sit on the ground and tend to them, sensing that they needed me. Nana would sit there, perched on her gardening stool, looking at the tomatoes in the same way.

"Nana," I asked one day, "should I take off all these little yellow flowers?"

"Why would you take the flowers off?" she asked gently.

"Well, I thought they might attract the bugs and then the bugs might eat them."

"No, darling," she said with a little laugh, "those flowers will turn into zucchini soon."

"Really?"

"You just wait. Soon you'll see that little things can turn into wonderful things. You should remember that."

"Little things can turn into wonderful things," I repeated.

"That's right," she said.

Every Sunday I returned to the garden to check on the zucchini plants, and each time I saw more and more zucchini.

"Do you think there are so many because I take good care of the plant?" I asked.

"Yes," Nana said, "when you look after things, good things tend to grow. You should remember that."

"When you look after things, good things tend to grow," I repeated.

"That's right," she said.

I looked after the zucchini plants even better after that. I removed brown leaves, and if one of those tiny tendrils couldn't reach the lattice, I moved it a little closer. Nana did the same to the tomatoes. Then one Sunday I watched as she took the clippers and cut off one whole branch of the plant.

"Nana!" I put my hand over my mouth in shock. "What did you do that for?"

"The plant isn't strong enough to have two good branches full of tomatoes," she said. "I had to get rid of one so the plant could make the most of the other one."

"Oh."

"You might have to make the same kind of choice some day," she said.

"What do you mean, I'll have to get something chopped off?"

"No dear," she said with a giggle, "but you might have

to make some decisions, because sometimes you just can't have everything."

"I'll remember that," I said.

For months I returned every week to Nana's to see how my plant was doing, and each time I was proud to see more zucchini. Until one day, when they stopped appearing, and a few weeks later, there were none.

"Nana, what's wrong with my plant?" I asked tearfully. "It's not growing anymore."

"That's what happens, darling. Things grow but then they stop. Nothing lasts forever."

"But I was so good to it."

"Yes," she said, "but things end so new things can start."

"And is there something I should remember?"

"Yes," said Nana. "Seasons change, but for everything that ends, something new will take its place."

"I'll remember that," I said.

I helped tend other garden plants, but one day I admitted, "I really miss the zucchini plants."

"I know, darling."

"I was thinking, Nana, what if we got Poppy to make a greenhouse? Then we could have zucchini plants all year."

"I don't know," she said. "Maybe we should just wait for the right season."

"But can we just try? Can I just ask Poppy? Please Nana."

"I guess we can try," she said.

Poppy agreed, and the next week I arrived to find a greenhouse constructed. The best part about it was the inside of the walls: there was lattice from top to bottom.

"This is the perfect home for zucchini plants," I said.

"And tomatoes," Nana added.

We planted zucchini on one side and tomatoes on the other. Week after week, the zucchini plants looked better and better. Nana's tomatoes were just as good. Then the fruit came, and we both realized that this greenhouse worked perfectly.

"Look, Nana," I said. "I have a little zucchini here and hundreds of flowers. These plants are going to be the best ever."

"What a fabulous idea you had," Nana said, squeezing my hand.

"Nana," I said, "I think you should remember something."

"What's that?"

"There is always a way if you want something bad enough."

Nana turned and looked at me. I saw a tiny tear in her eye and for a moment, I thought she was going to cry. Then she smiled the biggest smile I have ever seen. She shook her head slightly and squeezed my hand again.

"Thank you, darling," she said. "I will remember that."

Shelley Ann Wake

Love's Labors Found

Life isn't a matter of milestones, but of moments.

Rose Kennedy

I was feeling horribly rejected. Spurned.

My grandson Isaiah, a feisty seven-year-old with a mind and will all his own, had decided he was too old to hug and kiss his grandmother. For that matter, Zay, as he is universally known, was too old even to bother with me.

When my husband and I made the two-hour round trip to see him in a school play for his two-minute walk-on, or made sure to be at his karate class for his (ahem) graduation, Zay would greet us with a grin—but keep his distance.

Once, when I forgot the mandate and hugged him in a public place, he reminded me of the ground rules: no hugging anywhere, especially not in public.

When I'd try to spend time with him before he went to bed, Zay seemed eager for me to leave so he could play with his "guys," those strange creatures kids call "action figures."

I needed advice and a little sympathy, so I turned to

Zay's mother, my daughter Jill, the same person who used to turn to me for solace. "What should I do?" I asked this daughter, who knew how much I was hurting.

Wise Jill assured me that seven-year-old boys often struggle with issues of independence and boundaries.

So I waited it out, just as Jill advised. I kept my distance from Zay and lavished my hugs on his sister and his younger cousins, who all hugged me back.

But it was downright painful to leave Zay's room feeling that I was an unwelcome intruder. And waving goodnight to him from the safe distance of the doorway almost made me weep.

This wonderful little boy with the dark brown eyes who had once begged me to read him *Goodnight Moon* ten times in a row—who had pleaded with me to stay in his room long after the light went out—was testing my endurance for rejection.

On a recent visit, I was braced for the usual from this seven-year-old master of the rebuff. When I met Zay at his bus stop, to my surprise and delight he rushed toward me, and for the first time in too long I saw real delight on his face. I willed my arms not to dare reach out to him, but felt his hand grabbing mine even before the bus pulled away.

I didn't dare show my surprise—or my soaring elation. This was the old Zay, the pre–seventh–birthday Zay. It was wonderful to have him back. Still, I was not going to be taken in by beginnings. I figured at home he would once again play the tough guy who didn't believe in public displays of affection.

And I was half right.

Zay didn't join in the ice cream party in the kitchen, a tradition that usually marked my visits, and he didn't choose to join us in a spirited game of Go Fish. But at dinner, he begged to sit next to me. And at bedtime, he scrambled into his pajamas and brushed his teeth knowing that the payoff for speed was extra story time with me.

When I sat down on his bed, it was almost like old times. He asked for a "mouth story," his way, years ago, of telling me not to read from a book but to invent one for him. As I began my tale, it was almost nostalgic, if one can be nostalgic with someone who's only been on this earth for only seven years.

We laughed a lot in that mouth story, making up characters named "Clotilda" and "Bongi." And when it was clear that he was ready to surrender to sleep—when those brown eyes fluttered a few times—I was ready to tiptoe out when Zay pointed to his cheek.

I got the message.

I leaned over and kissed him for the first time in too long.

Zay smiled. And so did I . . . for a week.

Sally Friedman

God's Hands

You do not really understand something unless you can explain it to your grandmother.

Albert Einstein

Following her granddaughter's baptism, my friend asked the youngster, "Why don't you draw me a picture of what happened to you in church?"

Judy drew a large pair of hands with a child standing in the middle of them. Grandma was impressed.

"Oh, did they sing 'He's Got the Whole World in His Hands'?"

Judy shook her head seriously. "No, Grandma. That's a picture of what Daddy said to Mommy. 'Now that Judy is baptized, God is sure going to have his hands full!'"

Shirley Pope Waite

God's Good Time

Where children are, there is the golden age.

Novalis

A few Christmases ago, I opened a gift from my son and daughter-in-law and was mystified to see a diaper nestled in holiday paper. Turning it over I read, "I love you, Grandpa and Grandma. See you in July." Talk about fireworks! I instantly became a first-time grandmother-in-waiting, with all my time references revolving around that due date.

I told everyone I knew, and those who were grandparents all gave me the same glowing response. I would will my eyes not to glaze over while I listened to these sage words over and over again. "Just wait. You can't imagine the joy and love of being a grandparent."

Of course I could imagine! I had five children of my own, four nieces and seven nephews. I'd been there. I knew what it was all about. In fact, I already loved this baby.

June took more than its fair share of summer, and then July trudged into August, forgetting to leave us a grandchild along its way. "Everything in God's good time," I had always taught my children, but now I was really beginning to wonder if God might just need a calendar.

Every time the phone rang I jumped up thinking, *This is it!* If I was away from home I checked for messages every half hour. Cheryl, the mother-to-be, was kind and patient with me. I did try to limit my "How are you doing?" calls to no more than four or five or six times a day. I took her to lunch, matinees, craft sales, garage sales, anything to move the days along and hoping, just maybe, I would be with her when it happened.

If you noticed all creation sang in harmony on August 4, 1998, it's because that was the day Joshua was gifted to this world. He was wonderful beyond words, and I was captivated by his every sound and motion, his very scent. And the first day of his life didn't pass before I heard myself say to a grandmother-in-waiting, "Just wait. You can't imagine it." I'm not sure, but I think I saw her eyes glaze over.

When Joshua was three months old that little family moved two hours away. My husband and I saw him as much as possible, but it was never enough. We'd call each other Papa and Grandma just to hear the words.

Of course, Joshua learned to say "Papa" long before he said "Grandma." On the phone he'd squeal "Hi, Papa!" all through the conversation.

He could say "coo-kee" and point to my cookie jar. He said "pease" for please and included the sign language gesture his mother taught him. He said "bite," "ball," "show," "touchdown," "cracker," "outside," and the list went on and on.

But no "Grandma."

When Jason and Cheryl asked us to care for Joshua while they traveled to her brother's wedding, we couldn't say yes fast enough. I was reminded of the "We've Got Annie" musical number in the movie *Annie.* You know, tap dancing down the grand stairway, singing and twirling bed sheets in the air as we prepared his room. Okay, I admit, I do exaggerate a little—our stairway is more functional than grand.

Our four days together rushed by with swings, slides, choo-choos, playing trucks and reading stories. Joshua delighted us with kisses and reminded us to pray before each meal.

When we paraded him into church he pointed out every picture of Jesus. "Jethus love me," he'd announce with absolutely no doubt about his lovability.

At home he'd stand eye to eye with the statue of Jesus in our living room. "Hi'ya, Jethus," he would say, trying to shake hands or get a high five.

But still no "Grandma."

The last night of his stay came too soon. I was in my bedroom folding his little clothes fresh from the dryer and packing them for home. I was missing him already when a scraping sound coming down the hall broke my thoughts. I looked out to see Joshua struggling to pull the statue of Jesus behind him. When he saw me, he righted the statue and flung his arm around its shoulders.

He smiled up at me. "Look, Gamma. I bring you Jethus!"

My heart filled until my joy spilled over into tears. God truly uses the simple to confound the wise.

Cynthia M. Hamond

"My grandma did the cutest thing the other day. . . . "

Jenny's Antique

Grandmas are just antique little girls.

G. W. Curtis

My six-year-old granddaughter stares at me as if she is seeing me for the first time. "Grandma, you are an antique," she says. "You are old. Antiques are old."

Not satisfied to let the matter rest, I take out Webster's dictionary and read the definition. "An antique is not only just old, it's an object existing since or belonging to earlier times . . . a work of art . . . a piece of furniture. Antiques are treasured," I tell Jenny as I put away the dictionary. "They have to be handled carefully because they sometimes are very valuable. In order to qualify as an antique, the object has to be at least one hundred years old. I'm only sixty-seven," I remind her.

We look around the house for real antiques. There is a bureau that was handed down from one aunt to another and finally to our family. "It's very old," I tell Jenny. "I try to keep it polished, and I show it off whenever I can. You do that with antiques." When Jenny gets older and understands such things, I might also tell her that whenever I look at the bureau or touch it, I am reminded of the aunt, so dear to me, who gave me the bureau as a gift. I see her face again, though she is no longer with us. I even hear her voice and recall her smile. I remember myself as a little girl leaning against this antique, listening to one of her stories.

Our tour of antiques continues. There is a vase on the floor that's been in my house a long time. I'm not certain where it came from, but I didn't buy it new. And then there is the four-poster bed, sent to me forty years ago by an uncle who slept in it for fifty years.

"One thing about antiques," I explain to Jenny, "is that they usually have a story. They've been in one home and then another, handed down from one family to another, traveling all over the place. They've lasted through years and years. They could have been tossed away or ignored or destroyed or lost. But instead, they survived."

I point to a picture on the wall purchased at a garage sale. It is dated 1867. "Now that's an antique," I boast. "Over one hundred years old. Of course, it is marked up and scratched and not in very good condition. Sometimes age does that," I tell Jenny. "But the marks are good marks. They show living, being around. That's something to display with pride. In fact, sometimes, the more an object shows age, the more valuable it can become."

For a moment Jenny looks thoughtful. "You *are* my antique," she says. Then her face brightens. "Could I take you to school for show-and-tell?"

Jenny's antique lifts her up and embraces her in a hug that will last through the years.

Harriet May Savitz

Sandwich Generation

Children have more need of models than of critics.

Joseph Joubert

I am a member of the "sandwich generation." I'm forty-two, my children are fifteen and twelve, and I visit my eighty-two-year-old debilitated mother three to four times a week.

Widowed, she lives alone in her condo six miles from my home. She no longer drives and is dependent on others for transportation and social activities. I get very bogged down running two households. I'm either taking her to my home for a visit, to the grocery store or for a haircut, or I'm driving her around with me on my errands just to get her out of the house. She appreciates very much every small thing I do for her and tries hard to understand my busy schedule.

One particularly hot Texas day in July, I was driving my daughter from one errand to another when I realized I was running behind—again—and needed to call Mom and tell her I would be late picking her up. As I sped down the road, I called her on my cell speakerphone. I told her we were coming by to get her but that we were behind schedule. Her Irish lilt filled the car. "I'll be ready whenever you come." Then we ended our conversation with our daily, "I love you. See you soon."

As I hung up, my precious twelve-year-old said, "I was just imagining that I was you and that my daughter was sitting next to me in the car and we were talking to you, the grandma, on the phone." I was stunned. My prayers were being answered. As hard as it is sometimes, with all the running and juggling schedules, I am modeling something for my children after all, teaching them that nothing matters more in this world than the time we spend with those closest to us.

Yes, I may very well be old, one day, and all alone. I hope my daughter will then say, "I love you. See you soon."

Tricia Short

Secret Weapon

Life affords no greater responsibility, no greater privilege, than the raising of the next generation.

C. Everett Koop

In 1965, when I was a little girl, my family moved to a picturesque neighborhood in Pennsylvania. We were stunned to find a petition had been circulating to bar us from settling there. The neighbors, upon learning that a family with seven kids was elbowing its way into their territory, feared the worst. Perhaps they had envisioned seven times the mischief—churned-up flowerbeds, battered mailboxes, their sleepy lives unraveled by gleeful shrieks of children peppering cars with rocks and tripping up the elderly.

The petition was denied.

And so we moved into the colonial-style house, my parents' first home after fifteen years of transitioning from one army housing complex to another. What a luxury it was, owning a brick structure with two stories that we did not have to share with other families. The backyard, stretching on for what seemed like miles, tugged at my exploring spirit.

As one month flowed into the next, the neighbors held their breath. Finally, there was a collective sigh of relief as they began to see that their world would remain intact after all.

Then they began to wonder why. Why was such a large family so quiet? Even during Dad's tour in Vietnam, there was not a single hiccup.

What the neighbors didn't bank on was Mom's secret weapon—a weapon that would have brought Genghis Khan to his knees. Flattened evil empires. Rewritten history.

Her secret weapon, for lack of a more technical term, was "the look."

I believe there was a patent pending on it at the time.

This is how it worked.

First, the eyebrows arched. Then the lips tightened into one thin, rigid line. The eyes, narrowed and unflinching, turned to glass.

Whenever I was caught in mid-mischief, there she was, armed with that baleful stare. I was a fish about to be slapped onto butcher paper if I dared twitch. None of my brothers and sisters had the nerve to challenge "the look," so I could only imagine the consequences of crossing that line. I was certain that it meant being hauled away to a dark, damp place for bad kids, where a cackling witch pinched their fingers to see if they were plump enough to be on the menu. You can be assured that I never once attempted to confirm this.

There were even times Mom had the eerie ability to foresee mischief barely hatching in my brain. One look in my direction whittled my plans, along with my constitution, to sawdust. Like the Nat King Cole song, my only alternative was to straighten up and fly right—for the time being.

As it always is with army life, after three years and one more sibling added to the family, we followed Dad to his new assignment, where we were once again placed in generic housing on post. To this day, my parents cherish the friendships they collected while living on that tree-lined street in Pennsylvania. I've never forgotten the sweet man next door who always seemed to have a pocketful of butterscotch candy for us when he mowed his lawn.

A few years ago, my three-year-old niece was acting bratty at the dinner table, which solicited a five-star glare from her grandmother. Our forks poised in midair, we waited awkwardly for the little girl's reaction. Then . . .

"Grandma!" she said, giggling. "You're funny!"

We gasped.

She had breached the rules and . . . and she was still living!

Even more shocking, though, was what I detected on my mother's face. A trace of defeat. Just enough to make me appreciate how precious that tool must have been to her all these years, the pride she must have felt to be able to discipline a caravan of kids in church, in the store, the park, libraries and museums—all with just one look. Especially in one particular neighborhood that dreaded our arrival.

It's been said that Mom was the only one in her family who successfully adopted her mother's glare to control the kids. It must be genetic. The other day my two-year-old was whizzing around at top speed on the Sit-N-Spin during naptime when I opened the door quietly and zeroed in on him with that look. He braked with his heels, hopped off and quickly crawled into bed.

Hmmm. Maybe it's not too late for that patent after all.

Jennifer Oliver

The Wooden Spoon

Be ever gentle with the children God has given you. Watch over them constantly; reprove them earnestly, but not in anger.

Elihu Burritt

My son and daughter-in-law decided before their children were born that they would not spank. Both had been brought up with disciplinarian parents who believed in using the rod rather than spoiling the child."

My granddaughter, Jessica, went to Montessori school for a year, and of course they are against corporal punishment as well. Her punishment was mainly time-outs.

One day little Jessica had pushed her mom as far as she could. Carrie was so upset she went to the kitchen and pulled out a wooden spoon from the drawer. Lifting it in the air she said, "Do you see this? This is what my parents used for me."

Little four-year-old Jessica looked at her with big blue eyes. "They cooked you?"

Beverly Houseman

Out of the Mouths of Babes

It is the will, and not the gift, that makes the giver.

Gotthold E. Lessing

Some things never change. Take, for instance, the capricious nature of desire. *Will I never learn?* I wondered once more, remembering.

I had been pushing a shopping cart with my almost-four-year-old granddaughter through Target when Tiffany squealed, "Looky! There are shoes just like Dorothy's!"

Unmistakable excitement filled her voice. My eyes followed Tiffany's emphatic, pointing finger. There they were, a whole rack of them: ruby slippers sparkling as if sprinkled with scarlet fairy dust. Magical footwear transported straight from the silver-screen Land of Oz. There were gold and silver ones, too, but it was the ruby ones that mesmerized my granddaughter. Naked desire flared in Tiffany's eyes. When we stopped before the shoe rack, Tiffany reached with longing for a ruby slipper. She turned it over and over with reverence and wonderment.

I could so easily visualize my darling Tiffany dancing a

regal waltz in them, dipping and twirling off into that elusive world of dress-up and fantasy that she so often inhabited. Tiffany was a luminous little girl who loved everything swishy and swirly. Glittery and glamorous. Tiaras, high heels, angel wings, taffeta and tulle skirts, feather boas, and sparkling jewelry of every description.

I had already bought Tiffany's birthday gift only days before. Dedicated to nurturing my granddaughter's appreciation for the more important things of life, I aimed always—well, almost always—not to overdo the materialistic. But in this case, I pondered, how often does one get such an easy opportunity to fulfill a childhood desire?

Believe it or not, for three days I wrestled with this dilemma. Finally, I returned to the store for the ruby slippers that would surely fulfill Tiffany's heart's desire.

Standing at the cash register waiting for my change, I was so delighted that it took an enormous act of will to restrain myself from breaking into a spontaneous tap dance. I couldn't stop smiling. Strolling out of the store, clutching my precious package as if it contained the crown jewels, I felt absolutely triumphant. Surely there were springs in my shoes. This was one time an unquestioning certainty guaranteed I had found the perfect gift.

On Tiffany's birthday, I could hardly wait for my granddaughter to open the box containing the slippers. When at last she tore away the bright wrapping paper, the light flooding Tiffany's face said it all. In an eager instant she slipped her little feet into the sparkling shoes. It was as if they had a life of their own. Suddenly Tiffany minced. She swayed. She strutted. She sashayed. On and on she danced, oblivious to everyone. From all appearances, she couldn't help herself. She was lost in their spell.

All afternoon Tiffany wore the magic shoes. She couldn't tear her eyes from them as she played. As the day waned, it was as if she had drained every last bit of magic from them. Every last bit of wonder and joy.

At last dusk descended. Finally wearied by all the excitement, Tiffany crawled into my lap, as she so often did, snuggling close and giving me the best of little grand-daughter bear hugs.

"You really enjoy those red slippers, don't you, honey?"

Tiffany nodded slowly, an expression of sudden gravity sobering her dear little face. Then she paused to ponder for a bit before offering her carefully considered answer.

"Actually, it was the gold ones that I really wanted."

Jane Elsdon

6

GRANDMA'S LESSONS

*The sacred books of the ancient Persians say:
If you would be holy instruct your children,
because all the good acts they perform will
be imputed to you.*

Montesquieu

Granny's Journey

To know how to grow old is the master work of wisdom.

Henri Frederic Amiel

Deep in my memory as a teenager is my grandmother's attempt to shake me awake on Sunday mornings. "Oh! Granny, please," I'd plead. "I'm so tired and sleepy. I'll go next week. Promise." At that age, getting in early from a Saturday night date so I could stay awake in church on Sunday morning wasn't on the top of my priority list.

But she'd taunt me, "Well, young lady, why am I not surprised you're weak from fatigue? Funny thing to me, you're not too tired to carouse around on Saturday night, but you can't give the Lord your time on Sunday. Come on now, it won't do to be late. Get up and get dressed." And I would.

Grandmother Nora was a tall, handsome, fashionable woman. When she came to live with my mother, older sister and me, she was active, creative, determined and eighty years old. She'd made a fine reputation for herself as a talented tailor in the early 1920s. It paid the bills as she raised her three daughters. In those days there were few elegant department stores and no boutiques available to women of fashion. Their in-vogue wardrobes came from talented seamstresses like my grandmother.

She still loved sewing and seemed always to be working on a project. She told me she had one more heart's desire, to make choir robes for her church and give them as her final gift before she died.

Tension reigned with three generations in one small apartment. Granny and I, the oldest and the youngest, became a support team for each other. But even then we often disagreed. Her rules and traditions didn't fit my generation. At times there was real door-slamming tension between us. I realize now it was because we were so much alike. She saw herself in me and used any effective means, from pressure to bribes, to ensure that her look-alike granddaughter would be equipped with God's rules. Over time, we formed a truce of love and respect. We were quite a combination: a teenager yearning to fly and a granny whose wings had been clipped by age.

My mother, newly divorced, was also trying to make the best of several difficult situations. Returning to the workforce after many years away, raising two daughters alone and the irritation of her mother's sewing mess severely tested her patience.

One evening, arriving home later and more frazzled than usual, she looked at Granny's strewn fabric and with a stern expression said, "Mama, you must quit all this sewing. I simply won't come home every evening to this mess. Can't you just enjoy retirement and rest?"

Granny didn't want an argument. Peace was her game. Without a word, she winked at me and quietly went about cleaning up the room, putting away her sewing machine and packing up fabric. The next day she called a taxi and moved to the rooming house of a lady she knew from her church.

When Mother read the brief note Granny left her, she was shocked and saddened. Although they patched things up, Granny never came back, thinking it best to remain independent as long as she could.

During the next few years, spending many hours with her, I began to experience and understand the great lady as never before. No one else could have prepared me to meet life's opportunities like she did. I'd go by after school, and later, when I began to work as a model at Neiman Marcus, she was eager to hear all the exciting details of the clothes and fashion shows. As we shared our lives, I watched her finish twenty-seven heavy, faille burgundy robes with fluted backs for her church choir on her old treadle sewing machine. Listening to the details of her difficult life and her love of her Lord made a great impression on my young mind and guided many of my decisions.

Years later when Granny was diagnosed with cancer, she moved to a small town in Texas where another of her daughters could care for her at home. By that time I'd married, moved to Colorado and had a four-month-old baby.

Granny's illness was long and extremely agonizing. In those days there weren't many miracle drugs for pain. Mother kept me posted on my grandmother's shocking weight loss and described her terrible suffering. Yet, through it all, her faith remained constant.

When the end was near Mother told me Granny wept, saying, "I'm ready to go, but I've seen everyone except Ruthie. I must see her." I was the only one in the family who had found it impossible to make the trip to say good-bye.

Late one night, at home in Colorado, I was jolted awake and found myself sitting upright in bed. Someone had called my name aloud, yet my husband remained asleep beside me. It was Granny's voice I'd heard. Then I saw her standing in the corner of my dark bedroom. I could see her quite clearly. A shimmering radiance of light shone upon her. She looked just as I remembered her years before, smiling, healthy and vibrant. The love in her eyes for me was a hug that would last through the years. The vision lasted long enough for me to know I was fully awake and reminded me of a quote by Frances Bacon, "If the hill will not come to Mahomet, Mahomet will go to the hill."

I did not sleep much more that night, my mind occupied with memories of her.

When Mother called me the next morning to tell me Granny had died in the night, I wasn't surprised. I didn't tell her for quite some time that Granny had stopped by to see me as she ended her earthly journey. I was savoring it as my own private moment with someone who had sewn in me seamless faith and love.

Ruth Hancock

Confidence

Much wisdom often goes with fewest words.

Sophocles

Grandmothers have a way of uniting families through traditions. Some pass down favorite recipes and others share their sewing techniques, but the tradition my grandmother gave us was very different. Her favorite T-shirt read, "This is No Ordinary Grandma You're Dealing With!" And that said it all. Grandma was known by everyone to be an outgoing, witty and feisty woman. So, as you might expect, the tradition she passed on to our family was equally unique.

The summer after my high school graduation was the first time she told me the advice she gave to all the girls in our family. She had taken me shopping in preparation for my first semester of college. As we started toward the department store register with the cart full of everything a dorm room would need, we walked past the lingerie section and she stopped.

"Do you have your red underwear yet?" she asked.

"What? No . . . why?" I stammered, puzzled and embarrassed.

"It's important for every woman to have at least one pair of red underwear." She glanced at the appalled look on my face. "To wear on those days when you need that extra bit of confidence. When you have a test, a speech, a job interview or any time you need a self-assurance boost." Grandma went on to explain her philosophy, that when women have their own personal secrets about their "sassy" red underwear, they somehow feel more powerful and self-assured.

"Only you will know this tidbit of information about yourself, and it will give you a little extra edge of confidence," Grandma counseled.

Standing in the store discussing my underwear choices with my grandma was extremely embarrassing. I assured her I didn't need any underwear and convinced her we should leave.

Months later, after my roommate and I had been up all night studying for our first set of final exams, I stumbled into anthropology class and saved her a seat. She hurried in and sat down beside me with a package under her arm. "I picked up the mail on the way to class and we got another package from your grandma!" We were both excited because Grandma often sent us care packages with cookies and goodies, so I ripped open the parcel right there—and yanked out a pair of red underwear! Her note simply said, "Thought you could use these. Love, Gram."

Classmates snickered and whistled as I desperately tried to stuff the contents back in the package, my face as red as the panties.

Many times after that, when discussing an important upcoming event, one of the girls in our family repeated Grandma's advice without hesitation, "Don't forget your red underwear!"

Ten years later Grandma's time on earth came to an end. As we made plans for her funeral service we decided on a final farewell to honor such an inspiring lady. Her daughters, nieces, granddaughters (and even my college roommate) all shared a common secret that day. The music played softly as we gathered together, holding hands in prayer before entering the chapel. We winked at each other and giggled, then walked down the aisle—each with that "extra edge of confidence."

Jody Walters

The Pine Tree

Whatever you would have your children become, strive to exhibit in your own lives and conversation.

Lydia H. Sigourney

The Pine Tree Restaurant was a landmark in Bangor, Maine, for over forty years. Located in the heart of downtown and adjacent to the Greyhound bus station, it served regulars and transients from all walks of life. Boasting typical diner fare, the restaurant's food was good. The desserts were homemade and ample. However, many years after the Pine Tree closed, I learned that the customers didn't always visit for the food.

Natalie Greer was a tall, rail-thin waitress. Her uniforms were white and crisply starched and always adorned with complementing handkerchief and pin. She wore long sleeves year-round, as her skinny arms made her self-conscious. Proficient at her job, she worked at the Pine Tree for twenty-seven years.

Widowed in her forties, Nat raised six children on her wages and tips. Never one to complain, she provided her family with their needs and more. A smile always graced the face of this attractive waitress, and gentlemen frequently asked her out on dates. Never even considering remarrying, she turned them down with a smile and a style and grace generally reserved for those of a higher social stature.

Kindness was this waitress's forte. From the wealthiest of customers to the lowliest of kitchen help, Nat treated everyone the same. She looked after those who had difficulty with their jobs there, and she often stayed late teaching them tricks of the trade. In performing this kindness, she made countless friends.

When Nat was finally forced to retire due to complications from asthma, her many friends she'd made throughout the years came to visit her frequently, bearing homemade treats or invitations to go out to lunch or for a Sunday drive. She cherished these moments as she had cherished these friends.

"How about a nice hot cup of tea and a cookie?" was her standard greeting to those who called.

For years she kept in touch with customers and fellow employees from the Pine Tree. Even in old age, she remained close to many of them. Strewn throughout the Bangor area, they managed to get together occasionally, thanks to one of Nat's daughters and the introduction of senior citizens' transit to the region.

When Nat died in December, 1999, at the age of eighty-two, a few of those same customers and employees attended her funeral. After the service, some offered a few kind words to the family.

"You know," one elderly gentleman said, "the food was never that great. But Nat could make you feel like a million bucks."

"I'll miss Nat," a well-dressed lady said. "She could brighten anyone's day."

"Didn't she always look nice, with her hair fixed just so, and those pretty pins she wore," another said.

"I liked to go in on rainy days," a portly gentleman remarked. "She could make me feel the sun through all the clouds."

The comments continued in cards and letters.

"When I was broke, Nat would always remind me that if I had my health, I had everything. As I got older I understood how true her words were."

"It's not how much you have, it's what you do with it that counts. Nat gave so much from having so little."

Nat never owned a home and she never drove a car. In fact, she never acquired much in the way of material wealth at all. She was, however, richer than most of us will ever be—for she knew how to look at the positives in life, and she found them in so many unexpected places.

One of the places she found them was in me, her granddaughter. And for many years, I, too, was a waitress. Using the lessons my grandmother taught me, I refused to look at my job as one of triviality, and instead used it as an outlet to reach out to others. I made wonderful friends. I helped people who needed a hand in a variety of situations. And I gained a self-confidence and ease with myself that years later allowed me to pursue my dreams.

My grandmother didn't leave me a trust fund. She didn't leave expensive jewelry or heirlooms I'll pass from generation to generation. What she left me is worth so much more. She instilled in me as a very young child that a person's worth isn't determined by the money they have or the job they perform. It's in the person. No matter how rich or poor, or how highly educated, everyone deserves the dignity of being treated with kindness and consideration. I hope I leave to my children and grandchildren but a fraction of the legacy my grandmother left to me.

Kimberly Ripley

Grandma's Cake

Is not wisdom found among the aged? Does not long life bring understanding?

Job 12:12

"Let's go on a walk," Grandma suggested cheerfully while twisting her wavy, snow-white hair into a bun. The rest of the family was busy in the fields harvesting hay, and it was my responsibility to watch Grandma.

"Oh, no," I cautioned. "Last time you stepped in a big mud puddle and Mom was very upset."

"Oh, posh," Grandma replied. "I'm not going to sit and rock all day. Idle hands are the devil's workshop. Let's make a cake.

"Grandma, we can't make a cake. You can't see," I reminded her anxiously.

She laughed. "You can do anything you want to if you just try," she said. "God gave us five senses and seeing is just one of them." She pulled herself up from the rocker, and I guided her to where her apron hung on the wall. "Now, get a kitchen chair, child," she directed.

I pushed the chair up to the counter in our big, sunny

pantry. Following Grandma's directions I carefully retrieved a teacup from the cupboard. Putting one chubby hand on Grandma's shoulder, I nestled the cup in her hand. Then I found a big bowl and placed it in front of her. Deftly, she measured two level cups of flour in a big bowl. In amazement, I watched as she blindly searched the containers in the cupboard.

"Now find me the baking powder," she commanded.

"But Grandma, I can't read," I stuttered.

"You can taste, can't you?" she replied tartly.

I found a can and handed it to her. She screwed the top off, licked her finger, dipped it in the powder and tasted it. "Oh, no, that's baking soda," she declared. "Now you try it." It tasted bitter and fizzy.

The next container I found was not quite so bitter, and Grandmother announced that it most certainly was baking powder. I found the sugar and flour, and Grandma said we could tell which was which by tasting or feeling.

We identified vanilla easily by its smell. Grandma made sure that the lids were replaced on every container and that the containers were put back where they belonged. Then she showed me how to crack an egg properly and let me help beat the cake. By now the pantry was showing the effects of our cake-making.

Grandma ran her hand over the countertop. "Lands, child," she laughed. "We have made a mess. Never mind, we will have it spick-and-span in a jiffy." I got a dishpan of sudsy water and wiped the counter vigorously with the dishcloth. I watched as Grandma carefully ran her hand over the counter, feeling to see if it was clean enough. She had me wipe the counter again and then again. Finally she declared it was thoroughly clean.

Just as I wondered how we would be able to fire up the cook stove, Mom walked into the kitchen. She added kindling to the coals and a little later carefully opened the oven door and stuck her hand inside. She announced that the temperature was just right. I proudly carried the cake to the wood stove, and Mom popped it into the oven.

Grandma eased herself back into the rocker and said with a smile, "Someday you will face difficulties. Don't be too blind to look around and see how you can overcome them. Use the materials and abilities that God gives you. Count what you have, not what you don't have."

I don't remember how the cake turned out, but I have never forgotten the making of it.

Norma Favor

Frozen Water . . . Melted Hearts

Kindness is more important than wisdom, and the recognition of this is the beginning of wisdom.

Theodore Isaac Rubin

When my grandmother repeatedly left pots of water on the stove, dangerously simmering away unattended, the reality was there. The time had come to move her to an assisted-living facility.

It ripped our hearts from our chests to move this usually sweet but now angry woman into her "new home." I reassured myself, *She is forgetting too many things and could really hurt herself or others.*

Back at her house we began the arduous task of cleaning her home of twenty-seven years. I was given the assignment of cleaning the refrigerator and freezer. So many memories of life with my grandmother flooded my mind: Thanksgiving and Christmas dinners, summers canning fruits and vegetables, and special times spent delivering home-cooked meals to those in need.

I was jolted from these pleasant memories when I

discovered thirty tiny juice bottles filled with frozen water. More evidence of my grandmother's senility. Not wanting to add to my aunt and uncle's heavy heart, I quickly threw them in a large trash bag. *It must be tough seeing your own mother slowly losing her mind,* I said to myself. *I don't like seeing it either.*

A protective covering formed over my heart as I completed my assigned task. Like the ice lining the freezer, I hardened my heart so the pain would not overtake me. I heard laughter coming from the other rooms of the house as family members cleaned and reminisced. Those sounds that for years fittingly filled my grandmother's home now seemed out of place. "How can they laugh at a time like this?" I murmured as I shoved the last item into the plastic garbage bag.

My mind drifted to the memories of my grandfather, who had passed away several years earlier. Grandmother doted on him. After he died she turned her attention to her children and grandchildren. I always enjoyed going to Grandmother's because she knew just what each grandchild liked to eat. She lovingly prepared our favorite dishes and placed them in the freezer just in case we came to visit.

Smiling at the recollection, I headed for the door, wanting to leave with a good memory fresh in my mind.

Before going to our own homes, my sister and I stopped at Grandmother's new one to visit her. Before we left she showed us pictures of her beloved home and garden. In an almost therapeutic way she shared stories of the people in each photograph—when suddenly she halted. She stared at a picture of herself and a large man with dark skin standing by her rose-covered trellis. With a wrinkled forehead and set jaw, she turned to me, demanding, "Who's taking care of Melvin?"

"Who's Melvin, Grandmother?" I asked, almost afraid of the jumbled answer to come.

"He's the garbage man. I always leave a frozen bottle of water for him, tied to the post by the garbage can. Somebody needs to take care of him now that I'm gone."

My heart melted. While we thought she was forgetting important things, she was still remembering the most important ones.

Cheri Lynn Cowell

Nana

Becoming a grandmother is wonderful. One moment you're just a mother. The next you are all-wise and prehistoric.

Pam Brown

She was a wild woman of the west. Unlike any woman you've met, she left an impression on you that you'd never forget. She wore crazy earrings, loved the desert and looked like she walked right out of a Louis L'Amour novel. Her name was Waneene, my husband's grandmother, and we called her Nana.

Nana was eccentric, feisty and spicy. And at the same time she was one of the kindest, most softhearted women who ever walked this earth. Accepting everyone as they are, she loved you completely and made you feel like you were somehow more special than anyone else. It was her way, a gift with her. She never let a conversation with me end without saying, "I love you, darlin'."

A child of the earth, Nana preferred the outdoors and hungered for it like a firefly for a summer night. The most remarkable thing about her was that she lived as she pleased and didn't give a hoot what anyone thought. "True to herself" is the best way I can describe her. She taught me that and reminded me often to embrace life and love and to live with all my heart. "Life is short, don't waste a second of it," seemed to be her mantra, as she repeated it to me often and emphatically. She not only said it, but she lived it too.

When the Utah winters slowly melted away, Nana would give her landlord notice, pack up her apartment and move into a tent for the summer. She loved the mountains; she loved the desert; she loved anything and anywhere outside. Camping and hunting were as natural to her as cookie baking to most grandmothers. Swearing she had the spirit of a Native American, I could picture Nana squatting near a campfire, making an aloe medicine concoction from scratch and weaving a basket. With her own pistol and a love for jerky, venison and cold river water, she could easily have fit in during the wild days of western migration. I can visualize her winning a shooting contest with Billy the Kid and then telling him to mind his manners.

Our family spent many happy summers camping with Nana and learning the ways of nature. She personally taught me how to cook a full meal for six over a campfire with nothing more than flour and weird spices. Whenever we ate Nana's cooking, we usually whispered discreetly to each other, "What the heck is this?"

The first summer I met her, we attended our first Mountain Man Rendezvous, where we ate fried bread dripping with honey and joined an Indian pow-wow. Nana, head thrown back in laughter, eyes sparkling as she joined in the Native American dance of friendship, her sun-catcher earrings glinting in the firelight, showed me how to really live. Over the years, Nana's lessons in living impacted me, and I began to remember to cherish each little miracle in my own life. I remembered to say "I love you" more often, to stop and watch the clouds float by, and to accept others with a wide-open heart, always feeling Nana prompting me.

My husband told me of amazing childhood memories of living in a ghost town in Arizona with this woman who was part gypsy, part cowgirl. She taught him how to pan for gold, and together they fed wild burros that had long ago been abandoned by silver miners. They watched weekend "shoot-outs" on the dusty, dirt-covered main street of the tiny western town, a pocket of history alive in the Arizona desert. His childhood was painted with adventures with Nana, wherever she happened to be living at the time. She taught him to love God and nature, and our children were blessed to have these values passed on to them. At times I can see glimpses of the earthiness of Nana in my children's spirits. My oldest son loves nothing more than to sleep under the stars and catch his own meals in the cold, flowing stream. Just like Nana.

"I'm here for you, honey," she said when my sister died of a brain tumor. I didn't know that only three weeks later I would be giving the eulogy at Nana's own funeral.

On Mother's Day, Nana was absent from our traditional family dinner. My gift to her lay unopened, the card sealed. She didn't feel well enough for the one-hour drive out of the mountains where she lived. We called her that night and made plans to drive up soon for a visit. I told her how much we all loved her, and she told me that it was important to her that I understand that she knew. Her last words to me were, "I love you, darlin'."

The following Sunday, as my family was driving home from Palm Springs, where we had spent the week, the car phone call came. Nana had died. Suddenly and without warning, she was gone.

I wish I had hugged her one last time and thanked her

for teaching me to be true to myself, to love unconditionally and to live life with zest and passion. I miss Nana, but her spirit remains eternally. I see her in the sunset, in the untamed desert of the west. I see her in the mountains of Utah and the dancing fields of wildflowers. I see her in every bit of beauty that God has blessed us with, and forever I will see her in the eyes and spirits of my children.

I love you, darlin'.

Susan Farr-Fahncke

Grandmother's Quiet Addiction

I cannot but remember such things were, that were most precious to me.

William Shakespeare

My grandmother was perfect in most ways. Like other prairie mothers she had worked hard, raised her kids, attended church and crops with equal importance, and sewed and mended umpteen pairs of britches. She baked for bake sales, helped birth babies and calves, and never said a swear word, even when things were really bad. Only one thing kept her from being perfect. Grandmother had a quiet addiction that only we knew about: her relentless obsession with jigsaw puzzles.

There was never a time I can remember that a half-finished tiger or Eiffel tower didn't grace her kitchen table. Amid canning jars or supper plates laid the quiet addiction. The box with the jumble of pieces was set on top of the icebox when company was over to keep it away from prying fingers that might be dirty or elbows that might launch it. During supper a fresh tea towel would cover and conceal a work in progress. But once the meal was over it would be uncovered, and Grandmother would be at it again.

It was Grandfather's fault in the beginning. He got her the first one from the Sears Roebuck Christmas catalog. He figured it would give them something to do during the cold prairie nights before bedtime. It was either that or shell out dollars for one of those newfangled televisions Grandmother had hinted for but that he could not afford.

So he got one pretty puzzle with flowers on it by some fellow named Van Gogh. Grandmother took to it like a chicken to scratch, forgetting about the silly television and spreading out the pieces like trinkets of gold upon the clean kitchen table. Grandfather never got the hang of it, his thick fingers not able to pry apart the little pieces and his puzzle ability leaving a lot to be desired. So he retired to the den and his paper and she to her jigsaw. They spent many a peaceful evening in separate rooms this way.

But jigsaws soon became an obsession. After a while all her egg money was going to buy newer, harder ones. She became a puzzle expert, knowing the best brands and searching for them at church bazaars and cast-off sales.

Her nighttime habit soon became her morning and afternoon one as well.

One day she lost track of time and heard Grandfather roar home on the tractor. She realized she hadn't even started supper yet! She dashed to the kitchen and put an onion in a frying pan, giving the aroma of a home-cooked meal on its way to maturity. Grandfather never could figure out what smelled so good when he got in, or how it turned into cold beans and Spam.

We children loved Grandmother's quiet addiction, especially me. Our days with her always included a jigsaw puzzle, though she called it "learning." History was taught by completing a puzzle of the *Mayflower*'s landing, nature by doing one on sunflowers, art appreciation by completing the masters like Van Gogh, Rembrandt and Whistler. Social studies involved completing maps and pictures of foreign countries. Through it all Grandmother would talk. Did I know that the first jigsaws were actually invented by John Spilsbury, who produced a cut-up of an old map in 1762? That Chinese rice was grown in wet paddy fields and Indians used canoes to harvest wild rice? That tigers live alone but lions live in families called prides?

I learned my math: "Twenty pieces left in a thousand-piece puzzle means how much have we done?" Solving abilities. "Always do your frame first, then match colors." And to never neglect chores: "Nancy! Bring the broom! The cat's got into the puzzle and we need to find three pieces!"

After years of fighting for elbow room on the kitchen table and missing her company by the fire, Grandfather built Grandmother a puzzle table, just the right size to do her jigsaws in the parlor. He took some ribbing for feeding her "quiet addiction," but he shrugged his shoulders and said, "T'aint much of a fault in a woman. Besides, I'm the one who started it all." In later years, he sat beside her, going through her puzzle box for errant pieces when her eyesight started to dim. "Here's the blue bit you've been looking for," he'd say, and she would smile and press it in its place.

I wonder if Grandmother knows the legacy she left me. Upstairs in my daughter's room one of those three-dimensional puzzles sits half finished in a protective tray her father built to keep the cats out. Boxes of foxes, lions, sunsets and famous paintings line the upstairs shelves, waiting for a power outage, a cold rainy afternoon or a visit from friends. Tucked away by the dining room table is a puzzle mat rolled up with a half-finished treasure inside it.

I'll take it out once my husband goes to work and smile. And just in case I get carried away with my own "quiet addiction," I'll have an onion close at hand by the frying pan.

Nancy V. Bennett

Like the Turtle

Honor the old. Teach the young.

Old Danish Proverb

My grandmother is one of the kindest, most giving and beautiful people I know, but never, at least during my lifetime, has she ever been called "athletic." The colorful dresses and vintage suits stored carefully in dusty garment bags in the spare room's closet give testament to both of my grandparents' younger lives as sparkling social butterflies and first-class swing dancers, but as time passed I knew them as the relaxed and smiling retirees I always liked to visit.

As my grandfather got older he had blood pressure problems, and with them came the trimmed diet and regimented exercise program that doctors recommended. I can say without hesitation (though perhaps not without reluctance) that he is more physically fit than I. I was once outpaced by this cool and casual senior citizen when he motored past me as I panted up a steep hill in West Hollywood. By contrast, my grandmother had to be pestered to take a five-minute walk around the block a couple of times a month.

In the summer of 2002, our family took a thirteen-day trip to China. We expected Grandpa to fare better than Grandma, and for the most part this was true—until we visited the Great Wall.

The Great Wall is just that: great in every possible sense of the word. We traversed stairs of jagged stone, two feet high and three inches wide, ascending hillsides that make a mockery of San Francisco. There were towers with tiny staircases so narrow that only one small person could pass through them at a time.

My young niece and nephew were, of course, undaunted. They ran at full tilt back and forth along the straightaways and gamely clambered up steps more than half their own heights. When we made it about halfway to the tourist checkpoint, my great-uncle and grandfather turned back—the altitude, heat and sheer aggression of the Wall had defeated them. My own quads were burning and so were my lungs; my brother, two years younger than me and quite a bit stronger, wasn't faring much better. As we struggled to keep up with our niece and nephew, eventually it occurred to us that we'd lost Grandma. Unworried but curious, we used our walkie-talkies to triangulate her location.

She was at the far-end checkpoint. Buying a souvenir. A little plaque that commemorated one's stamina and fortitude in making it that far along the Wall. Many energetic and athletic young couples, armed with water bottles and expensive walking shoes, had endeavored to make it this far and failed.

We were amazed. My grandfather was astounded. "I was like the turtle," was my grandmother's simple, almost laughing explanation. And indeed she was; as the rest of us had scrambled to keep the younger generation in sight, we'd been completely unaware of Grandma's steady progress toward the far-end checkpoint—a place, by the way, that neither my niece nor nephew had the energy to overtake in the end. I fought my way, exhausted, to also get a plaque. Grandma wasn't even breathing heavily.

To this day I still don't know how she did it. Neither does my grandfather. Maybe she's been hiding her physical fitness all this time, though that seems unlikely. Maybe her Chinese ancestors imbued her spirit with some unnatural strength to conquer the Wall they had built. Or maybe—and more likely—the will we all knew was strong carried her along.

Erin Hoffman

Nan

Perpetual pushing and assurance put a diffi-culty out of countenance, and make a seeming impossibility give way.

Jeremy Collier

Nan was my bonus grandmother. By the time I reached the age of twenty-five, all of my grandparents had passed away, and when I married Jay and acquired Nan as part of the package, I was elated to establish a relationship with her.

She was a bright, unquenchable little spark, a whirl-wind of activity, a dynamo of energy, a formidable garage-sale shopper and an unending source of optimism and fierce determination. She didn't believe in just sitting around and crocheting, although she did even that with finesse.

Nan's apartment was a magical and enchanted place. My children and I would ride the elevator up to the ninth floor for afternoon tea and step out into the hallway to see her twinkling in the doorway of #914. She loved to wear long flowery skirts, shiny slippers, frilly blouses, sparkly belts, yards of chunky beads, dangling earrings, rhinestone brooches, lots of bracelets and numerous rings. Whether any of it matched was irrelevant. My sons, Barrett and Thomas, would enter reverently, eyes wide as saucers, with my warning "not to touch" ringing in their ears.

Every available inch of the apartment was adorned with antiques. The paintings she produced in astonishing numbers marched across the walls. Garage-sale treasures were crammed between expensive knickknacks. Clocks ticked and chimed and bonged and cuckooed. A canary sang in the corner. It was a dizzying, delightful celebration of who Nan was and what she loved.

Her energy seemed boundless. The apartment was not only immaculate, but entire rooms of furniture would be rearranged from week to week. I often wondered how she managed to negotiate midnight trips to the bathroom. Beds traveled from one bedroom to another. Dressers were hauled on strips of carpet from the pink room to the hall to the painting room to the blue room and then back to the pink room again. A huge cupboard of antique dolls vanished from the hall only to reappear in the back room. "Slow but steady, that's the secret," she would say sagely. "Pull, don't push, and just keep at it." Each visit was a bit of an adventure as well as an inspiration. I usually left with renewed resolve to dust and clean and smarten up my house.

I admired not only her outer, but her inner strength. I saw it surface often during her long, debilitating struggle with skin ulcers. It was a battle that lasted more than twelve years, yet as those horrible sores worsened and multiplied, her pluck and fortitude burned brightly. She was not inclined to complain or despair or quit. She kept on going even though the furniture didn't move quite as often, the paintings took longer to finish and the lure of garage sales lessened.

Shortly after Nan had been admitted to the hospital for

the last time, unaware that she would never leave, I ran into a friend there who had become a nurse. "Who are you visiting?" she asked. When I told her she exclaimed, "She is your grandmother? We just love her! She is so amazing."

For a long time Nan talked about getting better and going home, but the skin grafts were unsuccessful. Her appetite, meager to begin with, waned; she lost weight. I noticed clumps of hair on the pillow. Heavily medicated to cope with the pain, she drifted in and out of sleep. Sometimes, to reassure myself that she was still breathing, I watched the little pulse in her throat. Though her tiny frame seemed impossibly frail, that flicker of life beat strongly. "Slow but steady, that's the secret," I could almost hear her say.

Even then, on some of her worst days, when the agony of bedsores, infected graft sites and gangrenous ulcers crept through the morphine, her response to, "How are you?" was a whispered, "Oh, not so good and not so bad."

As her body weakened her smile grew sweeter. The reserve she had always cloaked herself in slipped, and she seemed to glow with a new tenderness and appreciation for people. Traversing that vast desert of adversity, she discovered the riches of relying on others.

One Saturday afternoon I spent some time with Nan. She was heavily sedated and semicomatose; my efforts to wake her were unsuccessful, so I read to her. Remarkably, as I held her hand and told her not to be afraid, that it was okay for her to go, her eyes fluttered open a few times. When I told her I loved her, her hand began to shake.

The next morning at approximately 5:00 Nan stepped over the threshold of death's door. I had longed to see her at peace, yet after that portal swung silently shut, the luster of this world seemed paler and its music off-key. I thought I was prepared. I thought her anguish had readied me. But there is no preparation. Ever.

From her life of quiet strength and impressive dignity in the midst of unrelenting pain and suffering, I carry these words and do my best to apply them when things become difficult: "Slow and steady, that's the secret. Pull, don't push, and just keep at it."

Rachel Wallace-Oberle

Gram's Garden

Nature and wisdom always stay the same.

Juvenal

My cousins Michelle and Joey and I were fortunate to live with our grandmother in her home during her final years. At ninety-three, her health declined, and we became homebound along with her. That was when the real heart work began. We knew we were going to keep Gram home and her spirit alive. She had given all of us so much, so our hearts opened up and accepted the direction our lives were meant to take.

Gram loved her garden and planted one every year. But this summer she was too weak and frail even to walk outside. Still she said, "I want to plan the garden like I always did, and help with the planting and picking, too." Her bedroom was on the side of the house on the first floor, where the sun shined bright every morning. The four of us decided to plant the garden right outside her bedroom window.

On that sunny morning, as we tilled the soil, Gram's head peeked out the window and her fingers pointed to the middle of the garden. "Plant the Italian pole beans right here." Then, "Hand some seeds to me, Joey." She tossed them out the window into the dirt. "There, I wanted to show you how to do it," she said, wiping her hands on her apron. "Now, plant the rest of the vegetables over there, and we will sit and watch them grow."

As weeks went by, Gram often walked the few steps from the living room into her bedroom and sat in the chair looking out the window, watching her garden coming alive.

Joey and I asked her once, "Gram, did we do okay with the planting?" Her arms stretched out, pointing to the garden, as she said, "Look how high the plants are!"

As the summer went by, Gram reveled in the joy of watching her garden grow. She never lamented about not going outdoors anymore.

When the beans were ready she told us, "Let me help you pick them."

Joey opened the window as she sat in a chair wearing her apron. He picked the beans, handed them to her through the window, and she gathered them in her lap. "There," she said, as she stood up with her apron filled with the beans, "I have some work to do now." She sat on the porch later and snapped them. "These are really good," she boasted, tasting them. "Not too stringy or tough." Joey and I relaxed on the porch reading the paper while Gram tended her harvest.

The tomatoes were her favorite. Joey pulled the six-foot vine close to the window, and she reached to pick one. With salt shaker in hand, she took a bite and juice squirted down her chin. "Not only are these plump and red, they are so juicy this year." We knew life couldn't get any better than this.

There were a few mistakes the first year we assisted with the garden. We didn't ask Gram how many zucchini seeds to plant. We checked them at first and saw they were small and few in number. Then one midsummer day Gram told us, "You should check on the zucchini, they are probably coming in by now." Joey and Michelle went out and the garden was full of them! Hundreds, it seemed! Joey kept walking in with more and more armfuls, gasping, "These plants are out of control!" Much to our surprise, they kept growing and growing. We gave many zucchini away that summer, and for weeks the three of us ate it fried, baked and sautéed, and in zucchini cakes and breads.

Little did we know how much closer we'd all become on this gardening journey of ours. Not only were we taking care of Gram, she was taking care of us, too. At the end of the day, I still rested my head on her lap and told her how much I loved her. A smile would come across her face while she rubbed my head and said, "I know."

Our love and closeness grew more abundant than zucchini.

Paula Mauqiri Tindall

Digging in the Dirt

In the name of God, stop a moment, cease your work, look around you. . . .

Leo Tolstoy

"Dig in the dirt with me, Noni."

My three-year-old grandson, Ethan, stood in the kitchen with pleading eyes and a big spoon. I had two large clay pots with soil that needed changing, and he needed something to do—a perfect match. After getting the necessary digging utensil from the junk drawer, he'd rushed to the deck and sent dirt flying everywhere. I could just imagine my daughter's reaction to his dirty clothes, but that was okay with me. As the grandma, I'm allowed to spoil.

It was hard to resist his invitation to play, but I had a meeting that night and I still had to fix supper.

"I can't right now, honey. Noni's busy."

Ethan hung his head and stared at his shoes all the way back outside. Guilt hovered over me while I chopped celery and onions for meatloaf. Some grandma! But, I reasoned, it's different being a grandmother these days.

I'm younger, busier. I don't have time to play like mine did when I was a child.

As I watched Ethan through the window, memories of a tea party with my grandmother surfaced. I remembered how Mammie filled my blue plastic teapot with coffee-milk and served toasted pound cake slathered in butter. She carried the tray as we walked to the patio and sat under the old magnolia tree that was full of fragrant, creamy-white blooms. I served the cake, poured the coffee into tiny plastic cups and stirred with an even tinier spoon. Our playtime probably lasted less than thirty minutes, and yet, after all these years, I still remembered.

Ethan saw me watching him and pointed to the pot. He had emptied it. I waved and nodded to him. Just then it dawned on me that my love for flowers came from Mammie. She had dug in the dirt with me. I recalled the new bag of potting soil and flower seeds I had in the garage. It would be fun to plant seeds and watch them grow with my little grandson.

I left my knife on the chopping block, found another old spoon and went outside.

"Noni can play now."

Ethan clapped his dirty hands as I plopped down beside him. What fun we had that sunny afternoon. Supper was on time, and so was I for my meeting.

I learned the important life secret that Mammie always knew: there's always time to play.

Linda Apple

The True Lesson of Homework

*He that will make a good use of any part of his
life must allow a large part of it to recreation.*

John Locke

She is a study in consternation. Hannah's brow is furrowed; she is squinting and biting her lower lip, sure signs of anxiety in this granddaughter.

The woeful mood is due to a second-grade scourge known as "homework."

Hannah has begged to play outside on this glorious day, but I am under strict orders from her mother that she must first attack her assignments. And as the babysitter-in-residence, I am pledged to follow instructions.

Never mind that I, a former teacher, have decidedly mixed feelings about the importance of missing a golden afternoon when the sun is winking off the back patio, the trees are dancing in a lovely breeze and nature herself is celebrating spring.

Hannah's work sheets are spread out in front of her. It's been a while since I've seen what second-grade homework looks like, so I sit near Hannah, careful not to disturb her, but fascinated by watching this child I love so much as she attacks word configurations on a printed page.

Her teacher wants Hannah to transpose some letters to make new words. Hannah is working on set number three—and has been at this for nearly twenty minutes. She had sailed through the first two sets—the easy ones, she'd assured me—but this third set was the killer.

So we sit together, a grandmother and a grandchild, and neither of us speaks. Once, Hannah throws down her pencil in frustration. Another time, I think I see the start of a tear in her chocolately brown eyes.

"Let's take a break," I attempt. I even offer to make her favorite apple/raisin treat, one that usually gets Hannah racing off to the kitchen with me. But this earnest child is resolute. "If I finish," she reasons aloud, "I can go outside and play with Julia and Trevor." And to make matters worse, we can hear their shouts and occasional laughter through the open window.

Minutes later, Hannah has symbolically climbed to the language arts mountaintop. The word work sheets are finished. Now only two pages of addition stand between Hannah and the great outdoors.

Once again, all goes swimmingly at the beginning of Hannah's math homework. The computations come so easily that she's lulled into eight-year-old cockiness. "These are SIMPLE!" she exults, almost offended, it would seem, at the lack of challenge.

But on the second math worksheet, toward the bottom of the page, Hannah collides with a tough set. And she has her comeuppance. No matter how she struggles, the instructions—and thus the solutions—elude her.

I feel a meltdown coming.

It's nearly five in the evening. Hannah has been up since six-thirty in the morning. She's put in a full day in school, including a play rehearsal that both delighted and drained her. Her little brother is on a play-date, and he doesn't have homework because Zay is, after all, only in prekindergarten.

The injustice of it all finally gets those tears spilling. "I HATE homework," Hannah sobs. And she means it.

This time, I ignore my pledges to her mother. I make an executive decision that my granddaughter and I are going outside to catch the last—and hopefully best—of this gift of a day.

For the next hour, I watch Hannah as she celebrates liberation. She runs and leaps and then climbs to the top of the jungle gym that is in the yard. I snap a photo of her as she performs feats of daring up there that still make me gasp.

Her cheeks are flushed, her hair is wild, and I wish that utter abandon and unbridled joy could last forever.

When my daughter comes home, Hannah is momentarily stricken. "I didn't finish my math sheets," she confesses at once.

I hold my breath. I watch my daughter as she looks at Hannah, at me, and at the day that is surrendering to dusk.

And Jill says the very thing I might have written in a script for her:

"You can finish your homework later," my daughter tells hers. "Play some more!"

And on a glorious spring day, I silently bless my daughter for her wisdom.

Sally Friedman

I Can Make It Grow

I have often thought what a melancholy world this would be without children; and what an inhumane world, without the aged.

Samuel Taylor Coleridge

My granddaughter Lydia, who was five years old, was visiting her grandpa and me one spring day when we all decided to go for a walk, taking Missy, our dog, with us.

Since I have multiple sclerosis, my legs have taken on wheels to accommodate me; I use a three-wheel scooter. Nonetheless, I enjoy the sunshine and the adventure of getting out and about like the rest of the family.

Now Liddy, as we call her, was taking in all her eyes would allow. As you may know, the eyes of a child spot things an adult's eyes may never see. So it was on this particular day. In the subdivision where we live, there are no sidewalks; everyone goes for their daily walks strolling down the middle of the streets. There is a slight embankment along the road, and it is in one of these shallow ditches that she spotted it.

"Look, Grandma," Liddy said eagerly.

I tried to muster enthusiasm for the little artificial flower that had somehow made its way into the drainage ditch. "Oh, that is nice, Liddy."

She held it tenderly. "It's a beautiful bouquet. Isn't it?"

"Oh, yes." I placed it in the basket on my scooter.

"I want to plant it when we get home," she informed me.

I couldn't bring myself to tell her it would do no good to plant an artificial flower.

"I know how to plant flowers. I planted some at Grandma Carolyn's house."

Grandma Carolyn was her grandma on her mother's side, and I never questioned her endeavors or abilities. After all, that grandmother was more able-bodied than me. Liddy spent more time there, staying overnight and bonding with her other grandma in a small rural community a few miles away. I was sure Grandma Carolyn had helped Liddy plant real flowers in her yard.

We continued on our walk, with the artificial flower surviving quite nicely in my basket. It sat there rather staunchly, as if it knew it had a mission.

As our home came into view, Liddy, too, had a mission. She was going to plant that flower.

"I can make it grow," she told me confidently.

She reached into my basket as we arrived at our house. I thought to myself, *How am I going to tell this sweet little child that this is a flower that will not grow when planted?*

"Liddy, you know that is not a real flower; it's artificial."

"I know," she said without batting an eye.

She told me she needed a shovel, then she picked out a spot beside the front walk leading to our porch.

"Grandpa, would you get Liddy a big tablespoon?" I requested of Bill, my husband.

I was not going to quash our granddaughter's spirit or her faith. She was sure she knew how to dig a hole, plant that flower and make it grow. She was adamant in her abilities and in that plastic flower's ability to sprout into an even more beautiful bouquet. She felt capable of achieving her goals. I wasn't going to deter her.

Liddy planted and watered her flower, proudly showing her daddy when he came. She had placed it in a spot where it wouldn't be missed on her next arrival.

Several visits and a multitude of rainstorms later, on one of her stopovers, Liddy, with a dejected look on her face, informed me that her flower was dying despite her loyalty. I couldn't stand the disappointment she faced.

One day a few weeks later, Bill purchased some flowers to plant in our backyard. A light went on in my brain.

"Bill, take one of those flowers and plant it by the walk in the front yard were Liddy planted that artificial flower."

On her next visit, Liddy's eyes sparkled when she saw the purple, flourishing flowers. Her faith was renewed. She continued to water that flower and care for it each time she came, declaring, "I told you I can grow flowers."

Sometimes nature and children need a boost in achieving their intended objectives.

Sometimes we just need to give a child hope in her dreams.

Sometimes we adults need to be encouraged to have the faith of a child.

Sometimes we need to replace our artificial lives with the real thing.

Other times, we need to water our hopes and dreams with effort, determination and will, having patience until they grow into being.

Most times, a child can teach us a multitude of things about ourselves and about life—if we just look at life through the eyes of a child.

Betty King

off the mark
by Mark Parisi
www.offthemark.com
WHEN I WAS A KID WE'D WALK TWICE AS FAR... ALL UPHILL AND AGAINST THE WIND... AND WE'D SPRINKLE TWICE, MAYBE THREE TIMES AS MANY SEEDS...
ATLANTIC FEATURE © 1995 MARK PARISI
offthemark.com
MARK PARISI
JOHNNY APPLESEED AND HIS GRANNY SMITH

Motherhood 202

What do we live for, if not to make life less difficult to each other?

George Eliot

At the age of eighteen, I became the mother of not one baby boy, but two. Being an inexperienced mom frightened me. I had never even held a brand-new baby before. The day I left the hospital the nurse placed a baby in each arm. Equipped with two care packages filled with formula and baby wipes, off I went to face an adventure of a lifetime. At that time, I didn't realize the sacrifices I would make and how much of my time these two beautiful babies would require.

Instead of going home, my husband and I stayed with my parents for a couple of weeks. *The more help we can get, the easier it will be,* I thought. Both of my parents worked during the day, so at night they were forced to get some much-needed rest. Sitting up most of the night with the boys as they took turns vying for my attention, then washing diapers while preparing formula during the day, was very exhausting, to say the least.

My wonderful grandmother, Mamma, came to help out. She walked inside, and love immediately poured from her heart as she gazed into the bassinets in which my tiny babies slept. I was so glad to see her. I threw my arms around her neck and held her close. I'll never forget how soft her hair was and how good she smelled that day. It reminded me of the times that she squeezed me tightly when, as a child, I needed a hug.

She smiled and said, "Babies raising babies, Lord. Now just what do you think about that?" By the expression on her face, I knew she still loved me, as much as ever. Suddenly I understood the sacrifice that she made when her girls were small and, later, while helping my parents to raise me. I also realized that I would always be a baby to her, regardless of my age.

During the next two weeks, Mamma and I spent a great deal of time together. While she rocked one baby, I changed the other. When I sterilized bottles, she folded mounds of diapers. I never imagined that two little babies could create so much laundry or drink so much formula. While I appreciated the efforts that Mamma put forward to physically help me get through the first two weeks of my babies' lives, I appreciated more the loving support. Just when I needed it most she said, "You're doing a good job, darling." She blessed me with instructions, giving me a crash course in Motherhood 202.

"Love them while you have them, darling," she said after we got both boys to sleep one morning. "Life is so short. Before you turn around good, they'll be gone." Of course, with them being less than two weeks old, the thought of them leaving home was the last thing on my mind—I was just concerned about making it through the next few days! But I listened and clung to every word she said.

"Always be positive," was a favorite hint that she repeated many times during our roundtable discussions.

"If you ever say 'no,' don't back down" and "Remember to say what you mean and mean what you say," were favorite lines of hers. "Sometimes it's better to say, 'Let me think about it' before answering. Never base your decisions on guilt, pride or obligation. Let love be your guide."

Mamma was never afraid to say what she was thinking. "Be willing to admit, even to kids, that you are capable of making mistakes, darling. Tell them you're sorry when you make a bad decision. They may be little, but remember that they have feelings too," she said as she kissed one of the baby's tiny cheeks.

"Never put them on the back burner of your life," she said. "God has given you two blessings. Pray for them daily, thanking him. Let them know you are praying for them too," she followed. "That is very important."

The two weeks passed quickly, and suddenly I turned around one day and the boys were walking, talking, and too soon they started school. A few years later, Mamma left this world behind. Through my tears, I watched as my little boys sang her favorite hymn before a chapel full of her friends and family. In my mind, I saw the love in her eyes as she gazed into their bassinets just a few years earlier. I knew in my heart that their sweet voices would make her feel very honored.

Over the years, as little storms crept into our lives, I never forgot Mamma's instructions. Many times I had to admit I'd made a mistake, and I told my kids I was sorry. When they became teens, I made some tough decisions. Like Mamma challenged me to do, I tried to base every decision not on guilt, pride or obligation, but on love. I am positive they have always understood how important they are to me. I realized life was short and they'd be gone in no time, so I spent quality time with them every single day.

When the boys grew into young men, I was elated as they walked across the university auditorium and accepted their hard-earned diplomas. I thought of Mamma and how proud she would have been of them both. When the dean called their names, in my heart I heard Mamma say, "Babies raising babies, Lord. Now what do you think of that?"

Somewhere, beyond the cheering, I also heard her say, "Good job, darling. I give you an A+ in Motherhood 202."

"Thank you, Mamma. You taught me everything that I know."

Nancy Gibbs

7

GIFTS FROM GRANDMA

*Presents which our love for the donor has
rendered precious are ever more acceptable.*

Ovid

Unexpected Gift

The heart of the giver makes the gift dear and precious.

Martin Luther

During 1956 and 1957 I worked in the various refugee camps near Linz, Austria. As a male volunteer under the auspices of the service arm of my denomination, the Church of the Brethren, I worked with people who had lost their homes and possessions in Eastern Europe during World War II or after the war when they fled from areas under Communist control. Although they desperately wanted to immigrate to a country where they could begin a new start in life, many were still stranded in dreary refugee camps.

My experiences with the survivors of World War II led me to enroll in college upon my return to the United States because I wanted to discover what had caused the terrible war that caused so much death, suffering and dislocation. In the summer of 1958 I organized and conducted a tour group of Americans visiting the tourist points of Western Europe, including Amsterdam, Paris, Rome and the Swiss Alps. In order to show these first-time visitors another side of European life, I also took the tour group, which included my mother and aunt, into a refugee camp (Camp Haid) to visit one of the refugee families living there. I was both glad and sad to see an elderly woman with whom I'd worked two years before.

About a week later, on August 14, 1958, a portion of the tour group departed for home on a regularly scheduled KLM (Royal Dutch Airlines) flight. Tragically, this airplane was the first plane to go down in the Atlantic Ocean since World War II. Among the ninety-six casualties were twenty of my tour group, including my mother and aunt. I was devastated.

Two years later I took another tour group on the same itinerary. Although hoping that by this time all the refugees would have been permanently resettled and no longer living in a refugee camp, I again took the group into Camp Haid. When I knocked on the door of the family's area of the old barracks, I was again face-to-face with the same elderly woman with whom I had renewed a friendship in 1958. Upon seeing me, the color drained from her face and the ashen-faced lady whispered, "Herr Kreider, I thought you had died in that airplane crash."

I explained that only a portion of our group, including my mother, had been on that particular flight. I shared with her that tragic period, but then said I had much better news to share. I told her that I had just learned by telephone that very morning that my wife had given birth to a little girl in Kassel, Germany.

The refugee lady froze and just stared at me in apparent disbelief. *What was going through her mind?* She then turned and walked to the other side of the room. Reaching up, she grasped a white puppy made of yarn. The cute, hand-looped poodle was about ten inches high, with floppy ears, sharply defined eyes and a pug nose. She walked back, handed the puppy to me and said, "This is a gift to the little baby—from her grandmother."

What a flood of emotions swept over me. *How could this be?* She explained that back in 1958 when I was showing other parts of the refugee camp to others in the tour group, my mother had remained in this lady's home and admired her handiwork, a handmade puppy. Despite her inability to speak German, Mother had communicated with the lady, ordered a puppy to be made, paid for it, including postage, and left her address. The old lady heard of the fatal accident and, assuming the worst, never mailed the puppy.

Now, on the day her first grandchild was born, a gift from Grandma was presented to her little granddaughter.

J. Kenneth Kreider

Grandma's Attic Treasures

The manner of giving shows the character of the giver, more than the gift itself.

John Caspar Lavater

"I don't want to go. You're not being fair."

My mother glared at me. Her tan cheeks flushed with crimson.

"I won't go!" I hollered.

"You will, and that's final."

"But . . ."

"Final," she said as she walked out of the room.

The ride from our home to Grandma's was lengthy, but the hours of silence intensified the dreary trip. I couldn't find joy in the book or music I had brought to occupy my time. My parents sat silently in the front seat. The hum of the car on the road and my brother's rhythmical snores were my only companions.

I looked at my watch. By now my friends were on their way to the jazz concert, having fun. I rubbed my jaw, trying to relax the tight muscles.

For the next three days I worked quietly beside my

parents as we cleaned my grandparents' house so they could sell it and move into an assisted-living residence near us. The dust, mold and musty smells were pungent, but not as foul as my attitude.

How could my mother treat me like this? Why would she insist I spend the most important weekend of my life doing such a rotten job? Most of my friends would graduate in three weeks, so this would have been our last chance to go to a concert and hang out together. Sweat rolled down my back as I scrubbed the kitchen cupboards, but the steam boiling in my heart was hotter than Grandma's perking teakettle.

My arms ached every night from the day's work, but my jaw ached even more from the tension built up in me. My only reprieve was following my grandparents up the rickety attic stairs to browse through the years of history stored on shelves and in boxes.

From antique dressers to handmade cedar chests, old papers, Christmas ornaments, dishes and toys, the attic was full of wonderful treasures. With every item I picked up, Grandma had a story to tell about it. I couldn't wait for our day of cleaning torture to be over so I could vacation in the past with my grandma.

Though the attic was an excellent distraction, my jaw tensed each time I thought of my friends at the concert.

As we packed to leave, Grandma tiptoed and placed a gentle kiss on my cheek. "Thank you for helping us," she said.

"You're welcome," I muttered. Her tender gray eyes sparkled. My sacrifice had meant a lot to her. "You're welcome," I said again, hugging her.

Three weeks later we moved my grandparents close by, and I was able to see them regularly and enjoy the vanilla wafer cookies and milk Grandma offered me. Their new home was cozy, but I couldn't ignore the dreamy look in Grandma's eyes when she talked about her home on the beach. Together we reminisced about the objects we had seen in the attic, and Grandma's familiar smile added happy wrinkles on her face.

When Christmas arrived, Grandma and Grandpa came with wide smiles and arms full of gifts. I enjoyed having my older sister and brother home from school. And though I knew the majority of presents under the tree were for my three-year-old brother, this year was special because we were all together.

It wasn't the bright lights on the Christmas tree or the multitude of presents hugging the trunk that caught my attention—it was the porcelain doll snuggled into the red and green plaid skirt surrounding the tree. Her hands were primly folded on her white, flowing dress. The pink satin bow around the waist and hem of her dress were bathed in the Christmas lights.

This precious gift was the last one to be handed out. Would my older sister receive this porcelain princess? Oh, how I wanted to hold it.

Grandma's curly hair bounced when she nodded her head at my mom, who tenderly picked up the doll . . . and placed it in my lap.

Silence. Even the background music seemed to sense this blessed moment. My tears fell onto the doll's fluffy white dress as I sat on the couch. "Thank you, Grandma."

"You're welcome, dear."

I noticed a tear trace down a wrinkle, falling onto her shoulder.

"Did you want to keep her?" I asked, stroking the doll.

"No."

"Then why are you crying?"

"I knew you would enjoy a treasure from the attic."

I was grateful I missed the concert, for I received priceless treasures from Grandma's. Not just the doll, but her stories and her smile, permanently etched into my mind.

Anne Johnson

A Quilted Life

*Remembrance is the only paradise out of which
we cannot be driven away.*

Jean Paul Richter

There is a quilt on every bed in my grandmother's battered farmhouse. Most of the patchwork blankets are generations old. Their bindings sport holes of wear. Newer
quilts flaunt their fresh, rich colors in Grandma's room.
My first attempt at quilting hangs on her wall. The colors
are bright, but the shapes are ever-so-slightly askew.
Nevertheless, every uneven stitch holds meaning. Each
crooked patch tells a story.

Years ago, during our annual family reunion at
Grandma's farm, my cleaning project was the musty linen
closet. I discovered a vibrant quilt top while sorting
through the handmade towels, table clothes and bedding.
It was patterned in a radiating star, the Star of Bethlehem.
My head reeled with the stories this quilt might tell.

I brought the top to my grandmother. She would
remember. "It was given to Annie," she said, a 1930s-era
barter for the medical services of my great-aunt. The

quilter spent hours cutting tiny pieces and then hand-stitching them together. For the maker, the quilt was a means to health care during the parched days of the Depression.

Later that weekend my grandmother placed her meditations book into my hands. She pointed a shaky finger to the day's lesson: "Opening your heart and home to those in need." Then she shared old stories of how abolitionists used quilt code to signal slaves. Quilts displayed ciphers hidden in the Log Cabin, Hourglass, Drunkard's Path and North Star patterns, among others. They were maps to freedom seen by all, understood by few. Quilts made with black cloth and featuring log cabins beckoned from clotheslines in front of houses that promised fugitive slaves warm meals, beds, safety and friendship. They meant home.

It dawned on me at that moment that every quilt is someone's story, a colorful history coded into a bright array of patchwork. The Depression quilt and the safe-haven quilts tell stories of survival. It was then I decided to make a quilt that told my grandmother's story. Hers is also a story of survival.

My grandmother spent her life caring for others. She made her home a welcoming haven. Family member, friend, neighbor and even stranger could count on a warm meal and bed at the farm. The Watkins man conveniently chose mealtimes to peddle his trove of spices, mixes and flavorings at the farm. And he was always given a place at the table. Even during the Depression, there was always an extra plate, though the homestead was not a place of wealth.

The family lived day to day, like most did, always dependent on the next rain for the crops to come in. In the Dust Bowl years, the children wore hand-me-down clothes from the neighbors and feed-sack creations.

Grandma would remake the hand-me-downs, carefully pulling stitches at the seams and refitting the clothes to ever-growing children. My aunt Kathryn loved her Nutrena pellet food-sack coat. The orange of the feed sack washed out to leave a jaunty print behind, fitting for a young girl's wardrobe.

Grandma used every scrap of fabric and put away every piece of metal or paper for another time. Years of pack-ratting resulted in closets and crawl spaces filled to the rafters with *Saturday Evening Posts,* vegetable remedies and bitters, and even wooden clogs, aprons and dresses from the Old Country. Farm animals had long abandoned out-buildings, crowded out by discarded furniture, broken down Fords and tractors, and even horse-drawn wagons. Hence each reunion was a virtual treasure hunt for antique goodies, as well as a nostalgic trip down memory lane for all sixty-four of my grandmother's descendants.

Unlike my ancestors, I don't depend on Grandma's farm for subsistence of body. For me it means a warm meal and safe bed for my soul—subsistence of spirit.

I remember annual vacations at the farm. It was the most carefree time I have ever known. I ran wild with my cousins. We plucked mulberries from the trees, snuck into Grandpa's candy drawer and ate fresh-baked cinnamon rolls during the days. We climbed into the featherbeds upstairs and told ghost stories at night. Our parents reminisced in the kitchen below us, their laughter eventually lulling us to sleep.

I take my own family to the farm now. I spend the days making repairs, cooking, cleaning and occasionally short-sheeting a bed or two. My son runs with his cousins, experiencing the freedom of spirit that I still feel in this old house. I tuck him into bed, and it's my turn to laugh until midnight with my cousins, aunts and uncles in the kitchen.

I have more good memories of my time at the farm than from any other period of my life. It's there that I return my focus to living every moment, not worrying about tomorrow or next week. It's there that I find my peace and my soul. I find rejuvenation to go home, to create a story for myself that may end up on a quilt someday.

My grandmother created not just a house, but a home— a place of shelter for the body and spirit, not only for her children and grandchildren, but for neighbors and strangers alike. Her life was hard, backbreaking at times. But I do not have to ask her why she worked so hard. I can see why when she watches her great-grandchildren play at her feet. Her gentle smile and sparkling eyes are affirmation enough. This is the story her quilt tells.

Julie Dunbar

Sister Said

He gives not best who gives most; but he gives most who gives best.

Arthur Warwick

No two words in the English language could send our household into more of a tizzy than those two words, "Sister said." So when I announced shortly after Thanksgiving that the nuns at my elementary school said I was going to be one of the angels in the Christmas play, it set the wheels in motion for the most frenzied of activities. My grandma rummaged through a trunk of yard goods, looking for the whitest of white scraps, while my father measured me shoulder to shoulder, neckline to shoe top. My mother searched the drawers and cupboards for the little bit of gold ribbon Sister said we were to wear around our waists. My father outlined wings on huge pieces of cardboard, wings that Sister said were to measure fourteen inches long and ten inches wide at the center. My daily messages of "Sister said" brought occasional moans and groans from my dressmakers as plans were changed and sleeves had to cover our fingertips, not stop at the wrist as those on my robe did. Another day, Sister said the hem should be at least four inches deep and we should wear a pink slip under the robe, not a white one such as my grandma had just finished making.

When my brother Tom came home one night two weeks before Christmas and said that *his* Sister had said that our family had to come to the Scout meeting that night, my father groaned the loudest and said, "But tonight I'm supposed to cut out those wings because Sister said Jeanie had to hand them in tomorrow for inspection!"

"Now, Raymond, you know perfectly well that I can cut out those wings," Grandma said. "You all go right ahead to that meeting, just like Sister said."

"Well, I don't know," my mother said. "You've been so tired lately. And you've taken that angel robe apart so many times the material is almost as worn as you."

"I'll be just fine," Grandma snapped. "Every stitch of the angel robe is made of love, and that's what keeps me going."

For the next few days and nights, my parents were too caught up with the Scouts' Christmas program to help much with the creation of my angel robe, so when, late one Friday night, I said that Sister said the angels had to wear white shoes, my grandma promised, "We'll go right downtown tomorrow, Jeanie, just the two of us, and shop for those shoes. You parents have put enough wear and tear on their car for the time being."

Even though my mother exclaimed that the real wear and tear was more apparent on my grandmother, Grandma Thomas would hear none of it. Once again, she recited her line about every stitch of that robe being made of love.

Eight days before the play, Sister said it would be nice if all the angels had curls in their hair the night of the play, but not *too* many curls. Out came Grandma's bag of rags and each night before bedtime, she rolled up my hair, practicing, hoping to find that fine line between curly and not *too* curly. She listened patiently, too, as I sang "O Little Town of Bethlehem," a song Sister said we had to sing every night until we had the words down pat.

Each ensuing evening I had new and often contradictory tales of what Sister had said that day in regard to the angel robe. In their struggles to comply, my parents' nerves were often set on edge. Was it any wonder that when I came home four days before the play and tearfully said that Sister said I couldn't be an angel after all because I seemed too fat, my father thundered, "That does it! That does it! Too fat? Why, if you weighed an ounce less, you'd BE an angel, I fear. I do not *ever* want to hear 'Sister said' again in this house!"

"There must be some mistake," Grandma Thomas said softly.

"No, no! I *know* that's what Sister said," I cried.

"You march right up to Sister tomorrow, Jeanie," my mother said, "and get this straightened out. I'm sure there is some mistake. You are not too fat and you never will be."

"I can't do that," I sobbed. "Sister *never* makes mistakes."

"Perhaps if I went . . ." Grandma began, but my father said, "Absolutely not!"

"Jeanie must learn to stand on her own two feet," my mother said. "After all the work, all the love you put into that robe—why, I am sure there has been a mistake."

Thinking about all that love and how heartbroken my grandmother must have been kept me awake most of the night. The next morning I waited until the very last minute before leaving for school, hoping my grandmother would defy my parents and go with me. Or perhaps my father would not be as angry and would take matters into his own hands. Surely my mother would see I had not slept well. Maybe she would say, "You poor thing. You must stay home today. I will go talk to Sister myself."

But none of those dreams came true, and I ended up standing on my own two feet beside Sister's desk, asking, "Sister, why did you say I seemed too fat to be an angel?"

"Too fat!" Sister said, truly taken aback. "I never said— oh, I think I understand. Jeanie, I never said you seem too fat. I said you 'sing too flat.' Besides, I want you to be the narrator. You have a good strong voice and read very well. Will you do that part for me?"

Sing too flat! Not seem too fat! And now I was going to be narrator! The narrator's part was the best of the whole play!

"Oh, Sister," I said in a rush. "Oh, Sister, I'll do my very best. I'd much rather read than sing, you know."

"Don't I know!" Sister teased kindly.

"But . . . but, Sister," I asked, "What does the narrator wear?"

"Anything you want," Sister said. "You must have a special outfit you want to wear. Think it over and tell me about it when school is out."

I didn't need to think it over long, for school had barely begun when I knew the only outfit I wanted to wear. Now if only Sister would say yes, I prayed as the day dragged on.

When the bell rang at 3:30, I stood before Sister's desk once more.

"Have you decided on your outfit, Jeanie?" Sister asked as she straightened out her desktop.

"Yes, Sister, I have."

"And what is it made of? Cotton? Rayon? Velvet?"

Cotton? Rayon? Velvet? I didn't know! I only knew one thing my outfit was made of. Would Sister understand?

I drew a deep breath before I poured out the story of my outfit. At the story's end, I said, "So you see, Sister, all I know is that every stitch of my outfit is made of love. SO will that be okay?"

Sister bent down, picked me up and hugged me close as she tenderly whispered her reply.

My father wasn't home yet, so I could safely say "Sister said" without listening to him groan. It's too bad he wasn't there, because he didn't hear me shout as I came in the front door, "Sister said I can wear the angel robe! Sister said it's made of exactly what Christmas is made of! Lots and lots of love!"

And you know Sister. Sister *never* made a mistake.

Jean Jeffrey Gietzen

Gifts of the Heart

Every gift, though it may be small, is in reality great if given with affection.

Peter Pindar

My eleventh birthday was just a week away when we arrived in the refugee camp on that bleak and cold November day in 1947. My grandparents, who were raising me, and I had fled our Soviet-occupied Hungary with only the clothes we were wearing. The refugee camp, called a displaced persons camp, was in Spittal, Austria.

To cold and hungry people like us, the refugee camp was a blessing. We were given our own space in a barrack, fed hot soup and given warm clothes, so we were grateful. But as for my upcoming birthday, I didn't even want to think about it. After all, we had left our country without any possessions or money. So I had decided to forget about birthday presents from then on.

My grandmother, the only mother I ever knew, had taken over my care when I was a baby because her only child, my mother, had died suddenly. Before the war intensified, my birthdays had been grand celebrations with many cousins in attendance and lots of gifts. The cake had always been a *dobosh torte,* which my grandmother prepared herself.

My eighth birthday was the last time I received a bought gift. Times were already hard, money was scarce and survival the utmost goal. But my grandmother had managed to buy me a book. It was a wonderful book, full of humor and adventure, and I loved it. In fact, *Cilike's Adventures* had transported me many times, from the harshness of the real world of war and strife to a world of laughter and fun.

After that, birthday presents were usually crocheted or knitted items, made lovingly by my grandmother—but there was always a present. However, in the refugee camp, I was resigned to the inevitable.

On November 25, when I woke in the barrack, I lay there on my little cot beneath the horsehair blanket and thought about being eleven. I was practically a grown-up, I told myself, and I would act accordingly when Grandma and Grandpa awoke. I didn't want them to feel bad because they couldn't give me a present.

So I dressed quickly and tiptoed out quietly. I ran across the frosty dirt road to the barrack marked "Women's Bathroom and Shower," washed, combed my hair and took my time, even though it was chilly, before returning to the barrack. But finally, I returned.

"Good morning, sweetheart. Happy birthday," Grandfather greeted me.

"Thank you. But I would rather forget about birthdays now," I replied, squirming in his generous hug.

"You are too young to forget about birthdays," Grandmother said. "Besides, who would I give this present to if birthdays are to be forgotten?"

"Present?" I looked at her surprised, as she reached into her pocket and pulled something out.

"Happy birthday, honey. It's not much of a present, but I thought you might enjoy having Cilike back on your eleventh birthday," she said with tears in her eyes.

"My old Cilike book! But I thought it was left behind with all our other things," I exclaimed, hugging the book to my chest, tears of joy welling up in my eyes.

"Well, it almost was. But when we had to leave so quickly in the middle of the night, I grabbed it, along with my prayer book, and stuck it in my pocket. I knew how much you loved that book; I couldn't bear to leave it behind. Happy birthday, honey. I'm sorry it's not a new book, but I hope you like having it back."

"Oh, thank you, Grandma. Having this book again means so much to me. So very much," I said, hugging her, tears streaming down my cheeks. "It's the best birthday present I ever received!"

And it truly was, because I realized that day how blessed I was.

Gifts of the heart are always the best gifts. They are true gifts of love.

Renie Burghardt

Marking Time

*Dost thou love life? Then do not squander time,
for that's what life is made of.*

Benjamin Franklin

I was late. Again. My fancy digital watch was losing twenty minutes a day. I'd made three trips to the store that week and every time forgot to buy a new battery. A mom on a constant schedule, I needed an accurate time-piece, so I grabbed the only other watch I owned, a delicate silver one my grandmother left me when she died.

Nana's watch was small with a diamond-encircled face and a sliver of a band. It was beautiful and petite, just like she was. I'd always loved it but rarely wore it. It was the old-fashioned, battery-free kind that needed winding each night. For me, a person who had trouble remembering to feed the cats, wearing a watch requiring any degree of upkeep was a bad idea.

The first few days I wore Nana's watch, I kept forgetting to wind it and still ended up late for everything. But by week's end, its elfin face and ticking second hand were as familiar to me as the feel of Nana's hand in mine when I was a child.

Wearing the watch wrapped me in memories of her. She used to take regular walks around the yard, just to see the loganberry trees in bloom. After dinner, she and Grandpa would walk me down to the 7-11 for a packet of M&M'S. We spent countless afternoons strolling downtown, window-shopping, and dreaming of things to buy and adventures we'd have someday.

Nana appreciated the value of time. Her son, Bobby, died when he was eight, in a tragic accident that left a measure of perpetual sadness in Nana's eyes. In 1976, Nana herself slipped through death's grasp when she had a brain tumor removed successfully.

So Nana refused to waste a second of the extra time granted to her. She taught me piano, asked about every school day, and waded with me through boxes of photographs and memories, trying to imprint legacies on an eleven-year-old girl who couldn't know then that time would ever feel short.

Years later, when she passed away, Nana left me the watch. In the busy-ness of my life with a husband, two kids, two cats, a dog, a job and a house, I often forget to slow down and really see the little things around me. Bread is store-bought, self-scrubbing bubbles clean my bathrooms, and my car is a mobile office between soccer games and Brownie troop meetings.

When Nana's watch stopped one day—because I'd forgotten to wind it again—I was lost. The children and I were shopping, on our way to an important appointment. I stopped in the middle of Wal-Mart and looked around for a clock, muttering to myself, annoyed. The children started whining about missing some show on TV. Spying an opportunity, my son darted across the aisle to a toy and my daughter headed for some books nearby. I had melting ice cream in the cart, cranky kids and someplace I had to be. I didn't need another frustration.

I tapped the watch with the futile hope that it would magically start again. A memory slammed into me with the force of an electrical jolt. Nana, my mother and I were strolling in the sunshine at a sidewalk sale. We bought a book for a dime and a drink from the soda fountain. Twenty-five years later, I still remember it as one of the best days of my life because every moment seemed to last forever.

I realized I'd been letting schedules and errands swallow those mini-moments in my own life, ruled by the ticking of a clock that weighed heavy on my shoulders. I abandoned the cart and joined my kids, bending down to see the toys. I marveled at the latest Buzz Lightyear and a colorful new Harry Potter book. Hand in hand, the kids and I ambled through the aisles, poking at this toy, pushing the buttons on that one, dreaming of Santa and birthdays to come. We wandered by the pet department, made friends with a hamster and chatted with a parrot.

We arrived home much later, carrying a puddle of ice cream in the grocery bag and one new goldfish. I'd missed my appointment, but it didn't matter. After dinner, we explored our neighborhood on foot, hunting for squirrels and rabbits in the summer evening light. We fed the ducks at the pond, soared through the air on swings and played a rousing game of tag. We were exhausted but laughing. And we all had another happy memory to hang onto.

That night, while I turned the tiny knob to wind Nana's watch, I realized why my grandmother had left me this particular piece of jewelry. Her legacy wasn't a million-dollar home on a hill or a priceless art collection. Her gift was much simpler, one we often forget in our calendar-driven lives. She gave me the gift of time, wrapped up in a watch that needs daily attention, a continuous reminder that our days pass as fast as summer storms.

In its tiny silver face, I see Nana, and in the ticking of its second hand, I hear the running journey of my life. That's when I turn off the phone, close the calendar and take the kids outside to greet the first daffodils of spring.

Shirley Jump

Green Ink

If there be any truer measure of a man than by what he does, it must be by what he gives.

Robert South

The rush of Christmas was again upon me. I was opening a stack of Christmas cards, glancing quickly at photos of friends' children while listening to my four-year-old daughter rehearse the *Little Drummer Boy* for her preschool Christmas program. My mind swirled with commitments, cookie recipes and carols, and then it froze.

Staring at the letter in my hand, I couldn't draw oxygen. My ears burned as if I had just come out of the December cold into a heated house.

I opened the envelope to find, not a Christmas card, but a letter signed by Helen's four children letting me know of the unfortunate passing of their beloved mother. Forty-seven years had passed since Helen Tibbals walked into my mom's living room. I dropped to my kitchen floor, shaking, while tears flowed down my face for the loss of this angel. And then I smiled. Helen was in heaven where she had always belonged and from where she certainly had come.

My mom has told her tale so many times I can still smell the scent of spruce and hear the clang of ornaments in the living room of their house on Hollywood Place:

We heard the echo of someone knocking. Grandma opened the squeaky front door of her small home, where my three brothers, my sister, my mother and I lived. A slim redheaded woman and her teenage boy stood smiling at us. I watched in awe as the two strangers carried armloads of packages wrapped in red with our names written on white tags in green ink. They also lugged a pine tree, strings of colored lights and glass ornaments, transforming the drab room from black and white to Technicolor. I backed against the threadbare couch to allow her and her son room to unload these treasures. They brought Christmas into our living room.

The woman in the green silk dress introduced herself as Helen Tibbals and her awkward-looking son as Todd Junior. She was a member of First Community Church, the same church we attended, and explained that she had taken a paper gift tag shaped like the star of Bethlehem off the Christmas tree standing in the church vestibule. It had our name on it. She was all lipstick and smiles and smelled like the department store downtown. The sharp scent of peppermint filled my nose as she opened a box of candy canes and invited us to join in decorating the evergreen. All the while, she asked questions about us kids as if we were her own. I had so many questions for her, but was too shy to ask them. Where had this angel and her elf come from, and why did she care so much about my family?

Helen was the gift of Christmas present, not past. A reminder that despite a father who had deserted us, a terminally ill mother and the fact that all five of us lived in a two-bedroom home with my mother and grandmother, God's hope and love lived in the world.

Helen became much more than a Christmas gift; she became a part of Mom's family. Until my mom and her siblings graduated from high school, Helen regularly brought them school supplies, new clothes and chocolates. She even sent them to summer camp each year. When my grandmother struggled with breast cancer, Helen brought candy bars and magazines to the small home as if she were Grandmother's sister. When my mom, aunt and uncles were in college, Helen wrote them faithfully, always using her signature green pen. She attended my grandmother's funeral, my mother's graduation from high school and my parents' wedding.

Helen's generosity expanded to the next generation as she adopted my brother and me as grandchildren, including us in her umbrella of selfless giving. She invited us to her home each summer for a feast and a stroll around her goldfish pond. Every birthday, gifts arrived at our house, our names written across the top in green felt-tip marker. I remember the excitement of seeing an envelope with my name scrawled in Helen's green ink every Easter and Valentine's Day. Poinsettias in December would bear her green signature, and even the place cards at the annual Christmas dinner at her club, where she made sure the waiter kept our Shirley Temples refilled, were written in green ink.

I was still weepy when my husband, Brett, came home from work. I pulled a boiling pot of pasta off the stove, placed it in the sink and scooped up our toddler, Max, whose hands reached to the sky. "Hold, Mama, hold."

I pointed to the tear-spotted letter on the counter.

Brett set his keys down and scanned the note. He turned and wrapped his strong arms around my quaking body. Soon I was able to exhale and push a smile onto my streaked face.

"Honey, can you get an extra name off the Giving Tree

at church this year?" I swallowed hard, then continued. "Helen came into my mom's life by picking her name from a tree. I would like to follow her example."

"Of course," he smiled and kissed me on the tip of my nose.

The next day when Brett came home from work, he pulled two yellow pieces of paper cut in the shapes of mittens from the pocket of his parka.

"The directions said to put our name on the half of the tag still hanging on the tree so the church would know who was responsible for that gift," Brett explained while easing his briefcase off his shoulder. "I guess that way no child will go unaccounted for."

I nodded while drying my hands on the holly-embroidered towel by the kitchen sink.

"I wrote B. Smith on this tag, our tag," he said, holding up one of the canary-colored cards. "And on this mitten," my husband's turquoise eyes twinkled, "I wrote 'H. Tibbals'— in green ink."

Laura Smith

Timeless Generosity

My grandmother's Social Security check was the high-light of her life. Everything depended on the arrival of her check. To this day, I have no idea how much it was, but she performed miracles with it. No matter what I wanted, she'd promise it to me, "when I get my check."

Her visits to our house were timed with its arrival. She could never come empty-handed. No sir, she came with delightful treats purchased with the money from that check. My dad would drive to Pittsburgh to bring her to our house two hours north. She'd emerge from the car laden with red licorice, cookies, chipped ham, potato chips, pop and her small blue suitcase. There was a small present for each of us, including my parents. After distrib-uting her gifts, she'd take out of her pocket a list of things yet to be purchased with the remaining money.

These items always were the same, but she made the list anyway. Pond's face cream, hairnets, Jergen's hand lotion, support hose, chocolate-covered raisins, writing paper and envelopes, and some "good cheese." My dad would drive us into our small town with my grandmother sitting happily in the front seat clutching her pocketbook and my brother and sister and me in the back. Our destination was the G. C. Murphy store where, instead of just looking at things, we would be leaving with treasures.

Grammie, as we called her, loved these trips. She took her time examining the support hose, the hairnets and the cold creams. We hung by her side as she made her decisions . . . always choosing the same items. Then we were free to pick out something. I always got a book, my brother a car of some sort and my sister usually got chocolate candy. Grammie would then pick out something for our other sister, too little yet to go on these magical shopping trips.

Next we'd go to the grocery store and she'd load the cart with anything we wanted . . . all the things my mother never bought. I can still hear her urging our dad to get something. "Go ahead, Buddy. I have enough to pay for it." We laughed at hearing him called by his childhood name.

I never saw my grandmother buy a new dress for herself, but she gave me money for my high school graduation dress. I never saw her buy new shoes or even a coat. She was always "making do" with her own things, but spending generously on those she loved. She lived with my dad's sister and her other grandchildren in Pittsburgh, and they experienced the same generosity.

The only month of the year she did not follow this ritual was December. She saved that check for Christmas presents. Each December she made yet another list . . . the list of what we wanted for Christmas. We had to give her three or four ideas so she could surprise us with one. Christmas was wonderful with the arrival of Grammie and all her mysterious, oddly wrapped packages.

Time moved on and I went off to college. By this time there were seven children in my family and some of my cousins now had children of their own. Grammie's check had to be stretched even further. The first letter she sent me at college read:

Dear Patti Jo:

My check came yesterday and I wanted to send you something, but I guess you have all the books you need there at college. Here are a few dollars so you can go out and have something nice to eat with your new friends.

Inside the folded sheets of the familiar writing paper I had watched her purchase time after time were three carefully folded dollar bills. This was the first of many such letters I received at college. Each letter during that first year contained folded dollar bills . . . my grandmother's love reaching across the miles . . . her check stretching very far.

And then I got the last one. She sent a five-dollar bill, a list of what I should get with it and instructions to save some too. The list was long. I laughed, knowing that it would never cover all that Grammie wanted me to have.

Before the next letter arrived, the news came that she was in the hospital. By the time I got to Pittsburgh, she had slipped into a coma. Sitting by her intensive care bed, I was besieged with grief, realizing that I would never talk to her again . . . never again witness her generosity and appreciation for the smallest of things.

My grandmother had no will, no bequests, nothing to leave anyone . . . she gave it all away to those she loved while she lived.

Not too long ago, I was out to dinner with my parents and I offered to pay.

"You're just like my mother," Dad said.

I've never ever received a nicer compliment. Grammie left me more than I ever realized.

Patti Lawson

"Now, now dear, I'm sure your mom is spoiling him because she loves him—not for revenge!"

Grandma's Surprise Party

When thou makest presents, let them be of such things as will last long; to the end they may be in some sort immortal, and may frequently refresh the memory of the receiver.

Thomas Fuller

A neon envelope glowed between magazine circulars. *Hmm, a letter,* I thought. Anything other than junk mail and bills in the mailbox was rare these days, since most of my communications came by telephone and e-mail.

I examined the square envelope. The writing was unmistakably Grandma Caryle's, but why would she send a card? My birthday wasn't for another two months.

What's she up to this time? I wondered.

I ripped open the envelope as I walked back to the house. Inside was an adolescent-looking party invitation with the words "Happy Birthday" on the front. Opening the card, I read:

You're invited
To a surprise party
At Grandma Caryle's house
On August 9 from 2-4 p.m.

Laughing out loud, I ran to the house. My eccentric grandmother always liked celebrating. In fact, her birthdays usually lasted all month, with many lunches, dinners and visits with friends and family members.

I dialed her number.

"Hi, Grandma, I got your invitation in the mail just now," I said.

"Oh!" she exclaimed in an exaggerated tone. "Did you call to RSVP?"

I giggled at her mock coyness. "Of course I'll be there. But it's customary that someone other than yourself host a surprise party when you're the guest of honor," I teased. "After all, you won't be surprised if you plan the party."

Grandma paused. "Well, you know how I love parties. I'm sure we'll have lots of surprises," she replied. "And if we don't, I promise to act surprised."

We both laughed and hung up the phone. Grandma had never planned a birthday celebration for herself and certainly never a surprise party, but then she'd never turned seventy-five years old either.

During the next few weeks, I tried to think of ways I could make Grandma's birthday special.

"Let me bake a cake," I offered.

"I already ordered one," she answered.

"What about decorations? May I decorate your house?"

"I'm using potted chrysanthemums," Grandma said. "Less to clean up, and I can plant them in my flower beds afterward."

Since she was planning the entire event, I wanted to do something extra to add an element of surprise. I decided to write on her driveway with sidewalk chalk and bring helium balloons. *That ought to surprise Grandma,* I thought.

Finally, Grandma's birthday arrived. I called that morning and sang "Happy Birthday." After the song, I playfully asked, "Are you surprised?"

"Oh, yes," Grandma said with glee.

Thirty minutes before the party, I chalked "Happy Birthday, Caryle" on her driveway. I attached balloons to the front yard trees and mailbox. Gifts and more balloons were unloaded from my car, and I rang the doorbell.

"Surprise," I shouted as she opened the door.

Grandma laughed. I put her gifts on the hall table and started into the dining area with the balloons. We always celebrated birthdays around the dining room table.

"Don't go in there," shouted Grandma as she blocked the doorway.

"I thought I'd tie the balloons to the dining room chairs."

"Take them into the living room. I don't want you to see the cake just yet," she instructed. "After all, this is a surprise party!"

Perplexed, I obeyed.

Soon, Grandma's best friend, sister-in-law, niece, stepdaughter, daughter-in-law and her other granddaughter, my sister Shelby, arrived. We sat in the living room, talked and snacked from party trays.

"Where's Dad?" I asked. My father, her only child, was conspicuously absent.

"Not invited," she replied. "It's a girls-only party."

We all laughed.

"Say, Caryle, I could see your yard decorations from down the block," remarked Aunt Gay.

Grandma looked confused.

"Come see," I said, gently taking her arm. We walked outside.

"Are you surprised?" I asked.

"Oh, yes!" answered Grandma.

Back inside, someone suggested opening gifts. Grandma sat down, and Judy, her daughter-in-law, handed over a gift bag.

"Open this one first," she ordered.

Inside was a rhinestone tiara.

"You're the birthday queen," proclaimed Judy.

Grandma's eyes glowed with excitement as she unwrapped the packages. Inside, I felt regretful that I'd never thought to throw her a party and that this one wasn't really a surprise.

Once the gifts were opened, Grandma announced, "We have cake in the dining room." She got up and led the way.

"That was abrupt," remarked my sister. "She must be hungry."

We filed into the dining room. On the table was a quarter sheet cake with the word "Surprise" on it and seven small boxes of various sizes.

We took our seats and Grandma began. "As you know, today is my seventy-fifth birthday and I've invited you here to celebrate with me. For many years, you've been a part of my life. I love you and although I'm not planning to die anytime soon, I want you to have something to remember me by."

We sat speechless.

"This is not a surprise party for me, but for you."

Grandma gave each of us a box.

"Stacy, you go first," she instructed.

I removed the lid. Inside was a diamond ring that I'd seen on Grandma's finger.

"It belonged to your great-aunt Hazel," she said quietly. "I inherited it when she died twenty-five years ago. I want you to have it."

Tears pooled in my eyes.

"Are you surprised?" mimicked Grandma in an attempt to lighten the mood.

"I thought sidewalk chalking was a big surprise," I said, hugging her neck. "Thank you so much. You're amazing."

On that, her seventy-fifth birthday, Grandma gave away her wedding ring set, her mother's strand of pearls, and several heirloom rings and bracelets. As each box was opened, she quipped, "Are you surprised?"

And indeed, we all were. Not only was the party a surprise for us, but a reminder of her generosity and love. Every time I wear that diamond ring, I think of Grandma Caryle and the legacy of fun I inherited from her.

Surprise!

Stephanie "Stacy" Thompson

A Grandmother's Gifts

If I cannot give bountifully, yet I will give freely, and what I want in my hand I will supply with my heart.

Arthur Warwick

Here's the math:

Six grandchildren. Eight days of Hanukah. One gift per child per day.

I wasn't going to provide that—not when our grandchildren were blessed with loving families who see to their needs, and then some.

So I've devised a quite different Hanukah plan. I get each grandchild a small purchased gift. One. It is never of such magnitude that I worry about the object being injured, maimed or destroyed. Mind you, four of the six are little boys under the age of eight.

Then I work on what I've come to think of as my "real" gift.

Because Hanukah is really about miracles, and because these six wondrous creatures are just that, I devote myself to this challenge:

I spend hours, sometimes weeks, preparing a letter to each child, even the two who are preverbal, to say nothing of preliterate.

I sit at my computer and secretly "talk" to it about Sam or Hannah, Jonah or Zay, Danny or Baby Emily. I chronicle who they are at this moment in their emerging histories. I catalogue conversations we've had, stories they've told me, names of their friends, their adored toys and stuffed animals, endearing habits, bedtime rituals, school anecdotes, even favorite articles of clothing.

Two Hanukahs ago, I actually decided to illustrate my ramblings with photographs, a motivation for "shooting" these adored little ones at every opportunity.

And then I stored it all away in what is becoming my bulging "Hanukah File." My vague sense is that the years of "gifts" will be delivered when each grandchild reaches thirteen.

So what does all of this have to do with Hanukah? And the gift-grab?

Nothing at all.

And everything.

Not now, but somewhere down the road, my grandchildren may understand why they didn't get the mountain of gifts their little pals did. Years from now, they may figure out why their grandmother asked them endless questions and sometimes frantically scribbled down their answers on scraps of paper, eager to get every word.

My Hanukah gift to these six is obviously not what they might expect. And because these are children exposed to the galloping gift frenzy of the season, they have shown and expressed disappointment. They want, in Hannah's immortal words as spokesperson for the clan, "cool stuff" for this eight-day potential gift bonanza. And they're not getting it.

I once heard Sam talking to a little friend and comparing

notes about the annual haul. His pal had gotten action figures and a scooter from his grandparents. Sam was left to
explain what he had—or in this case, hadn't—gotten.

He fumbled. He struggled to explain what he's been
told each year, that Grandma is creating something special for him, and that when he and his cousins are older,
they'll get something even better than "cool stuff." They'll
get memories, history, reminders of who they were at two
and five and eight.

Sam's friend didn't understand. Nor, I'm sure, does
Sam. Not quite. Not yet.

Does he wish he'd been handed a video game, a toy
with moving parts, a terrific computer accessory? You bet.

But for now, I'm hanging tough. I'm resisting the urge to
splurge on traditional grandmother gifts. I'm keeping my
credit cards locked in their compartment in my wallet and
using my loving memories as revenue instead.

This gift of my grandchildren's lives, frozen in time,
seems perfectly right for Hanukah, the season of history,
hope and miracles.

Sally Friedman

Star of the Week

The only way to pray is to pray; and the way to pray well is to pray much.

John Chapman

Joyce and Morgan Ilgenfritz are grandparents to twenty grandchildren. Fifteen in one family live in Pennsylvania, less than two hours from them. Two live in Colorado and the other three in West Africa.

Joyce and Morgan have also housed 370 people in their home over the last thirty years. In addition to those who are presently living with them, they are caring for Morgan's ninety-year-old mother, who has Alzheimer's disease. So their days are full.

Next to her relationship with the Lord, Joyce's top priority is her grandchildren. She is on the lookout year round for gifts and cards, and never waits until an occasion arrives to prepare for it. But she would be the first to admit that staying in touch takes some creativity.

Recently, Joyce was pondering what more she could do.

"I was in a store right after Valentine's Day," she explains, "and saw a picture frame and two heart boxes.

They were reduced in price, but I didn't buy them. That night," she continues, "I had a conversation with God. 'Lord, I have all these grandchildren,'" I said. "'How can I stay connected with them?'"

Joyce drifted off to sleep and soon awoke with a clear direction from the Lord. "He said to go back to the store and get the frame and boxes," she recalls. "Then he told me what to do with them."

Joyce could hardly wait for morning. She went to the store, made the purchase and placed the items on her kitchen windowsill. Then she collected pictures of each of her grandchildren and wrote all their names on pieces of paper, which she placed in one of the boxes.

Now each week she draws a name from the first box, puts that child's picture in the frame, and places the name in the second box for the next time around. That child is her "Star of the Week."

Immediately, she calls (e-mails to Africa) and informs the star of his or her status. Then she asks for prayer requests. The child gleefully anticipates hearing from her again during the week by way of another phone call, a letter or a package—or possibly all three.

Recently, five-year-old Moriah hung up from his phone call and announced loudly to any of his fourteen brothers and sisters within hearing distance, "I'm Grandma's Star of the Week!"

When six-year-old Ashley got her call, she told her grandma there was a girl in her class who was saying mean things about her.

"You just be nice to her and I'll be praying," Joyce responded.

The next time her grandma called, Ashley said, "That little girl has been so nice to me, and I know it's because you've been praying."

Being Star of the Week not only makes twenty

grandchildren happy, it fulfills the desire of their grandma's heart, allowing her to focus on one grandchild at a time, to pray specifically for that child's needs, and to surprise the "Star" with gifts of love.

Bonnie S. Grau

My Present

Miracles are the swaddling clothes of infant churches.

Thomas Fuller

I was ten years old when my mother's mother, my grandma Dolores, began losing her battle against breast cancer. She was only fifty-four and had always been the apple of my eye. . . . I felt like I was the pupil in hers. Grandma spent the last month of her life in the hospital. My little brother, Vernon, and I weren't allowed to visit her. Our parents thought that seeing her might frighten us because she'd lost one hundred pounds and hardly resembled herself. I missed her very much.

It was soon to be my eleventh birthday, and I told my parents that all I wanted for my birthday present was to see Grandma. They finally agreed, and on my birthday, May 30, 1954, we drove to the hospital in San Francisco, about thirty miles from our home. On the way my mother explained that Grandma was asleep and not to be surprised, that she was laying in an oxygen tent, that I was to be very quiet because she needed her rest, and that I wasn't to wake her. I wouldn't have understood then, being but a child, but the truth was that my grandmother had been in a coma for a week and wouldn't be waking up.

When we reached her room, I saw my relatives sitting on chairs everywhere. Everyone was quiet, unlike the happy noise I was accustomed to hearing when everyone got together at our family gatherings. My grandfather and great-grandma didn't even say hello to us. Neither did any of Grandma's younger brothers or sisters. I didn't realize it then, but they were all in a death vigil, waiting for my grandma to take her last breath. All I understood was that everybody was sad; my mother cried silently.

Grandma was lying fast asleep on the hospital bed, but I could see her clearly through the oxygen tent, which looked like a large, clear, plastic box extending from her waist to the top of the bed. She just looked like Grandma to me, and I was so happy to see her. I immediately went to the head of her bed—nobody stopped me, not even my mother or father.

Well, I tell you, my grandma just sat right up and pushed that tent aside and, smiling, said, "Barbara, come here and sit next to me, right here," as she patted the sheet on her right side. I pulled myself up and plopped down next to her, and she put her arm around me. "Barbara, it's your eleventh birthday and before I came to the hospital I got you a present—here." She leaned over and pulled out a little white box from a drawer near her bedside. I opened it and under a square of cotton was a turquoise tortoise-shell-covered compact. The cover was engraved with St. Christopher carrying the Christ child on his shoulders. When I opened the compact there was a mirror on one side and some light powder on the other. "Barbara, some day soon you will become a teenager, and when you do I want you to use this, and always remember that I love you."

I thanked Grandma and gave her a lively hug and a kiss. She chuckled and we smiled into each other's eyes. Then she told me that she was too tired to visit anymore and that she needed to take a nap. She slowly laid back and closed her eyes.

I hopped off her bed and a nurse came to reposition the tent around her. My father took me by the hand and, without saying good-bye to anyone in the room, the three of us left. That was that.

What I hadn't realized is that my parents and relatives had been unable to move or speak while watching Grandma and me enjoying my birthday together. They'd witnessed a miracle taking place right before their eyes— like seeing Lazarus rise from the dead. I can't imagine how it must have felt to everyone present, watching Grandma back to being fully herself while laughing with her little granddaughter, happily visiting together on a hospital bed.

My grandmother never opened her eyes again. She peacefully passed away one week later. I have believed in miracles ever since my grandmother woke up to attend my eleventh birthday party.

Barbara G. Drotar

Grandma Wanda

Life is short and we have never too much time for gladdening the hearts of those who are traveling the dark journey with us. Oh, be swift to love, make haste to be kind!

Henry Frederic Amiel

In the midst of her long and brave battle against cancer, my mother's spirits lifted with the arrival of her first grandchild, whom she welcomed as "a child from heaven." Better yet for Grandma Wanda, who'd been blessed with three healthy but raucous boys, there was finally a girl in the house . . . a beautiful, caring bundle named Kerry, whom Grandma Wanda adored. And Kerry adored her grandmother.

As a single father raising my daughter alone from the time she was two, I was grateful my mother and dad lived just two blocks away from us. It wasn't long before Kerry had beaten a path to their house for all the cookies, consolation and hugs that a little girl—particularly one being raised without a mother in the house—required of a loving grandmother.

My mother was deeply devout. For more than thirty years, until her illness forced her to retire, she was a church secretary. She took great pleasure on those occasions when Kerry accompanied her to work, where the friendly priests were always eager to hear about their latest adventures, whether it be a weekend journey to the shore, shopping for an Easter dress or baking cookies.

A favorite place for Kerry was her grandmother's lap, where she would curl up to listen to story after story. Most of all, they talked, just the two of them, endless conversations covering every imaginable subject. And then they hugged. Oh, how they hugged!

When it came time for Kerry to attend parochial school, my mother insisted, although now bedridden, on taking the measurements for her school uniform. Kerry literally stood on the mattress while her grandmother sized her up and down. Beaming with pride, Mother wanted it to "fit just right." When her dearest friend acknowledged her courageous fight against a disease that slowly and painfully consumed her from within, my mother reasoned, "I can't go anywhere yet; Kerry still needs me."

Three days before Christmas, the telephone rang. It was my mother, asking if I'd taken her wrapping paper. "The tea set I ordered for Kerry has just arrived," she said, her spirited voice as strong as ever, "and I want to wrap it before she sees it."

I promised to deliver the remaining few rolls of paper posthaste. But before I could leave my house the phone rang again. This time it was my father.

"The nurse just came downstairs," he said, his voice choking with emotion. "Your mom has only a few days to live."

This was hardly possible to believe when, moments later, I was watching Grandma Wanda, propped up on pillows, expertly wrapping the tea set before Kerry climbed the stairs and leapt into her arms. It had become obvious that my mother literally lived for such moments.

Christmas Eve arrived, and her condition grew worse by the hour. Still, as evening cast its shadows across her bedroom, she insisted I dress Kerry and continue our tradition of Christmas caroling. I could barely even look at my mother, whose breathing was very labored. Kerry was another story, gently hugging her grandmother and kissing her good night.

"Good night, angel," Grandma Wanda whispered back.

A silently grieving Santa Claus waited patiently for Kerry to drift off to sleep before placing her well-deserved presents beneath the Christmas tree. Outside, church bells called the congregations to midnight services, and as I filled Kerry's stocking with North Pole treats, I asked God that the beautiful chimes bring peace and comfort to my mother.

Earlier that Christmas Eve, Mother had expressed the wish to watch midnight Mass on television, celebrated by Pope John Paul II from the Vatican. As the clock struck twelve on this, the holiest night of the year, and my brother was helping my mother complete the Sign of the Cross, her battle ended. Outside, the church bells rang in celebration.

"It's Christmas, Dad, wake up!" Kerry shouted, grabbing my hand and leading the way to the Christmas tree. The very first present she opened was the tea set. She looked up at me and smiled, and I began to cry. And Kerry knew. She rushed to hug me, just like Grandma Wanda used to do. I knew then that the love my mother had showered on my little girl would always be there, and I was the lucky recipient.

John McCaslin

Rocks and Restoration

Pleasure is the flower that fades; remembrance is the lasting perfume.

Stanislas Jean de Marquis Boufflers

I slowly got out of the car at the end of a long, discouraging day. The February sky was gray to match my mood as I walked down our driveway to retrieve the mail. I looked at the neglected flowerbeds in our front yard. Busy with other pursuits, I hadn't planted any spring bulbs, mulched around the Japanese maple or cut back the English ivy, which threatened to choke out everything in its path.

As I approached the house, I reached down to move a large rock from a raised flowerbed. It hadn't hurt anything in the weedy spot, but there was something familiar about the rock itself. I smoothed the dirt off of its dimpled surface; then I recognized it. It had belonged to my grandmother, Essie May Brown, and I had claimed it from one of the rock borders she'd fashioned around the flowerbeds in her backyard. Holding that rock took me right back to the 1950s, to Grandma's garden on West Shadowlawn Avenue in north Atlanta.

"Why do you have so many flowers, Grandma?" I wiped the perspiration from my forehead, getting dirt on my face and in my curly red hair. At age four, I wasn't worried about a little dirt. Grandma smiled contentedly as she looked around her. "Flowers are my life," she said. "When I sit on the sewin' room floor hemmin' up a dress for Mrs. Alston or one of those purty young debs I sew for, I think about bein' out here in my garden, with all of God's beautiful flowers . . . and with you, my sweet man."

"I'm not a man, Grandma. I'm a girl," I grumbled, but I grinned up at her. She always called me that. Nobody in the family ever knew why she chose to call me her sweet man or "Luke," her other pet name for me (she hardly ever called me "Kathleen" unless she was reprimanding me), but I didn't really mind.

I spent a lot of time at Grandma's house while Mom accompanied Dad on frequent business trips, and Grandma and I were the closest of buddies. Grandma made everything seem like an adventure, from picking up pins in the sewing room to planting bulbs, as we were doing that day.

"Don't drop this'n on his head," she warned. "Dig him a little hole here—oh, that's a good'n. Now put him right there, and point his little head up so he can poke it out to the sun. Now don't cover him up too much. . . . That's right, maybe a little dab more. Let's give 'im some water now, he's thirsty. Give him a right smart more so he can start to grow. That's enough. He says, 'Thank you, ma'am!'"

"Why do we have to be so careful with each one, Grandma?" I asked.

"Now, Luke," Grandma said patiently, "God made rules for flowers just like he did for everything else. If you don't follow his rules, you won't grow any flowers. And if you put the bulbs in too far with their heads point'n' down at the devil, they won't ever see God's purty sunshine."

Most all of Grandma's bulbs grew lavishly into the sunlight. In the spring, her backyard was a gardener's dream. First the little white, yellow and purple crocuses unfurled their heads from green spiky leaves. Then came the nodding snowdrops, dainty snowflakes, sherbet-colored daffodils and narcissi, bold Dutch tulips whose bulbs had been special-ordered from Breck's, and yellow clouds of forsythia. Easter time would bring a snowstorm of pink and white dogwood blossoms, with elegant, lacy, white, pink and lavender hyacinths underneath. Irises would bloom later, like the pink Mobile azaleas whose tight buds were already swelling the bushes. In summer, big hydrangea bushes reared their blue and lavender mop heads, with fragrant climbing roses in the background. Lush, green, grassy paths were prone to invading violets, the one weed Grandma tolerated. She loved the violets' miniature purple and white faces, and admired their hardiness.

"Don't worry about him," she'd say. "You can step on 'im and he'll spring right back up!"

A charming white picket fence surrounded it all, like a frame around a lovely picture. And in the very center of the garden, a giant old pecan tree full of chattering squirrels and birds rose majestically, sprouting green leaf-buds, with a beautiful raised flowerbed at its base. A rock-border necklace encircled it with old-fashioned pansies, their cheerful faces upturned, peeking from its crevices. It was truly a paradise for a little girl who learned many of life's important lessons digging bulbs with her grandma.

I held a rock from that border now, forty-three years later. I'd taken it from Grandma's garden when the house was sold after her death in 1992. The new owners mowed everything down, tore down the old picket fence and installed a chain-link enclosure for their Doberman. Only the old pecan tree and the memories remain.

Well, I thought, *that's not really all that's left.* Grandma's favorite gifts to her family were, of course, flowers. Grandma gave me a Woburn Abbey rose bush that still out-blooms everything on our street.

I gently placed the old rock at the edge of my flowerbed and pulled up a weed. As I stood up I noticed something green under an overgrown holly. Pushing aside some pine straw, I instantly recognized the grass-like spikes: five mounds of Grandma's Star of Bethlehem!

The tears came as I grabbed a trowel and gardening gloves, and gently weeded and mulched around these symbols of my heritage. Just then the sunshine broke through the clouds and shone down on Grandma's flowers, still thriving after all this time. My grouchiness dissipated as I worked to restore the flowerbed, and my five-year-old son ran to hug me. "Whatcha doin', Mom?" he asked.

"See those little plants, sweet man?" I said, brushing dirt off my son's sweaty face. "Sit down here with me, and I'll tell you all about a special gift. . . ."

Kathleen Craft Boehmig

8

LEGACIES AND HEIRLOOMS

He that can only boast of a distinguished lineage, boasts of that which does not belong to himself; but he that lives worthily of it is always held in the highest honor.

Junius

Grandma's Words

Such as thy words are, such will thy affections be esteemed.

Socrates

My grandma's words were full of wisdom. "You know, dear," she was fond of saying, "you never stop learning." *You don't?* I wondered about this line a lot as a child. *Never? Even when you are as old as she is?*

Grandma was a great listener and wanted to hear all about my job as a kindergarten teacher. "You are a real teacher," she would tell me.

Regularly she asked, "Tell me, sweetheart, is there anyone special in your life?"

I would tell her about the man I was dating and somehow her words would make me question. "Trust your heart," she'd say. "Your heart knows." And sure enough, when I took Grandma's advice, no, he was not the one.

In her early nineties she moved into an assisted-living home. Her stories became the same story over and over, but just hearing her voice was soothing. It didn't matter that I'd heard it all before.

She told stories of leaving Russia as a child, alone, sent by her father to join his parents in America. "I got out," she said. "We had no idea what was about to happen. The rest of my family didn't make it, but for some reason, I did."

Her stories of those years were about eating her first orange on the boat, about her stern but kind grandparents in New York City, walks in the rain to the library. "I couldn't get enough of the books," she said.

The night Grandma had a stroke, at age ninety-seven, we thought that would be the end of her long life, but she lived another two years. The stroke left her unable to walk and talk. For the first time in her life my grandma was forced into silence. Visiting her was sad. I had never spent time with her in so much silence before.

"Hi, Grandma," I'd say.

"Uhnnnnn," was all she was capable of saying.

"My garden's doing well but something got the peonies. Maybe deer."

"Uhmmm, mmmmn, uhhh mmm," she would mumble.

I would nod and say, "Yes . . . yes . . . that's right," here and there. I knew she was giving me advice about the garden. She murmured and muttered. I nodded and talked. My heart broke from missing her words, her voice.

The next summer I met Andy. He became a great friend, and I was nothing less than thrilled when we began to date in earnest. I told him about Grandma and suggested we visit her. On the way to her nursing home I filled him in as much as possible about her condition and her wisdom.

"Andy, she was always filled with the most amazing words. She could stop me in my tracks and really make me think. You have to realize that the woman you meet is not really her. All she can do now is sit and murmur. But know that if she could talk, she would be saying something really wise."

"I understand," he said, but still I felt he was about to miss out.

We found Grandma sitting in her room.

"Grandma," I said, "I'd like you to meet Andy."

She looked up at us, first at me, then Andy. She studied him for quite some time. Sometimes she looked at me like that, only to close her eyes and drift into a long nap. But this time she lifted her gnarled hand, a great effort for her, and gave it to him. As he held her hand she continued to look deep into his eyes for quite a while. I felt embarrassed. Would she never let go of his hand? Would she ever look away? Would it be okay for Andy to drop her hand? I was trying to think of words to break this awkward silence, but the most unlikely person found them first. In a loud and clear voice my grandma said to Andy, "Welcome to the family."

Andy and I were married within the year.

Laura Mueller

Grandmother's Language of Love

A *thousand words will not leave so deep an impression as one deed.*

Henrik Ibsen

I didn't speak Polish and she didn't speak English, but we both spoke love. That's how I remember my grandmother, especially during one holiday a long time ago. On a very cold Christmas Eve in a Polish neighborhood in Detroit, I opened the door to my grandmother's house and ran right into her arms.

"Busha," I called, smiling with my whole body, delighted to see her.

She hugged me, then placed her soft hands on both sides of my face. Cupping my cheeks gently, she spoke lovingly to me with her eyes. Grandmother's face was inches from mine, and I loved looking into her beautiful eighty-year-old eyes—those eyes that said so much.

Bending over, she kissed my forehead. I stretched my six-year-old arms around her aproned front and inhaled her Christmas-cookie-dough smell. She motioned for me to hurry to the dining room. I fumbled around, trying to unbutton my scratchy wool coat with the silky lining. Grandmother came and helped me, then watched me stuff my earmuffs into a pocket and my hand muff inside the sleeve in the "don't want to lose it" spot. I remember feeling so happy to have earmuffs and not to have to wear a babushka, that old-fashioned scarf. My grandmother pointed me to the bedroom, where I put my coat on the bed, already piled high with the coats of my cousins, aunts and uncles. She caressed my new dress, took my hand and smiled. She twirled me around to get a good look, then we snugly walked to the dining room to join my cousins. I hoped they too would notice my new dress and shoes. They, being mostly boys, didn't notice. They were all sitting on the floor, impatiently waiting for my grandmother's clocks to chime. I gave up my ladylike pose, shrugged, sat down and wiggled in next to the only cousin who had red hair just like mine. Grandmother left me and went to the kitchen to be with my aunts.

I tucked my black, shiny, patent-leather shoes with the pokey buckle underneath me and joined the wait. Grandmother collected all kinds of clocks. I never knew all the types, but there were a lot of them and I believed they were magical. The chiming would start with the deep sound of the tall grandfather clock with the gold pendulum, then the small sound of the table clock on the buffet, then the bong-bong-bong sound of the skinny grandfather clock. Sound from the other clocks moved all around the room. The chimes didn't sound the same, but they all spoke "clock." Each of them was very special and had come from Poland, just like my grandmother.

The last clocks finished chiming, signaling us to follow my parents, aunts, uncles and cousins to the kitchen, where they sat chattering and laughing in Polish. I looked around at some of the special things my grandmother did to create Christmas magic. She knew the language of love.

There was the embroidered tablecloth draped across the table, the green smells-like-the-forest branches carefully placed all around the rooms, and the sound of the china clinking and the silverware clanging. My mom said, "All Grandmother's china and silverware came from Poland, too."

When the adults were ready, we began the *oplatek* ceremony. Grandmother motioned for me to stand up from the little bench I was sitting on and she gave me an *oplatek,* a wafer like the ones used in Communion in the Catholic Church. They had pictures of Baby Jesus, Blessed Mary and angels on them. My dad said that *oplateks* are known as the bread of love.

Grandmother started. Being the oldest, she held her *oplatek* out to me and I, the youngest, held mine out to her. She wished wonderful things for me. I know because my mother translated what she said. As Grandmother wished, she broke off my wafer—a small amount broken off for each wish. Then I wished my grandmother wonderful things. Again my mother translated, but this time in Polish. We put the broken wafers in our mouths and kissed. The ceremony continued throughout the family until my wafer was reduced to a crumb.

I loved all the kind things people wished. Sometimes it was all in Polish, sometimes in English and other times it was some kind of mixture of Polish and English. My aunt would wish, "Get good grades in school, stay healthy, and maybe you'll get that bike."

My mother would say, "Be good and we can talk about that puppy."

So many wonderful wishes—except for my brother's goofy wish, like, "I wish Trudy would get lots of toys for Christmas so she'll leave mine alone."

After the ceremony, my grandmother stacked my plate with dumplings filled with sauerkraut, cheese and potatoes called *pierògies*, cheese-filled crepes called *nalesnikies*, *chruscikies*—pastries sprinkled with powdered sugar—and apple strudel.

There were many other foods. Borscht, horseradish and sauerkraut were tasty, but I didn't eat everything—the pickled herring and mushrooms were yucky.

My grandmother sat at the head of the table on the other side of the room. She smiled at me with her eyes, and I smiled back with mine. She knew how to hug across a room. I felt loved all over, in Polish and in English.

Later, I fell asleep on a little bench off in the corner of the warm kitchen. Grandmother reached down and gently touched my face. As I woke and stood up she looked at me lovingly, reached over and hugged me. As we were getting ready to leave for church, she helped me with my coat and earmuffs. I left my hand muff on the bed. I didn't need it. She would keep me warm. I held her hand. She held my heart.

Trudy Reeder

Gutsy Grandma

Faith is the centerpiece of a connected life. It allows us to live by the grace of invisible strands. It is a belief in a wisdom superior to our own.

Terry Tempest Williams

It started with her name.

Luella Konstance Peterson Lovstuen.

At least, we thought that was her name . . . until she died and we saw her birth certificate. Then we found out she had been born Luella Caspara Peterson. She hated her middle name and changed it to Constance . . . with a K. She loved her initials, LKL, and changed her monogram on her handkerchiefs so that the K had the most prominent spot. That's the way she wanted it, so that's the way it was.

She just handled it.

She bore and raised six children, three boys and three girls, during the Depression era. She carried a heavy, pregnant belly during the furnacelike summer months, when temperatures stayed over one hundred degrees for weeks on end, working to sew clothes for her children, putting up preserves for the winter and helping on the farm. She cooked for threshers on a wood-burning stove in a small kitchen without air conditioning. I might have gone mad with the heat and the work.

She just handled it.

She struggled to keep her children warm in the harsh winters that still hold records. She bore her first child in February when the temperature had been at least fifteen degrees below zero for weeks, sometimes dipping to thirty degrees below at night. She worked to keep the stove going, often sleeping next to it. Wind chills on the flat Iowa fields were worse. She toiled to keep her family warm and fed despite the lack of necessary items during the Depression.

She just handled it.

When her husband reached his thirties he became very ill with paranoid schizophrenia. He wasn't like Russell Crowe's movie portrayal of a misunderstood genius. He was mean, nasty, delusional and a danger to himself and others. When the safety of her children was threatened because of the disease-induced hallucinations, she made sure that he was sent somewhere to get help. She also made sure that he couldn't threaten her children and her anymore.

She just handled it.

Times grew worse and the farm failed. She moved the six children into town, and she got a job at the local five-and-dime. She supported her family at a time when the term "single parenting" had yet to be coined. She still sewed all of their clothing and made sure that they were clean, churchgoing and well-loved. She didn't really have time to whine about the single-parenting dynamic; she was too busy ensuring that food was on the table and her children were growing up to be decent people.

She just handled it.

As her children grew up, they got jobs and tried to help out at home, but as time went on the boys joined the service and the girls left to get married or start lives of their own. With two brothers in town and the Depression over, things began to look better. Then her brother was struck with an excruciatingly painful disease. Medication didn't touch the pain, but it messed with his normal thought processes. In anguish he took his own life. She was devastated. None of us really knew how deeply it affected her until years later.

She just handled it.

When I reached middle age I sat talking with my grandma, who was in her late eighties, about her life. I commented on the trials and hardships she had endured. When she talked about her life, though, she talked about the joy, the blessings and the love. Problems were never the centerpiece of her conversations. This sweet, gentle woman still had such a tender heart. Mine, I fear, may have become bitter under those circumstances.

She just handled it.

"Grandma, how did you handle it all?" I asked as we talked, looking for the wisdom that would bring me through my own trials. She looked at me and the wrinkles grew deeper in her velvety skin as she smiled her sweet smile.

"I didn't," she said. "God did."

Karen J. Olson

Treasured Gift

Tell me a fact, and I will learn. Tell me a truth, and I will believe. Tell me a story, and it will live in my heart forever.

Indian Proverb

When I was a little girl, Christmas Eve was a time of family storytelling.

One of my favorite childhood stories was one that Grandma told every year. "Sometimes the best gifts come without ribbons or bows," she would say to her family before beginning this favorite story:

It was 1918, and Grandpa worked paving the roadways and laying railroad tracks in the city while Grandma worked part-time in the canneries. When Grandpa came home from work, he'd eat a hurried supper and then rush off to night school to get his education. After Grandpa graduated and attained his American citizenship, he went to work full-time on the cannery lines and part-time in a shoe-repair shop. He labored on the night shift so that his days would be free to take care of the children, thereby allowing Grandma to attend school and receive an education.

Grandma anticipated her first day of school in America as a very important moment in her young life. She knew that she needed an education to become a good citizen of her new country.

On the morning of her first class, Grandma excitedly rushed to dress. Though she didn't have much of a wardrobe, what she did own was clean and well pressed. As she slipped her feet into her best pair of long black stockings, Grandma's happy mood dissolved into sadness. Her stockings were riddled with gaping holes.

"Forget about your socks, Mama; you haven't time to mend them now," urged Grandpa. "You'll be late for class. And, anyway, I have a surprise for you!"

A moment later, Grandpa handed Grandma her old high-button shoes. Only now she hardly recognized her timeworn shoes—they had been transformed. They gleamed with brand-new leather soles and shiny black laces. She could see her reflection in their brilliant shine. While she had slept that night, Grandpa had secretly worked until the wee hours to repair Grandma's high-button shoes.

Grandma's eyes welled with tears of gratitude as she placed a kiss on her husband's cheek. "I will look like a fine lady in these wonderful shoes, Papa," she said.

"Hurry now, Mama, hurry. Slip your feet inside these beautiful shoes, and no one will ever suspect you have holey stockings. It will be our little secret," Grandpa promised.

Grandma had no time now to mend her tattered stockings. So she did as her husband had suggested and slipped her stocking feet into her high-button shoes. She quickly laced them up and rushed out the doorway, pausing only a moment for Grandpa to kiss her good-bye and to hand her two one dollar bills for her classroom tuition.

Arriving at school that morning, Grandma felt uneasy in

a classroom filled with strangers. Standing at the head of the class was a stern-looking teacher by the name of Mrs. Peabody. In her hand she held a long, ominous-looking pointer stick, which she used both for pointing and intimidation. She passed a large, empty bowl around the classroom and instructed each student to drop the tuition fees into the container. Every student complied. One of the more affluent students paid his fee with a bright two-dollar gold piece.

After collecting all the money, the teacher placed the bowl on her desk.

Later that afternoon, when Mrs. Peabody tallied up the tuition money, she discovered the gold coin was missing. Convinced that one of her students had taken the gold piece, she demanded that everyone in the classroom empty their pockets onto her desk. The students promptly obeyed, but no gold coin appeared. Angry and frustrated, the teacher took her search one step further and demanded that everyone in the classroom remove his or her shoes. A small gold coin could easily be hidden in a high-button shoe.

One by one, the students removed their shoes. Everyone, that is, except Grandma. She sat there frozen with embarrassment, hoping and praying the missing coin would be found before she had to slip off her shoes. But a few minutes later, when the coin failed to turn up, Mrs. Peabody pointed her stick directly at Grandma's shoes and demanded she remove them.

For what seemed like an eternity, the entire classroom stared down at Grandma's feet. Grandma, who had been so proud of her elegant shoes, just couldn't remove them now in front of her peers and expose her holey stockings. To do so would be a great disgrace.

Grandma's reluctance to remove her shoes convinced the teacher of her guilt. Mrs. Peabody marched Grandma off to the principal's office. Grandma, in tears, immediately telephoned Grandpa, who rushed down to the school. Grandpa explained to the principal why his wife was reluctant to remove her shoes. The understanding principal then allowed Grandma to remove her shoes in the privacy of his office. He soon discovered the only thing Grandma was hiding was a pair of unsightly, tattered stockings.

Grandma returned to her classroom, but all that day a shadow of suspicion hung over her.

Late that afternoon, just before the dismissal bell, Grandma was completely exonerated of any wrongdoing. When Mrs. Peabody raised her right arm to write the class assignment on the blackboard, the missing coin fell from the cuff of her sleeve and rolled across the room in plain view of the entire classroom. Earlier that day, as she counted up the money, the stiffly starched cuff of her dress had accidentally scooped up the small coin.

That afternoon, when Grandma returned home from school, Papa was waiting for her on the front porch swing. Exhausted from his night job, he was quietly napping. Cradled in his hardworking hands was Grandma's darning basket. Inside the basket were all of Grandma's old stockings that Grandpa had carefully and lovingly mended.

In later years, Grandpa would become a successful businessman. He took special pride in giving his wife stockings made from the finest silks and woolens.

Though Grandma appreciated these fine gifts, she often said they were never so dear to her, or so well-loved, as those old, tattered stockings, so lovingly mended by her husband's callused, hardworking hands.

Cookie Curci

More Than an Heirloom

The world does not require so much to be informed as reminded.

Hannah More

Fifteen of us crammed into my Grandma Chesser's tiny one-bedroom apartment a few days after her funeral. Even after her death at the age of eighty-one, her apartment was as it had always been—as neat as a pin. Grandma was quiet, austere; she dressed simply, almost plain, never drawing attention to herself. She hadn't cut her hair for years and wore it in a single braid wrapped around her head. Only at night would we see the long silver mane.

She was meticulous about her meager possessions, tidy to a fault, and practical about what she needed and didn't need. Because she had such a limited amount of storage, we thought that most of her keepsakes were thrown out or given away. But as drawers were opened and boxes searched, a whole mansion of memories unfolded before our eyes.

Grandma had utilized every available space in her tiny

apartment; we found boxes under her bed, hidden behind blankets and stacked in closets. Dozens of pictures and letters spilled out of small shoeboxes. I even unearthed some cards and letters with my childish handwriting, my first attempts at letter writing. Stacks of letters, cards and all kinds of papers included report cards from the 1930s, World War II ration books, postcards from forgotten vacations.

Cries of delight rang out when my sister and cousins found long-forgotten handmade gifts made fifteen to twenty years ago. Then I found practically all of the presents I had made for her, too. Simple boxes and trinkets most people would have thrown out one week later, she had safely tucked away for her pleasure.

All those gifts—needlework, shellacked plaques with trite sayings, macramé potholders and scores of other items made by her seventeen grandchildren—filled the spaces of her home. When I had given her gifts and crayon pictures, she had smiled pleasantly, never one to make a big fuss.

Box after box, we searched in wonder. There were crocheted baby hats, leaving us to wonder whose tiny heads they fit at one time. Seven sons had been born to my grandparents. She never said much about the two who died at young ages.

Nestled with the pair of wire-rimmed eyeglasses she must have worn as a teenager were Grandfather's rusted fishhooks. She had even saved his old shaving cup, razor and razor strap. His death came at the beginning of their "good years," after all the sons had left and life was slowing down. She stoically lived another twenty years without him, yet we always knew she missed him.

In her jewelry box, scattered among the costume jewelry, was a small, rough, gray rock. But it had my father's name on it, written in his own childish handwriting in black ink. As he rubbed and examined it, his eyes searched the stone for details of its past. He couldn't remember its importance, but she must have. He was her youngest son, the one she tended to spoil.

We laughed when we discovered a paint-by-number picture hidden behind a door. I claimed it as mine, but my brother said it was his. Why either of us would want to claim it, I don't know. It is the ugliest painting in the world, yet she saved it. From a distance, it looked like a dog; closer up, it was a swamp of mottled green and brown paint.

I saw the valentines first. It was like finding treasure. All different sizes of bright red cards, 1930s vintage. Chubby-cheeked children, angelic faces, with cute cartoon sayings: "How's chances?" and "You've got me all busted up over you!" Most were addressed to my father, each from a different girl. There were a few re-addressed to another brother, apparently some early attempts at recycling.

But most of all we found letters. Page after page that recounted everyday life, heartaches and unexpected joys.

"I think the kids have the flu."

"Guess we'll be coming home for Christmas."

"We're having pretty good weather today."

"I'm tired of camp and want to come home."

Grandma faithfully answered every letter.

I have heard many stories of families fighting tooth and nail over an antique bedroom suite, a piano or a diamond ring. Grandma wasn't able to hand down valuable heirlooms like that, but what we found were more precious than Victorian pianos. Her memories were her keepsakes, important enough to save for decades, even as long as fifty years.

I'm sure that on her loneliest nights, these treasures gave her—and now us—the greatest pleasures.

Susan Chesser Branch

A Leap of Faith

Life shrinks or expands in proportion to one's courage.

Anais Nin

In the early 1900s, when thirteen was, sadly, far from a tender age, my grandmother escaped the pogroms of the tsarist regime in the Ukraine with her father, baby brother and sisters for the "gold-paved" streets of New York City. It would be ten years before she would see her mother and her other brothers again.

To help her father begin to squirrel away enough funds to send for the remainder of the family, she endured the stifling summer swelter and finger-numbing winter cold, the severe eyestrain, and the loss of many precious days of her youth in the pursuit of piece work in the garment industry. What differentiated her from many immigrant girls and women in similar circumstances was the specific "sweat shop" in which she worked: the ill-fated Triangle Shirt Factory. For on March 25, 1911, shortly before her fifteenth birthday, my grandmother would become the instrument of her own survival, when the building would burst into flames, ultimately killing 146 of her coworkers. Almost seventy-five years later, I had the opportunity to learn more about this infamous day, right around the time I was facing major challenges in my own life that would test my mettle, resilience and courage—just as the great fire had tested my grandmother's.

In the mid-1980s, when my grandmother was nearing ninety, declining somewhat physically but still as sharp mentally as the needles with which she so lovingly continued to sew and repair our family's clothes, I read a human-interest article about the "last known" survivor of the Triangle fire. I knew the premise to be false, but rather than contact the reporter and diminish the fifteen minutes of fame of the brave subject of that story, I set out on a personal quest: to find out the details of the peril in which my grandmother found herself that day and the circumstances that enabled her to survive to enrich my mother's life and mine in so many ways for so many years afterward. I studied the history of the event and interviewed my remaining great aunts and uncles, but my best source of information was my grandmother herself. Although her short-term memory had declined over the years, her long-term memories were still intact and richly detailed.

They led me to a picture I hold deep in my mind's eye and in my heart: a young woman with long, auburn hair, strong legs and a determination to survive that led her veritably to leap across tall buildings in a single bound. I envision her with a heavy, patched apron, high black shoes and a set jaw as she refused to take the death leap like so many of the young girls with whom she worked. Following her instincts instead, she trusted the one supervisor in whose honesty and compassion she believed, forming a human chain with others from her work crew. I can see that chain weaving through the smoky haze as he led them around doors locked to "cut down on employee theft" to the one door they could force open and, ultimately, to the roof. There, she and her cohorts made the leap to the roof of the next building intact, defying their potential fate.

It was that image that sustained me when, at the age of thirty-five, I underwent heart surgery, and once again a month into my recuperation when I entered premature menopause and learned in my first year of marriage that I would never be able to conceive. And I would summon up her figure in midleap a year and a half later when I learned I had breast cancer, and throughout my year of ensuing chemotherapy treatments as well.

Now, at age fifty-four, a successful professional counselor, writer and adoptive mother of two young children, I know that my second mother and best friend, my inspiration and my rock, provided me with one of the most precious legacies a granddaughter could ever receive: the courage to take her life into her own hands with self-reliance and positive resolve.

Hannah Amgott

The Locket

*F*riendship is the shadow of the evening, which
strengthens with the setting sun of life.

Jean de La Fontaine

Lydia went up into the attic to get the old dehumidifier
for Grandma Ruth's bedroom. Once she'd opened the
trapdoor and climbed the rickety old ladder into the crawl
space, she couldn't resist rummaging through some of the
family heirlooms stored up there. Her attention was
drawn to an old locket resting on top of a photo collection,
stacked neatly in an attractive but faded hatbox. Lydia's
curiosity got the better of her, so she carefully picked up
and examined the tiny piece of jewelry. It didn't look
expensive, but it was well made and charming. She knew
it must have been a special present to a child.

She gingerly snapped the clasp open, taking care not to
break the delicate hinges. Hidden inside were two miniature photographs of smiling little girls, perhaps eight or
nine years old. One of the happy young faces looked
just like her Grandma Ruth. But who was the other
young lady? Could it be that Lydia had a secret, long-lost

great-aunt? Who was this stranger in the locket and what had become of her?

Forgetting the dehumidifier and clutching the locket, Lydia scurried down the ladder and burst into Grandma's sewing room. Grandma was busy at work on her entry in the town's annual quilting bee.

"Grandma," Lydia exclaimed, "look what I found. Is this you?"

Grandma slowly took the trinket from Lydia's hand and cupped it gently in her palm. She examined it quietly for a moment. A sad, wistful smile passed over her face. "It's me," she nodded.

"But who's the other little girl? You look so much alike. Was she . . . was she your sister?"

"Oh, no," Grandma laughed, "No . . . but we were as close as any sisters could be, Emma and I."

"But who was she?" Lydia asked eagerly.

"We grew up together right here in town. Went everywhere together—we wore the same clothes, rode the same bikes. We even got the same haircut. I remember the day these photos were taken, down at the old Imperial Theater—of course, that's a laundromat now."

"Sounds like you two had a very special friendship."

"We were like peas in a pod," Grandma agreed, "until Emma's family moved away to Akron. Her father was a doctor, and he took a job at a clinic in the city. We wrote every day, then every week, then a few times a year—all through high school, and even after I met your Grandpa Bill. But somehow we lost touch after that. It's been more than fifty years since I've heard from her."

Grandma's story made Lydia think of her own special friendships, how much they meant to her and how she would hate to lose touch with the "Emmas" in her own life.

"I wonder whatever happened to her," sighed Grandma, "I guess I'll never know."

But Lydia was never one to give up hope, and seeing Grandma's reaction to the locket, she was determined to find out. She spent the remainder of her stay poring over Emma's old letters—she didn't want to miss a single one. Fortunately, Grandma had saved many of them, pressed between the pages of a heavy copy of the young friends' favorite book, *Little Women* by Louisa May Alcott. Like the book, Emma's letters also told a moving story—the story of two great friends coming of age together. But the story of Ruth and Emma wasn't a tale of fiction; it was all true.

Lydia was struck by one letter in particular. It was among the latest in Grandma's collection, and it contained a clue she thought might help them learn of Emma's whereabouts. One of Emma's last letters announced that she had taken a teaching position at a school in the city. Perhaps that school still existed and might have some record of Grandma's old friend.

Some amateur detective work on the Internet quickly revealed that the school was still in operation, but had relocated to a new building in 1963. Lydia was worried. Had Emma's records survived the move? It was time to make some phone calls.

The principal was reluctant to share any details over the phone, but when Lydia explained the unique circumstances, she agreed to meet in person. Lydia bought a round-trip bus ticket and was on her way to Akron later that same week.

Lydia's meeting with the principal was more successful than she had dared to hope. Emma had retired before the principal had come to the school, but a few of the older teachers had fond memories of her. The French teacher still visited with her regularly. She could arrange a meeting.

Two weeks later, on the day of the annual quilting bee, Emma made the journey all the way from Akron, driven by her son Steve. Lydia had spent the morning calming Grandma, who paced nervously about the house, straightening and restraightening the doilies.

Emma entered quietly. "Ruth," she said with a shy smile.

Without a word, Grandma handed Emma the locket. No words were needed.

Emma's son Steve was an accomplished photographer, and his cameras captured beautifully the meeting of the two friends. When they left, he asked to borrow the locket. Nobody was quite sure why, until a package arrived at Grandma's house a few weeks later. Steve had enlarged, restored and framed the original photos of the young friends in the locket, and added two more—the old friends, reunited at last.

As for Lydia, she made a special lifelong friend of her own. She and Steve are expecting their first child this spring.

Tal Aviezer and Jason Cocovinis

Grandma's Necklace

*Memory is the diary that we all carry about
with us.*

Oscar Wilde

I ran up the stairs to Grandma Flemming's porch as fast
as my three-year-old legs would carry me. Slipping on the
wet porch, I fell and cut my eyebrow on a glass milk bottle waiting to be picked up by the milkman. Loving arms
enfolded me, "There, there, it will be alright. We'll make it
all better." Those are the first memories I have of my
mother's mother.

Not many years after that event my grandparents
moved away from Ohio to Indiana, where my grandfather
would pastor a succession of small churches until he
retired. Grandma remained a very special person in my
life in spite of the fact that I didn't see her as often as I
would have liked. I have many happy, poignant memories
of her funny, cackling laugh; her high nasal voice; spending several weeks with her one summer; the glass cabinet
where she kept her collection of knick-knacks and novelty
salt and pepper shakers; and her house near the railroad

tracks. One Christmas the rumbling of the train in the early-morning hours brought the nine-foot Christmas tree crashing to the floor!

Grandma died near the end my senior year of high school after a long battle with cancer. As the oldest grandchild and granddaughter, I inherited two things from Grandma: her wedding ring and a silver necklace given to her the year she was born.

When I got married only a few months after her death, my husband placed Grandma's wedding ring on my finger as Grandpa officiated. I wore the necklace rather reluctantly, only because it meant so much to my mother. The filigree daisy pattern had a diamond in the center. The chain was tarnished and tangled.

After our wedding I placed the necklace in a jewelry box and, quite honestly, I didn't think much about it for years. Then two things happened in rapid succession that made me reconsider the necklace: My older daughter, Susan, gave birth to her first child, Christine, and my marriage of twenty-four years ended.

Going through my things in the process of the divorce, I came across the necklace. For a minute I couldn't even remember where I had gotten it. Then I remembered Grandma. I bought a new chain to replace the tangled and tarnished one, and, had the pendant cleaned at the jewelers. I was amazed at the beauty of the little necklace. As I took off the wedding ring, I began wearing the necklace, and, I lovingly recalled my grandmother.

I saw my granddaughter often and baby-sat from the time I finished teaching until her mother came home from work at midnight, five days a week. She grew from an infant to a toddler to a little girl, and she loved the "flower necklace," as she called it. Since she is my oldest granddaughter, I let her know that, just as I had gotten the necklace from my grandmother, someday the "pretty flower" would be hers.

Christine is nearly twelve years old now, and growing into a young lady. I'm not going to wait until I die to pass this legacy on to her. The necklace will be one hundred years old the year Christine turns nineteen. I will pass her great-great-grandmother's necklace on to her, knowing she, too, will look back on happy, poignant memories.

Carol Spahr

A Sister's Visit

Gram and her sister, Acq, were close in age, and the bond between them was so strong they visited each other almost daily. But when she was ninety-three, Gram's health deteriorated, and she finally became homebound. Although they lived only sixteen miles apart, visits were no longer possible for them; they were both too ill to make the trip. I was privileged to be my grandmother's major caregiver, and I knew how desperately they missed each other and longed to be together again. It was always on my mind.

One cold winter day, Gram sat up in bed and said, "I want to see my sister." She was still weak from her last hospitalization; her face was pale and drawn from the weight she had lost.

"You can see her in the spring," I soothed.

Her eyes widened. "No, that's too long."

I knew Gram's time on earth was limited. She and Acq needed to see each other . . . but how? Then I had an idea. The next morning, I brought out the video camera.

"Gram, you can talk to your sister through this." I showed her how it worked. She threw her head back, laughed a little and said, "Okay." She went into the bathroom, washed her face and combed her hair. Then she held the camera and looked deeply into the lens. Gram spoke softly, "Acq, I'm too sick to come over and see you. . . . I miss you and we will be together again soon." Gram smiled. "When the garden is ready, I'll send you some of my tomatoes."

Her eyes sparkled and her voice became stronger. "Bye-bye, Acq."

I drove over to visit my aunt and told her I had a message for her. I helped her into the bedroom, where a picture of her and Gram sat next to the bed. I handed her the camera and turned it on. As soon as Gram started talking, my aunt sat up straight, excited, and answered her back. "Lizzie, you look good. I have missed you too, it's been so long." She sat back and listened to the rest of Gram's message to her. She looked at me as she wiped a tear from her eye. "If I talk, will Lizzie hear me?"

I told her yes, and she combed her hair just like Gram had, while displaying a renewed sense of spirit. When I pressed the record key, Aunt Acq's voice grew stronger. "Hi, Lizzie, it was nice to see you today." She turned to me. "Maybe she can't hear me." She held the camera with both hands and shouted, "I'd like some of your Italian beans from the garden, too."

We walked to her closet and opened the door while I continued to film. "You know my grandson Gerry's getting married in a few weeks. This is my new dress and shoes. I hope I'll be well enough to go."

As I left, I told my aunt I would return in a few days. I was not sure if either of them truly understood this method of communicating, but Aunt Acq hugged me and said, "Thanks for bringing Lizzie here to me."

Gram and I settled in on the couch, next to a picture of the sisters from last summer's family picnic. I draped my arm over her shoulder and showed her the whole video. When she saw herself talking, she giggled with excitement, "That's me!" We both laughed at the same time. When Aunt Acq started talking, Gram's eyes brightened and her whole face lit up. She reacted the same way my aunt had, holding the camera up close. "Hi Acq, it's good to see you again."

When Gram said that and looked up at me, tears streamed down my cheeks. At dinner that night, Gram said, "It was nice to see Acq today, she looks pretty good."

For the next few months they "visited" each other regularly. While they were never physically together again, they were "close" to the end.

Paula Mauqiri Tindall

The Wrecking Crew

God gave us memories that we might have roses in December.

James M. Barrie

It's difficult to watch a loved one wither. It's even harder to dismantle a life.

That's what I did today.

I disassembled the last bastion of my grandparents' home. Time is a cruel mistress. Grand is gone and Mammy is going. Two years ago, she moved into my parent's house after it became evident she could no longer live alone.

Last summer, we had cleaned out Mammy and Grand's house in a nostalgic whirl. We didn't just clean out the house. We decided which pieces of the puzzle that was my grandparents' lives were worth keeping and which were disposable. We passed judgment on every napkin, magazine and photograph. We dismembered their lives one item at a time. Every item brought a tale to mind. Some things we couldn't look at—we just quietly wrapped and packed away. Furniture was divvied up—dining room set to my brother, crystal to Mom, an old wardrobe for me. We decided what to keep, where it should go and what to do with the rest. Mom and I dove into the task like we were just spring cleaning, but when no one was looking, we'd stop and stare at nothing, trying to think nothing. It's the thinking that leads to remembering, and remembering is what gets you. As quickly as it hit, it was gone, and newspaper flurried over vases and lamps once more.

In a town where folks know what you're having for dinner before you do, it was no time at all before someone made an offer on the house. Months passed before Mom acted on it, but to the citizens of Honey Grove, it was a done deal. Once more, we trudged to Mammy's to clean out what was left. Mom told more than one curious neighbor that she didn't grow up in this house. *But I did,* someone tiny inside reminded me. So there's no sentimental commitment to keep it, Mom explained. She was, as the saying goes, putting on. I knew she was upset.

We sold it a few weeks ago to someone Mom knew all her life. He's going to tear it down and build a new house on the comfy corner lot. Perfectly sensible.

But today I went back.

Not out of curiosity or a trip down memory lane. I went to salvage the kitchen cabinets and inside doors for a workshop we're building. I got more than I bargained for.

As I pried fifty years of paint out of sixty-year-old screws so I could take the doorknobs off the doors, I stopped. Just stared at nothing and saw everything.

I saw myself running through the hallways, my sharp heels banging like cannon fire on the hardwood floors, my squealing little brother chasing after me. Behind him loped Grand, bare-chested and potbellied, whooping and hollering after us.

I remember the feel of the sheets, how they always felt cooler in Mammy and Grand's un-air-conditioned little house than in my waiting bed at home. The soft glow of the ship-shaped TV lamp we used as a night light—the very same lamp that now sits on my son's shelf, illuminating him as he dreams.

Standing in the rubble of what had been a large part of my childhood, I shrugged it off and marched inside, determined to get what I came for. My husband pried loose the cabinets with his trusty rusty crowbar while I piled up the broken remnants of shattered lives. He'd catch me standing around in a stupor every now and then, and had the sense not to bother me. Card games, dominoes, snacks and countless happy moments danced in my head as I stood in the dissected kitchen. I remembered the smell of Mammy's famous chocolate pie, and if I squinted just right and peeked into the dining room, I could see Grand sitting at the table finishing off one full half of it. I watched him get up, rub his belly, smile at me and walk into the living room. He sat down in his favorite chair—the one with his scrawny butt print mashed into it.

The one we sold last summer.

When I pulled out one of the sliding pastry boards in the countertop, I found a treasure beyond words. On the wood written in my brother's childish scrawl was "fart on Mammy." It was too much. I laughed and cried.

I stumbled around the house, supposedly making sure we didn't leave anything behind. We won't walk these halls again. Pretty soon no one will. The house will be torn down to make way for a new one. In my mind, I heard the hum of the box fan that sat in the window in the front bedroom at night. I felt myself squirm under the cool sheets, Mammy perched beside me, giggling like a child. My brother and Grand snoring in the other room. I wasn't leaving it behind. I just needed to see it again to make sure I could take the smells, the sounds, the love with me. I got what I came for.

K. K. Choate

More Chicken Soup?

Many of the stories and poems you have read in this book were submitted by readers like you who had read earlier *Chicken Soup for the Soul* books. We publish at least five or six *Chicken Soup for the Soul* books every year. We invite you to contribute a story to one of these future volumes.

Stories may be up to twelve hundred words, and must uplift or inspire. You may submit an original piece, something you have read or your favorite quotation on your refrigerator door.

To obtain a copy of our submission guidelines and a listing of upcoming *Chicken Soup* books, please write, fax or check our Web site.

Please send your submissions to:

Chicken Soup for the Soul
P.O. Box 30880, Santa Barbara, CA 93130, USA
Fax: +1 805-563-2945
Web site: *www.chickensoup.com*

We will be sure that both you and the author are credited for your submission.

For information about speaking engagements, other books, audiotapes, workshops and training programs, please contact any of our authors directly.

Supporting Others

Care where you can. Whether you are a grandparent or part of an extended family offering encouragement to young people in your neighborhood or local school, Generations United works on your behalf to support generations re-connecting.

Generations United (GU) is the membership organization focused solely on improving the lives of children, youth and older people through intergenerational strategies, programs and public policies. GU represents more than one hundred national, state and local organizations and individuals representing more than seventy million Americans. Since 1986, GU has served as a resource for educating policymakers and the public about the economic, social and personal imperatives of intergenerational cooperation. GU acts as a catalyst for stimulating collaboration and innovation between aging, children, and youth organizations providing a forum to explore areas of common ground while celebrating the richness of each generation.

GU works to build a world that values and engages all generations. Our mission is best demonstrated through two signature initiatives. First is GU's National Center on Grandparents & Other Relatives Raising Children. One in twelve children in the U.S. is growing up in a home headed by a relative. GU's Center provides training and technical assistance, develops publications and acts as a national voice for these important families.

GU also promotes the development of intergenerational shared sites. Shared sites provide programs and services to multiple generations and offer a venue for them to come together for care, enjoyment and life affirming activities. Examples include a school with an embedded senior center, an adult day care with child care or a community center that has activities for single age groups as well as opportunities for multiple generations to learn and play together. Intergenerational shared sites make sense and help resources go further.

Generations United honors all ages, supports all ages and engages all ages.

Generations United
1333 H Street, NW, Suite 500W
Washington, DC 20005, USA
Phone: +1 (202) 289-3979
Fax: +1 (202) 289-3952
E-mail: *gu@gu.org*
Web site: *www.gu.org*

Who Is Jack Canfield?

Jack Canfield is one of America's leading experts in the development of human potential and personal effectiveness. He is both a dynamic, entertaining speaker and a highly sought-after trainer. Jack has a wonderful ability to inform and inspire audiences toward increased levels of self-esteem and peak performance. Jack most recently released a book for success entitled *The Success Principles: How to Get from Where You Are to Where You Want to Be.*

He is the author and narrator of several bestselling audio- and videocassette programs, including *Self-Esteem and Peak Performance, How to Build High Self-Esteem, Self-Esteem in the Classroom* and *Chicken Soup for the Soul—Live.* He is regularly seen on television shows such as *Good Morning America, 20/20* and *NBC Nightly News.* Jack has co-authored numerous books, including the *Chicken Soup for the Soul* series, *Dare to Win* and *The Aladdin Factor* (all with Mark Victor Hansen), *100 Ways to Build Self-Concept in the Classroom* (with Harold C. Wells), *Heart at Work* (with Jacqueline Miller) and *The Power of Focus* (with Les Hewitt and Mark Victor Hansen).

Jack is a regularly featured speaker for professional associations, school districts, government agencies, churches, hospitals, sales organizations and corporations. His clients have included the American Dental Association, the American Management Association, AT&T, Campbell's Soup, Clairol, Domino's Pizza, GE, Hartford Insurance, ITT, Johnson & Johnson, the Million Dollar Roundtable, NCR, New England Telephone, Re/Max, Scott Paper, TRW and Virgin Records. Jack has taught on the faculty of Income Builders International, a school for entrepreneurs.

Jack conducts an annual seven-day training called Breakthrough to Success. It attracts entrepreneurs, educators, counselors, parenting trainers, corporate trainers, professional speakers, ministers and others interested in improving their lives and the lives of others.

For free gifts from Jack and information on all his material and availability go to:

www.jackcanfield.com
Self-Esteem Seminars
P.O. Box 30880
Santa Barbara, CA 93130, USA
Phone: +1 805-563-2935 • Fax: +1 805-563-2945

Who Is Mark Victor Hansen?

In the area of human potential, no one is more respected than Mark Victor Hansen. For more than thirty years, Mark has focused solely on helping people from all walks of life reshape their personal vision of what's possible. His powerful messages of possibility, opportunity and action have created powerful change in thousands of organizations and millions of individuals worldwide.

He is a sought-after keynote speaker, bestselling author and marketing maven. Mark's credentials include a lifetime of entrepreneurial success and an extensive academic background. He is a prolific writer with many bestselling books, such as *The One Minute Millionaire, The Power of Focus, The Aladdin Factor* and *Dare to Win,* in addition to the *Chicken Soup for the Soul* series. Mark has had a profound influence through his library of audios, videos and articles in the areas of big thinking, sales achievement, wealth building, publishing success, and personal and professional development.

Mark is the founder of the MEGA Seminar Series. MEGA Book Marketing University and Building Your MEGA Speaking Empire are annual conferences where Mark coaches and teaches new and aspiring authors, speakers and experts on building lucrative publishing and speaking careers. Other MEGA events include MEGA Marketing Magic and My MEGA Life.

He has appeared on television (*Oprah,* CNN and *The Today Show*), in print (*Time, U.S. News & World Report, USA Today, New York Times* and *Entrepreneur*) and on countless radio interviews, assuring our planet's people that "You can easily create the life you deserve."

As a philanthropist and humanitarian, Mark works tirelessly for organizations such as Habitat for Humanity, American Red Cross, March of Dimes, Childhelp USA and many others. He is the recipient of numerous awards that honor his entrepreneurial spirit, philanthropic heart and business acumen. He is a lifetime member of the Horatio Alger Association of Distinguished Americans, an organization that honored Mark with the prestigious Horatio Alger Award for his extraordinary life achievements.

Mark Victor Hansen is an enthusiastic crusader for what's possible and is driven to make the world a better place.

Mark Victor Hansen & Associates, Inc.
P.O. Box 7665
Newport Beach, CA 92658, USA
Phone: +1 949-764-2640
Fax: +1 949-722-6912
Visit Mark online at: *www.markvictorhansen.com*

Who Is LeAnn Thieman?

LeAnn Thieman is a nationally acclaimed professional speaker, author and nurse who was "accidentally" caught up in the Vietnam orphan airlift in 1975. Her book *This Must Be My Brother* details her daring adventure helping to rescue three hundred babies as Saigon was falling to the Communists. An ordinary person, she struggled through extraordinary circumstances and found the courage to succeed. LeAnn and her incredible story have been featured in *Newsweek* magazine's "Voices of the Century" issue, FOX-TV News, PAX-TV's *It's A Miracle, NPR, BBC* and countless radio and TV programs around the world.

Today, as a renowned motivational speaker, she shares life-changing lessons learned from her airlift experience. Believing we all have individual "war zones," LeAnn inspires audiences to balance their lives, truly live their priorities and make a difference in the world.

After her story was featured in *Chicken Soup for the Mother's Soul,* LeAnn became one of *Chicken Soup*'s most prolific writers, with stories in eleven more *Chicken Soup* books. That and her devotion to thirty years of nursing made her the ideal coauthor of *Chicken Soup for the Nurse's Soul.* Her lifelong practice of her Christian faith led her to coauthor *Chicken Soup for the Christian Woman's Soul.* All of the above earned her the honor of coauthoring *Chicken Soup for the Caregiver's Soul, Chicken Soup for the Father and Daughter Soul* and now *Chicken Soup for the Grandmother's Soul.*

LeAnn is one of approximately ten percent of speakers worldwide to have earned the Certified Speaking Professional Designation awarded by the National Speakers Association and the International Federation for professional speakers.

LeAnn and Mark, her husband of thirty-five years, reside in Colorado, where they enjoy their "empty nest." Their two daughters, Angela and Christie, and son Mitch have "flown the coop" but are still drawn under their mother's wing when she needs them!

For more information about LeAnn's books and tapes or to schedule her for a presentation, please contact her at:

LeAnn Thieman, CSP
6600 Thompson Drive
Fort Collins, CO 80526, USA
Phone: +1 970-223-1574
E-mail: *LeAnn@LeAnnThieman.com*
www.LeAnnThieman.com

Contributors

The majority of stories in this book were submitted by our readers' response to our call-out for stories. If you would like to contact any of the contributors for information about their writing or would like to invite them to speak in your community, look for their contact information included in their biographies.

Nadia Ali is an experienced freelance writer. She resides on the Caribbean island of Trinidad with her husband, Khaleel, and two daughters, Shazara and Raisah, who were the inspiration for this humorous story about their grandmother, Azmine Khan. Nadia can be reached at *nadia@freelance-worker.com.*

Hannah Amgott is the author of several poems, professional articles and the 2004 memoir *In the Year of the Ox.* She is also a career counselor and university administrator in the Philadelphia area, and holds master's degrees in counseling and German. Please e-mail her at *hannah.amgott@widener.edu.*

Gina Antonios received her bachelor's degree from CCSU and her master's degree from SCSU. She teaches kindergarten at Carrington School in Connecticut. She is married to her high school sweetheart and loves being a mom to her precious twins. She dedicates this poem to her mom, dad and maternal grandmother.

Linda Apple lives in northwest Arkansas with her husband, Neal, their five children and two grandchildren. She is a speaker for Stonecroft Ministries and contributor to *Chicken Soup for the Nurse's Soul, Chicken Soup for the Working Woman's Soul* and *Chicken Soup for the Soul Living Your Dreams.* E-mail *psalm10218@cox-internet.com.* Website: *www.lindacapple.com.*

Tal Aviezer and **Jason Cocovinis** are Manhattan-based writers who specialize in prose, scripts and copy of all kinds. Their work has previously appeared in *Chicken Soup for the Ocean Lover's Soul.*

Nancy V. Bennett lives in British Columbia, along with assorted cats, dogs and a rooster named Coburn. She enjoys history and sewing historical clothing. Her work has previously appeared in *Chicken Soup for the Ocean Lover's Soul.*

Susan Chesser Branch, a freelance writer, lives with her husband and three children in Lake Mary, Florida. She does a wide variety of writing: novels, memoirs, magazines and newspaper features. You can e-mail her at *mbranch@cfl.rr.com.*

Ellie Braun-Haley is the author of four books. She also has short stories published in *Chicken Soup for the Soul,* other books and a wide variety of online e-zines. She presents workshops to kindergarten teachers and others in creative dance and movement for children. Please e-mail her at *shaley@telusplanet.net.*

Renie Burghardt, who was born in Hungary, is a freelance writer. She lives in a beautiful rural area and loves nature, animals, hiking and especially spending time with her own granddaughters.

Bobbi Carducci lives in Round Hill, Virginia, where she writes a feature column for the *Purcellville Gazette*. Her series of character studies celebrates the unique personality of the area and its inhabitants. Bobbi dedicates "Deposition Stew" to her beloved children and grandchildren. Please e-mail her at *bobbi@bobbicarducci.com*.

Libby C. Carpenter is a freelance writer living in North Carolina. A former educator, she continues to challenge others to learn and grow through her inspirational writings. Married to Hugh, she is the mother of two daughters and doting grandmother to Taylor, Andrew, Madison and Will. E-mail her at *libbyac2@juno.com*.

K. K. Choate is a mother of two and business owner. She writes humorous stories on family and life in general. Currently she is compiling a collection of her stories. Please e-mail her at: *ladyname@aol.com*.

Elayne Clift, a writer and journalist in Saxtons River, Vermont, teaches women's studies at several New England universities and colleges. Her latest book is *Women, Philanthropy and Social Change: Journey to a Just Society* (UPNE/Tufts University, 2005). She is now working on her first novel.

Cheri Lynn Cowell, speaker and author, blends her messages with warmth and confidence, sprinkling them with just the right amount of homespun wisdom and practical application. Her let's-have-a-cup-of-coffee style endears her audiences to her and has them wanting a second cup. To learn more, go to *www.CheriCowell.com*.

Kathleen Craft Boehmig is an Atlanta native who enjoys writing about her southern heritage. She serves on the board of the Atlanta Writers Club, is a Georgia Master Gardener intern and is currently writing her first book. E-mail her at *pkboehmig@charter.net*.

Cookie Curci was born during WWII, and most of the articles she writes about are from in and around that time frame. For sixteen years she wrote a popular nostalgia column for her community newspaper, *The Willow Glen Resident* (Silicon Valley Metro Newspapers in San Jose, California). Her generational stories have appeared in several nostalgia books and newspapers across the country.

Barbara G. Drotar is a freelance writer whose short stories have been published in most of the San Francisco Bay area's newspapers. She is the mother of six grown children and grandmother of seven. She plans on publishing a book on storytelling soon. Please e-mail her at *dbdrotar@aol.com*.

Julie Dunbar is an photo editor and writer living in Colorado. She has published numerous essays and recently completed a historical novel. She enjoys traveling, hiking and hanging out with her sons. Julie can be reached at *julie_dunbar@msn.com.*

Jane Elsdon has published many short stories, a children's novel, a collection of poetry and four poetry chapbooks. A California Poet in the School, she taught experiential writing of poetry to K-12 for many years. She is the Poet Laureate of San Luis Obisipo, California, for the year 2005.

Emily Erickson is a fifth grader in Loveland, Colorado. She won first place in the Colorado State Writing Contest in fourth grade. Besides writing stories, she enjoys playing basketball and tennis. She would like to thank Delores Doyle (Nana) for inspiring her to use her imagination and writing her thoughts.

Susan Farr-Fahncke is the author of *Angel's Legacy* and coauthor and contributor to numerous books. She is the founder of 2TheHeart.com (for writers and readers of inspiration) and Angels2TheHeart.com (sending hope to critically ill people) and can be reached at *Susan@2theheart.com.*

Norma Favor, a widow, attended Bob Jones University and Clinton Junior College. She served as a pastor's wife for twenty-five years. She plans to write about her family during the 1900s and her life as one of twelve siblings. She enjoys time with her children and twenty-two grandchildren. Please e-mail her at *2mranch@hisurfer.net.*

Carolyn Mott Ford lives at the Jersey Shore and loves spending time with her grandchildren—she has seven, ranging in age from a beautiful newborn baby to a thoughtful young adult. Carolyn writes stories for young readers as well as poetry and essays, and volunteers in a grade-school reading program.

Sally Friedman, a New Jersey essayist, is a graduate of the University of Pennsylvania. A freelance writer for three decades, her work has appeared in national magazines. Her favorite subjects are her husband, a retired judge, her three daughters and seven grandchildren. She is an admitted workaholic and chocoholic. E-mail: *pinegander@aol.com.*

Nancy Gibbs is an author, editor and motivational speaker. She has had approximately seventeen stories in *Chicken Soup* books. She has written four books and contributed to numerous other publications. Nancy and husband Roy have three grown children, Chad, Brad and Becky, and three granddaughters, Hannah, Halle and Katie. *Nancybgibbs@aol.com* or *www.nancybgibbs.com.*

Joanie Gilmore is retired from an executive assistant/public relations career of twenty-five years. She is the published author of *North Whidbey Pioneer Schools*, reminiscent stories of the early pioneers and schools of North Whidbey Island, Washington, where she lives. She enjoys writing, golf and snowbirding in Arizona.

Jean Jeffrey Gietzen is a poet and family essayist whose work has appeared in dozens of secular and religious magazines. She is best known for her Christian gift book bestseller *If You're Missing Baby Jesus,* published by Multnomah in 1999. She spends winters in Arizona and summers in Wisconsin. E-mail: *octodon31469@cs.com.*

Bonnie S. Grau is a freelance writer who enjoys reading, cooking, traveling and spending time with her three young grandchildren. She and her husband live in York, Pennsylvania.

Andrew Grossman is the founder and director of the online cartoon service *CartoonResource.com.* Under various pen names he has contributed cartoons and cartoon features to many of the leading print outlets in the United States and Europe.

Janet Hall Wigler enjoys her work as a dramatist, writer and director, and she is pleased the *Chicken Soup* series has chosen her work for several publications. You can reach Janet at *actingjanet@hotmail.com.*

Cynthia M. Hamond, SFO, has numerous stories in *Multnomah's Stories for the Heart* and the *Chicken Soup for the Soul* series. Her stories are in major publications including *Woman's World* and King's Features Syndications. She received two writing awards, and her short stories "Goodwill" and "Friends to the End" are TV favorites.

Ruth Hancock has been published in magazines, hospice journals and several books in the *Chicken Soup* series: *Volunteer's Soul, Grieving Soul* and *Caregiver's Soul.* Her stories are based on her life and interests as a hospice volunteer, ombudsman and widow of an Episcopal priest and her extensive fashion career. E-mail: *ruthhancock@att.net.*

Speaker-artist **Bonnie Hanson** is author of several books for adults and children, including the popular *Ponytail Girls* series, plus hundreds of published articles and poems. Her family includes husband Don, sons, grandchildren, cats, birds and possums! Contact: 3330 S. Lowell St., Santa Ana, CA 92707; (714) 751-7824; *bonnieh1@worldnet.att.net.*

Maria Harden lives and works in Winnipeg, Manitoba. She writes for newspapers, magazines and Web sites, sharing her life experiences. In her spare time she enjoys traveling, playing the piano and spending time with her family, especially her grandson. Contact Maria at *mharden@mts.net.*

Emily Sue Harvey's upbeat stories appear in women's magazines, the *Chocolate* series, *Chicken Soup for the Grieving Soul, From Eulogy to Joy* and *Caution: Children Praying.* Her mainstream fictional novel, *God Only Knows,* about an all-too-human preacher's family, is with the Peter Miller Agency in New York. Her current project, *Sunny Flavors,* is about Sunny, a mill hill girl, and her quest to overcome her family's shame. Please contact Emily at (864) 439-5358 or *EmilySue1@aol.com.*

Jonny Hawkins' cartoons in *Chicken Soup for the Grandmother's Soul* are dedicated to his beloved Grandma Hawkins.

Barbara Hibschman is a writer and speaker. She is the author of eight books and a contributing author to thirteen inspirational books. She speaks for women's groups, churches and seminars in the United States and abroad. She enjoys team-teaching at marriage retreats with her pastor-husband, Jim. Contact: *jbhibschman@cs.com*.

Born in Michigan and raised in Texas, **Renee Hixson** now resides in beautiful British Columbia with her husband and four children. She has taught Sunday school and high school English and written early childhood curriculum. At the moment Renee is working on a romantic adventure novel. Please e-mail her at *rhixson@telus.net*.

Erin Hoffman is a freelance writer and designer currently residing in Los Angeles. She dedicates this publication to her grandmother, Dorothy Asakawa. Erin was born in San Diego, California, and graduated from Rensselaer Polytechnic Institute in 2003. She specializes in fantasy and young adult fiction. For more information, visit *www.erinhoffman.com*.

Alaska's long winters give **Valerie A. Horner** plenty of time to write and quilt. She runs a bed and breakfast, catering to guests from around the world. She loves traveling, boating and gardening. She is known for her great cooking and has published a cookbook. Her e-mail is *sealad@bearsrun.com*.

Beverly Houseman is a retired registered nurse. She has published a book about her son, Rusty. Beverly is a contributor to *Chicken Soup for the Nurse's Soul, Chicken Soup for the Caregiver's Soul, From the Heart* books 1 & 2 by Kendall Bell. She is a pro-life counselor with Osceola Pregnancy Center in Kissimmee, Florida. Please e-mail her at *harhousman@earthlink.net*.

Sheila S. Hudson is published in the "Chocolates for Women" series, including "God Allows U-Turns," "Stories from the Heart—Volumes 1 and 2," "Taking Education Higher" and "God's Vitamin C." She is a columnist for *Athens Banner Herald*, contributor for the *Christian Standard Magazine* and president of Southeastern Writers of America.

Anne Johnson earned a bachelor of science degree and is a registered nurse in Nebraska in an intensive care unit. However, her most rewarding job is being a wife and mother. Writing is her way of relaxing.

Louise Tucker Jones is a Gold Medallion award–winning author and popular speaker. She holds a master's degree in creative writing and is author and coauthor of three books. Her work has been published in numerous magazines and compilation books, including *Guideposts* and other *Chicken Soup* titles. Louise resides in Edmond, Oklahoma. E-mail: *LouiseTJ@aol.com*.

Shirley Jump spends her days writing romantic comedies with sweet attitude for Kensington Books (*The Bachelor Committed Pastry*, February 2006) and Silhouette Romance (*The Marine's Kiss*, August 2005) to feed her shoe addiction and avoid doing housework. Visit her Web site at *www.shirleyjump.com*.

Kathryn Kimzey Judkins, LVN, has lived in California since 1962. Since retiring in 1998, she spends much of her time writing poetry and short stories. Married fifty-eight years, she has three children, six grandchildren and three great-grandchildren.

Betty King is an author, newspaper columnist and speaker. She is a wife, mother and grandmother and has lived with the disease MS for thirty-eight years. She is read in publications worldwide. Her Web site is *www.bettyking.net* and e-mail is *baking2@charter.net.*

Jean Kinsey, a native Kentuckian, enjoys traveling, camping and writing. Her personal experience stories have been published in *Chicken Soup, Reminiscence, Live* and e-zines. American Syringomyelia Alliance Project has published twelve of her profile columns. Jean hopes to finish soon her novel *Brightest Star,* about a boy who has syringomyelia. E-mail: *kystorywriter@yahoo.com.*

Roger Kiser's stories have been publsihed in seventeen books in five countries. Roger will never forget how he was treated as less than human while living in a Jacksonville, Florida, orphanage. Roger's story is at *www.geocities.com/ trampolineone/survive/noframe.htm.* Contact Roger at *trampolineone@webtv.net.*

J. Kenneth Kreider is professor emeritus of European history at Elizabethtown College (Pennsylvania). He received his Ph.D from the Pennsylvania State University and is author of *A Cup of Cold Water: The Story of Brethen Service* (2001). He conducts tours and has traveled in over ninety countries and seven continents.

Margaret Lang received her bachelor of arts degree from Brown University in 1963. She teaches women and children's groups in California. Margaret has one story accepted for publication and others under consideration. Her daughter is a physician/missionary, her son a youth pastor, and she has one granddaughter.

Patti Lawson is an author, lawyer and public speaker who lives in Charleston, West Virginia, with her dog Sadie. Patti and Sadie write a newspaper column, "Dogs . . . Diets . . . Dating," for the *Sunday Gazette-Mail.* Patti's first book, *The Dog Diet,* will be published in 2005. Visit her Web site at *www.thedogdiet.com.*

CLASS graduate **Delores Christian Liesner** of Racine, Wisconsin, delights in sharing her faith-walk with eight grandchildren, radio audiences (Chapel of the Air; Renaissance Racine), by written word *(Woman's World, God Answers Prayer, Renaissance, CBN Internet, Health and Wellness,* etc.), speaking inspirationally or creating personalized poetry. Contact: *www.deloresliesner.com* or *delores_liesner@yahoo.com.*

Patricia Lorenz is the proud grandma of Hailey, Hannah, Zachary, Casey, Riley, Chloe, Adeline and Ethan. She's an art-of-living speaker, author of five books and a top contributor to the *Chicken Soup for the Soul* books, with stories in twenty-five of them. To hire her as a speaker, e-mail *patricialorenz@juno.com* or visit *www.patricialorenz.com.*

Alice Malloy is a recently retired social worker from Long Island, New York. Besides writing, her new life consists of long walks by the ocean, good books and, of course, Tuesdays with her grandchildren. Please contact her at *aqmalloy@optonline.net.*

Bettye Martin-McRae, writer's mentor, founder of Writers' Ongoing Workshops, has been freelancing since 1972, including daily newspapers, *Guideposts*, Focus on the Family, *The Christian Reader*, Texas Folklore Society; national columns in *Mules and More Magazine*, and author of eight western humor and inspirational books. Please contact: *www.BunkhouseBooks.com; bunkhouse@wtconnect.com*; (325) 235-9969.

John McCaslin is a nationally syndicated political columnist and author based in Washington, D.C. He's seen regularly on national television discussing the latest White House and Capitol Hill gossip. In his spare time, he enjoys writing travel articles for numerous publications. Mostly, he relishes time spent with his daughter, Kerry.

Janet Lynn Mitchell is a wife, mother, author and inspirational speaker. She is the coauthor of *A Special Kind of Love, For Those Who Love Children with Special Needs*, published by Broadman and Holman and Focus on the Family, 2004. Janet can be reached at *Janetlm@prodigy.net* or by fax (714) 633-6309.

Laura Mueller lives in southern Vermont with her husband, Andy, and their two young children. Laura has published numerous essays, is writing a novel about teenage girls and has recently finished cowriting a play called *Mommy Talk* with playwright Adriana Elliot. Laura can be reached at *limeyfoe@sover.net.*

Motivational humorist **Jennifer Oliver**, a former El Pasoan, resides in central Texas with her husband and four kids. Author of *Four Ears: Works of Heart*, her stories have appeared in *Chicken Soup for the Soul, Don't Sweat the Small Stuff, Heartwarmers, Stories for a Woman's Heart* and *Half Full.*

Karen J. Olson is a writer and columnist from Eau Claire, Wisconsin. She writes two columns regionally as well as inspirational magazine articles on local, regional and national levels. She enjoys reading, bicycling and scrapbooking. You may reach her at *kjolson@charter.net.*

Rachel R. Patrick writes Bible studies and teaches in her church's women's ministry. Married nearly thirty years to Al, she has a grown son, three nearly teen granddaughters and a toddler grandson. Encouraging women to apply biblical principles to their lives is her life's goal.

Denise Peebles is a happily married mother of two children, Ashley, age twenty, and Jonathan, age ten. She and her husband, Keith, enjoy traveling and watching their son play sports. Denise dreams of publishing a children's book someday. Please e-mail her at *SPeeb47489@aol.com.*

Dr. Debra D. Peppers, a retired English teacher, was inducted into the prestigious National Teachers Hall of Fame. Now a university instructor, Emmy award–winning playwright, radio and television host, Debra is also a member of the National Speakers Association. Dr. Peppers is available for bookings at (314) 842-7425, *drp@pepperseed.org*, or visit her Web site at *www.pepperseed.org*.

Teresa Pitman is the author or coauthor of ten published books and a regular contributor to *Today's Parent* magazine. As the single mother of four children and the grandmother of two, she loves writing about parenting—and now grandparenting.

Shirley Pope Waite has had fillers, articles, poems and devotions in over 150 publications and twenty-four books, including her own *Delight in the Day*. She has taught at writers' conferences and currently writes a weekly column and teaches a class helping seniors write their life stories.

Trudy Reeder has a Ph.D in psychology from the University of Denver, a master's degree in education from Wayne State University and a bachelor's degree from Eastern Michigan University. She loves people, psychology, teaching, art and writing, and she worked at Loretto Heights College, the University of Northern Colorado and in Poudre School District. E-mail her at *trudyreeder@hotmail.com*.

Carol McAdoo Rehme, one of *Chicken Soup's* managing editors and most prolific contributors, compares grannyhood to homemade happiness—life's natural sweetener. Carol directs a nonprofit organization, Vintage Voices, Inc., which brings interactive programming to the vulnerable elderly. Speaking engagements and storytelling gigs fill her spare time. Contact: *carol@rehme.com; www.rehme.com*.

Kimberly Ripley is a wife and mother of five from Portsmouth, New Hampshire. She is the author of six books, including *Freelancing Later in Life*. Visit her Web site at *www.kimberlyripley.writergazette.com*.

Michelle Rocker is a mother of two boys and two girls. She is passionate about music and addicted to reading. She loves writing, has written several children's programs and is currently working on a women's inspirational book. Please e-mail her at *mmrocker@netzero.com*.

Stephen D. Rogers is a stay-at-home dad who is late with his own thank-you notes. Please e-mail him at *sdr633@hotmail.com*.

Harriet May Savitz has had twenty-two books published and an ABC-TV "Afterschool Special" produced by Henry Winkler. Her recent book of essays, *More Than Ever—A View from My 70s*, is available through *Authorhouse.com*. Visit her at *www.harrietmaysavitz.com* or reach her by e-mail at *hmaysavitz@aol.com*.

Ann Kirk Shorey lives in southwestern Oregon with her husband, two cats and a dog. She's had articles printed in various regional publications and is currently at work on her second novel. She can be reached at *ashorey41@msn.com*.

Tricia Short received her bachelor of science degree from the University of Texas at Austin. She has a master's degree in reading from Texas A & M at

Commerce. She teaches English as a Second Language at a college in Dallas, Texas. Tricia enjoys reading, exercising and time with family and friends. She plans to do mission work overseas with her husband one day.

Deborah Shouse is a writer, speaker, editor and creativity catalyst. Her work has appeared in *Reader's Digest, Newsweek, Woman's Day, The Washington Post, Family Circle* and *MS*. She is the coauthor of *Making Your Message Memorable: Communicating Through Stories*. Deborah frequently does programs for Alzheimer's caregivers, families and friends. Deborah's Web site is *www.thecreativityconnection.com*.

Sharon Ozee Siweck is an international speaker and Personality Plus trainer; graduate of CLASS in Albuquerque, New Mexico. A widow and cancer survivor, she enjoys travelling, writing and speaking to churches and professional groups. She is now writing a book from her years of journaling. Please contact her at: *sharonsiweck@hotmail.com*.

Laura Smith is the author of the children's book *Cantaloupe Trees* and of numerous inspirational stories appearing in the *God Allows U-Turns* and *God's Way* anthologies. She graduated from Miami University with a bachelor's degree in marketing. Laura lives in Oxford, Ohio, with her husband and their three children.

Carol Spahr received her B.S. in Elementary Education in 1990 and her B.A. in English and History in 1991 from Atlantic Union College in Massachusetts. She teaches English for grades 7–9. She enjoys reading, music, and traveling and is currently working on several writing projects. Please e-mail her at *cspahr8@msn.com*.

Marcia Swearingen is a former newspaper editor and columnist now freelancing full-time. She and her husband, Jim, enjoy teaching young marrieds at Hixson United Methodist Church near Chattanooga. They are the parents of a daughter currently serving in the U.S. Navy.

Angela Thieman-Dino was a young teen when she wrote her story about her great-grandma. Today she is a cultural anthropologist living in Denver, Colorado. Angela, her husband, Brian, and their son, Dante, eagerly await the arrival of a new sibling for Dante in summer of 2005.

A first-time mom at forty-one, **Stephanie "Stacy" Thompson** and husband Michael enjoy the antics of their two-year-old daughter Micah. An inspirational writer, newspaper columnist, radio host and speaker, Thompson founded State of Change, an organization disseminating stories of hope and action. Reach her at: P.O. Box 1502, Edmond, OK 73083, or *stephanie@stateofchange.net*.

Melodie Lynn Tilander transitioned from a corporate career to pursue her dream of writing. She resides in Oregon, earning publishing credits in several media. Melodie enjoys being near the water and creating stained glass/stone design. She is coauthoring an inspirational book on God's ministering angels.

Please reach her at *lynnmelodie@hotmail.com.*

Paula Mauqiri Tindall is a registered nurse and resides in South Florida with her toy poodle, Lucy. After many years of taking care of her grandmother with her cousin Joey, she is completing her first book on their life during that period. She can be reached at *lucylu54@aol.com.*

Pam Trask resides on a lake in Fairview, Oregon, with her husband, David. She is the mother of three grown children and six grandchildren. Pam's special niche is writing and she meets once a week with her writing group "The Magnificant Seven." She finds inspiration for much of her writing while boat-camping with her husband on the Columbia River near her home. Her family is high on her priority list and in her leisure time she loves playing the piano and working with her flowers.

Diane M. Vanover writes from her home in Tucson, Arizona, where she shares her love of stories with her five terrific grandchildren: Travis, David, Amanda, Alexis and Mishelle, who are superb and inspirational storytellers. You may contact her at *dmvanover@aol.com.*

Shelley Ann Wake has a master of arts degree in professional writing, and degrees in science, business and commerce. She is a professional writer with publications including essays, articles, children's novels and nonfiction books. She is also the co-owner of Twenty Twenty Publishing. She can be contacted at: *shelleywake@ozemail.com.au.*

Rachel Wallace-Oberle has an education in journalism and radio/television broadcasting and writes for numerous publications. She also works in radio and for a foundation that provides assistance to Haiti's poor through sustainable development. Rachel loves walking, classical music and canaries. She can be reached at *rachelw-o@rogers.com.*

Jody Walters graduated from Colorado State University with a degree in construction management. She is a project manager with a general contractor in Fort Collins, Colorado. Jody enjoys spending time with her husband and eleven-year-old son, as well as hiking, biking and traveling.

Phyllis W. Zeno recently retired after twenty years as founding editor of *AAA Going Places.* She is currently the editor of *Marco Polo Magazine,* an adventure travel magazine. Her mother, an inveterate traveler, was the inspiration for a lifetime of travel with her daughters, Linda and Leslie. You may contact her at *Phylliszeno@aol.com.*

This Ain't No Bull. Reprinted by permission of Joan Rae Gilmore. ©2004 Joan Rae Gilmore.

Everything but the Kitchen Sink. Reprinted by permission of Nadia Ali. ©2004 Nadia Ali.

Trying Times and Dirty Dishes. Reprinted by permission of Cynthia Marie Hamond. ©2003 Cynthia Marie Hamond.

A Thank-You Note to Grandma. Reprinted by permission of Gina C. Antonios. ©1996 Gina C. Antonios.

A Holy Moment. Reprinted by permission of Sheila S. Hudson. ©2002 Sheila S. Hudson.

Grandma's Prayers. Reprinted by permission of Ann Sharon Ozee Siweck. ©2004 Ann Sharon Ozee Siweck.

Angel in the Clouds. Reprinted by permission of Melva Jean Kinsey. ©2004 Melva Jean Kinsey

Parting Gifts. Reprinted by permission of Marcia McDonald Swearingen. ©2004 Marcia McDonald Swearingen.

A Teenager's Song for Gramma. Reprinted by permission of Angela Lea Thieman Dino. ©1986 Angela Lea Thiemann Dino.

Love and Water. Reprinted by permission of Emily Sue Harvey. ©2000 Emily Sue Harvey.

The Perspective of a Pansy. Reprinted by permission of Laura Lynn Smith. ©2000 Laura Lynn Smith.

Red and White Carnations. Reprinted by permission of Barbara Jean Hibschman. ©1987 Barbara Jean Hibschman.

The Feeling. Reprinted by permission of Margaret Eleanor Braun-Haley. ©2000 Margaret Eleanor Braun-Haley.

Picked Just for You. Reprinted by permission of Bonnie Blanche Hanson. ©2001 Bonnie Blanche Hanson.

Shiny Red Shoes. Reprinted by permission of Bettye Martin-McRae. ©1991 Bettye Martin-McRae.

Monday Night Tea. Reprinted by permission of Delores Liesner. ©2004 Delores Liesner.

Outing with Gram. Reprinted by permission of Delores Liesner. ©2004 Delores Liesner.

Grandma Days. Reprinted by permission of Maria Harden. ©2003 Maria Harden.

Afternoon Delight. Reprinted by permission of Diane Marie Vanover. © 2004 Diane Marie Vanover.

Two Dedicated Grandmas. Reprinted by permission of Janet Lynn Mitchell. © 2004 Janet Lynn Mitchell.

Go-Cart Grandma. Reprinted by permission of Patricia Lorenz. © 1982 Patricia Lorenz.

Surf's Up, Grama. Reprinted by permission of Pamelia D. Trask. © 2004 Pamelia D. Trask.

Grandma and the Snowbank. Reprinted by permission of Ann Kirk Shorey. © 2004 Ann Kirk Shorey.

Grandma's River. Reprinted by permission of Melodie Lynn Tilander. © 2004 Melodie Lynn Tilander.

Journey Home. Reprinted by permission of Renee Willa Hixson. © 2004 Renee Willa Hixson.

Travels with Grandma. Reprinted by permission of Phyllis W. Zeno. © 2004 Phyllis W. Zeno.

Going Places. Reprinted by permission of Carolyn Mott Ford. © 2004 Carolyn Mott Ford.

Will He Remember? Reprinted by permission of Maria Harden. © 2003 Maria Harden.

Love Never to Be Blinded. Reprinted by permission of Nancy V. Bennett. © 2001 Nancy V. Bennett.

Pennies from Heaven. Reprinted by permission of Emily Erickson and Rebecca Erickson. © 2004 Emily Erickson.

Dusting in Heaven. Reprinted by permission of Denise Peebles. © 2002 Denise Peebles.

Healing. Reprinted by permission of Jennifer Ilene Oliver. © 2004 Jennifer Ileene Oliver.

I Will Remember. Reprinted by permission of Shelley Ann Wake. © 2004 Shelley Ann Wake.

Love's Labors Found. Reprinted by permission of Sally Friedman. © 2003 Sally Friedman.

God's Hands. Reprinted by permission of Shirley Pope Waite. © 1995 Shirley Pope Waite.

God's Good Time. Reprinted by permission of Cynthia Marie Hamond. © 2003 Cynthia Marie Hamond.

Also available from Vermilion

Chicken Soup for the Soul

Stories may be *the* most powerful teaching tool available to us, especially when the subjects being taught are love, respect and values. In this book the authors share a collected wisdom on love, parenting, heroism, death and the overcoming of obstacles.

Price: £8.99   ISBN: 9780091819569

Chicken Soup for the Mother's Soul

This book pays tribute to motherhood – the vocation that requires the skills of a master mediator, mentor, cook, chauffeur and counsellor. These heartwarming stories celebrate the defining moments of motherhood – from birth to letting go as your children leave the nest.

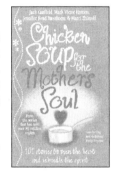

Price: £8.99   ISBN: 9780091819767

Chicken Soup for the Teenage Soul

Including important lessons on the nature of friendship and love, the value of respect for yourself and others, and dealing with tough issues like death, suicide and the loss of love, this is your handbook for surviving and succeeding during these exciting but sometimes difficult years.

Price: £8.99   ISBN: 9780091826406

Order these titles direct from www.rbooks.co.uk/chickensoup

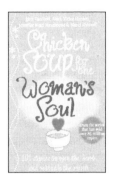